Program Budgeting
for Urban Police Services

Donald C. Shoup
Stephen L. Mehay

Published in cooperation with
the Institute of Government and Public Affairs,
University of California, Los Angeles, California

The Praeger Special Studies program—
utilizing the most modern and efficient book
production techniques and a selective
worldwide distribution network—makes
available to the academic, government, and
business communities significant, timely
research in U.S. and international economic, social, and political development.

Program Budgeting for Urban Police Services

With Special Reference to Los Angeles

PRAEGER SPECIAL STUDIES IN U.S. ECONOMIC, SOCIAL, AND POLITICAL ISSUES

Praeger Publishers   New York Washington London

PRAEGER PUBLISHERS
111 Fourth Avenue, New York, N.Y. 10003, U.S.A.
5, Cromwell Place, London S.W.7, England

Published in the United States of America in 1972
by Praeger Publishers, Inc.

Library of Congress Catalog Card Number: 72-83009

Printed in the United States of America

For the last few years a number of scholars at the University of California have been engaged in research on local government program budgeting under the co-direction of Werner Z. Hirsch and Harold M. Somers. The research has been concerned with both theoretical and applied issues, often in relation to a specific program--police, education, recreation, health, and welfare services. This volume is the first in a series of published reports.

In this report on police services, Donald Shoup and Stephen Mehay discuss some objectives of police activities, in operational terms, and develop alternative budget structures for the Los Angeles Police Department. Program analyses are presented for traffic law enforcement and for crime deterrent patrol, utilizing multivariate regression of existing data in the first analysis and controlled experimentation to produce new data in the second analysis. Emphasis is upon the question of police service production functions. Evaluations of costs and benefits are described for the enforcement and patrol programs and an examination of intergovernmental aspects of the distribution of police services is included. A summary of the methodology and findings is provided in an abridgment.

It is a pleasure to acknowledge the invaluable cooperation of the Los Angeles Police Department in this study of program budgeting for police. The authors are particularly grateful to Deputy Chiefs Roger Murdock, James Fulton, and Robert Gaunt; Inspectors Thomas Janes and Sidney Mills; Captain Robert Vernon; Lieutenant Robert Mammen; Mr. Fred Kumagai, and Mr. Thomas Berg. Captain Vernon inaugurated the traffic law enforcement experiment described in Chapter 3 and aided the authors well beyond the call of duty. Mr. Gary Fisher of the UCLA Institute of Traffic and Transportation Engineering helped greatly in the difficult task of assembling the accident statistics for computer use.

While much of the research relates to issues of concern to municipal and county government in metropolitan Los Angeles, the analytical approach and techniques employed here no doubt have relevance for all local governments.

The Institute of Government and Public Affairs is pleased to present this volume in continuing cooperation with Praeger Publishers.

Werner Z. Hirsch
Director
Institute of Government
and Public Affairs

SPECIAL ACKNOWLEDGMENTS

This report of research on local government program budgeting has been made possible by a grant from the Ford Foundation, whose financial support is gratefully acknowledged.

CONTENTS

		Page
FOREWORD		v
SPECIAL ACKNOWLEDGMENT		vii
LIST OF TABLES		xii
LIST OF FIGURES		xvi

Chapter

1   INTRODUCTION   3

2   POLICE GOALS AND THE PROGRAM BUDGET
    STRUCTURE   11

    Minimizing the Cost of Illegal
      Activities   15
        Violations of Property Rights   16
        Violations of Individuals' Rights   24
        Violations of Regulations Relating
          to Moral Conduct   26
        Collective Civil Violations   28
        Traffic Violations   30
    General Community Services   31
    Police Program Budget Structures   33
    Estimates of Program Expenditures   48
        Expenditure Estimate for the
          Traffic Program Structure   49
        Expenditure Estimates for Total
          Police Program Structure   58
    Integrating Program Budget Structure
      and Program Analysis   61
    Supplement 1: Method for Crosswalking
      from Line-Item to Traffic Program
      Structure   64
    Supplement 2: An Estimated Program
      Budget for the Detroit Police
      Department   70

　　　Supplement 3:　Judiciary and Law
　　　　Enforcement Aspects of the Program
　　　　Budget of Philadelphia, 1970/71   73

3　　PROGRAM ANALYSIS FOR TRAFFIC LAW
　　　ENFORCEMENT   80

　　　Traffic Law Enforcement Production
　　　　Functions   87
　　　　　Statistical Data   95
　　　　　Engineering Data   95
　　　　　Experimental Data   96
　　　An Experimental Investigation of
　　　　Traffic Law Enforcement Production
　　　　Functions   99
　　　　　Background of the Experiment   100
　　　　　The Experiment Design   102
　　　　　Valuation of Benefits and Costs
　　　　　　of Traffic Law Enforcement   108
　　　　　Details of the Traffic Law
　　　　　　Enforcement Experiment   117
　　　　　Effect of Traffic Law Enforcement
　　　　　　on Traffic Accidents   124
　　　　　Effect of Traffic Law Enforcement
　　　　　　on Crime Rates   138
　　　　　Effect of Traffic Law Enforcement
　　　　　　on Speed of Travel   141
　　　Summary and Conclusion   146
　　　Supplement 1:　Detailed Analysis of
　　　　the Costing Effort   151
　　　　　Determining Activities   151
　　　　　Salary Costs   152
　　　　　Vehicle Costs   152
　　　　　Office Equipment Costs   153
　　　　　Administrative Overhead Costs   153
　　　　　Cost Units   154
　　　　　Costing the Activities   154
　　　　　Spreading the Costs   154
　　　Supplement 2:　Traffic Volume,
　　　　October-June, 1964-69   157
　　　Supplement 3:　Traffic Speed   158

Chapter   Page

4   PROGRAM ANALYSIS FOR POLICE PATROL
     SERVICES   159

     Production and Distribution of Crime
       Deterrent Patrol Services   163
     A Production Model for Crime
       Deterrent Patrol Services   172
     A Statistical Analysis of Patrol
       Services   179
         The Measures of Patrol Output   181
         Description of the Patrol Input
           and Environmental Variables   193
     Results of the Regression Analysis   197
     Evaluation and Conclusions   208
         A Benefit-Cost Evaluation of
           One-Man versus Two-Man
           Patrol Units   211
         Statistical Analysis in Program
           Budgeting   222
     Supplement   226
         Sources for Column 1, Table 4.12:
           Personal Losses for Selected
           Offenses   226
         Sources for Column 2, Table 4.12:
           State of California Criminal
           Justice System Costs per
           Offense   229

5   INTERGOVERNMENTAL ASPECTS OF POLICE
     SERVICE DISTRIBUTION   231

     The City-County Conflict over Police
       Service Finance in Los Angeles
       County   233
     The Lakewood Plan of Contract Services   236
     The Effects of Intracounty Subsidies   239
     Police Service Finance in the Unin-
       corporated Area of Los Angeles
       County   244
     Police Service Costs in the Unincor-
       porated Area of Los Angeles County   247
         Other County Service Costs   255
         Formation of Subordinate Taxing
           Areas   257

Police Service Costs in the Contract
Cities of Los Angeles County   258
Conclusion   272
Supplement 1: Allocation of Vice
Bureau Expenditures   276
Supplement 2: Allocation of
Detective Division Expenditures   277

6   SUMMARY OF METHODOLOGY AND FINDINGS   278

Goals of the Police   278
Police Program Budget Structures   279
Estimates of Program Expenditures   281
Integrating Program Budget
Structure and Program Analysis   283
Program Analysis for Traffic Law
Enforcement   284
Traffic Law Enforcement Produc-
tion Functions   284
The Experimental Investigation of
Traffic Law Enforcement Produc-
tion Functions   286
Summary of Results of the
Experiment   297
Program Analysis of Crime Deterrent
Patrol   298
A Production Model for Crime
Deterrent Patrol   299
A Statistical Analysis of Patrol
Production   301
Results of the Regression Analysis   304
Intergovernmental Aspects of the
Distribution of Police Services   310
The Lakewood Plan of Contract
Services   312
Geographical Distribution of
Sheriff's Police Services   313
Subsidies to Contract Cities
and Unincorporated Areas   314
Implications of the Intergov-
ernmental Analysis   317

NOTES   319

ABOUT THE AUTHORS   342

LIST OF TABLES

Table		Page
2.1	Major Police Program Categories	35
2.2	Police Program Structure: Major Goals Expressed in Quantifiable Terms	38
2.3	Crime Commission Police Program Budget	40
2.4	Example of Divisional Breakdown of Distribution of Police Services in Los Angeles	43
2.5	Police Program Structured on a Geographical Basis	50
2.6	Traffic Bureau Program Structure	52
2.7	Cost Data for Proposed Traffic Bureau Program Structure	55
2.8	Los Angeles Police Department Traffic Bureau Budget Crosswalk, 1967/68	66
2.9	Detroit Police Department Resources Allocated toward the Control of Specific Criminal and Noncriminal Activities	71
3.1	Base Period and Experimental Period Data for Traffic Beats	104
3.2	Hypothetical Traffic Enforcement Experiment Data	105
3.3	Cost of Traffic Accidents	116
3.4	Correlation Coefficients between Number of Accidents per Month in Experimental and Nonexperimental Hours, January 1, 1964, to September 1, 1968	118

Table		Page
3.5	Traffic Volume, 1964-69	121
3.6	Enforcement and Accidents on the Experimental Beats	125
3.7	Input-Output Rankings on Six Experimental Beats	126
3.8	Surface Street Traffic Accidents, Los Angeles, 1967	127
3.9	Injury-Accident Equivalent Cost	128
3.10	Enforcement Costs and Accident Costs on the Experimental Beats	129
3.11	Tradeoff between Alpha Error and Beta Error	134
3.12	Effect of Traffic Law Enforcement on Crime	142
3.13	Summary of Costs and Benefits of Experimental Patrol Changes	147
3.14	Cost Estimates of Traffic Enforcement Division	155
3.15	Cost Estimates of Accident Investigation Division	156
4.1	Patrol Bureau Formula for Crime Deterrent Patrol Allocation	169
4.2	Average Field Response Time for Crime Deterrent Patrol	171
4.3	Police Personnel for Urban Areas (Median), 1967	180
4.4	Actual and Reported Crime Rates for the United States	188
4.5	Actual and Reported Crime Rates for 13 Western States	189

Table   Page

4.6   Regression Equation on FBI Crime
         Rates per Capita in 1968, for
         Cities in Southern California   198

4.7   Regression Equation on California
         Crime Rates per Capita in 1968,
         for Cities in Southern California   199

4.8   Regression Equation on FBI Crime
         Rates per Capita in 1968, for
         Cities in Southern California,
         Employing Additional Police
         Input Variables   201

4.9   Regression Equation on Total Crime
         Rates per Capita in 1968, for
         Cities in Southern California   202

4.10   Regression Equation on Arrests per
         Capita in 1968, for Cities in
         Southern California   206

4.11   Estimated Numbers of Crimes Deterred
         by 1 Percent Increase in One-Man
         Patrol   214

4.12   Social Costs for Selected Offenses   216

4.13   Social Benefits of a 1 Percent
         Increase in One-Man Patrol   217

4.14   Dollar Losses per Property Crime   219

4.15   Social Benefits of 1 Percent
         Increase in One-Man Units   219

4.16   Annual Measures of Demands for
         Police Services in St. Louis,
         1948-66 Inclusive   223

4.17   Regression Summaries of Demands for
         Police Services in St. Louis,
         1948-66 Inclusive   224

Table   Page

4.18   Projected Demands for Police Services
         in St. Louis, 1975 and 1980   224

4.19   Motor Vehicle Fatality Losses--Total
         Population: Number of Deaths and
         Earnings Lost, by Age, 1968   228

5.1   Station Costs of Los Angeles County
         Sheriff's Department, 1968/69   264

LIST OF FIGURES

Figure   Page

2.1 Minimizing Cost of Illegal
    Activities   15

2.2 Supply and Demand for Entrance into
    Crime   20

2.3 Criteria for Allocating Urban Police
    Resources   46

3.1 Accident Rate as a Function of the
    Level of Enforcement   90

3.2 Accident Rate Reduction as a Func-
    tion of the Level of Enforcement 91

3.3 Accident Rate Reduction as a Func-
    tion of the Level of Two-Wheel
    and Four-Wheel Enforcement   93

3.4 Hypothetical Traffic Enforcement
    Marginal Product Curve   106

4.1 Effect of a Correction Factor for
    Reported Crimes   190

5.1 Map of the County of Los Angeles 238

5.2 Expenditures and Internally Raised
    Revenues for Local Police Services 241

5.3 Effect of Intergovernmental Subsidy 243

5.4 Effects of Subsidy on an Unincor-
    porated Area   246

5.5 Effects of Below-Cost Provision of
    Police Services   267

Program Budgeting
for Urban Police Services

Since 1960 almost all statistical indicators of social and economic well-being in cities have shown an improvement--except statistics on crime.[1] As examples of how crime statistics have behaved, between 1960 and 1968 the national reported rate of forcible rape per 100,000 population increased 65 percent, that of aggravated assault 67 percent, and that of robbery 119 percent.[2] While reported crime rates were rising, so were expenditures by government on police protection: between 1960 and 1965 federal, state, and local expenditures for police protection rose by 39 percent.[3]

This is surely a challenging combination of trends. Improvements in the measurable conditions of welfare--for instance, increases in median income, decreases in unemployment, decreases in the number living below the legally defined poverty line, and increases in the proportion of students completing high school--all seem to be factors that should tend to decrease crime. Similarly, increases in public expenditures on police protection should be expected to decrease the incidence of crime. Yet the opposite occurred. Part of the problem may, of course, lie in the unreliability of national crime statistics in that increases in the reported crime rate may arise from more complete reporting of formerly unreported crimes.[4] Despite this potential source of overstatement of the upward trend of crime rates, there is widespread feeling that the problem

of crime has worsened, and concern for personal
safety has become an important political issue, especially in urban areas. More recently, the methods
used by the police in dealing with crime and civil
disorders have also become prominent topics.

The responsibility for providing police protection is largely at the local level; local governments account for 79 percent, state governments 13
percent, and the federal government only 8 percent
of all expenditures for police protection.[5] Thus,
although the problem of crime has been the subject
of national debate, the burden of providing a police
response falls mainly on local governments. One
form of response that has been widely recommended,
and tried, is to spend more on police. Another form
of response, the one explored in this study, is to
look for ways of using the resources devoted to providing police protection more effectively. More
specifically, the application of program budgeting
to the provision of police protection by local governments will be examined.

Program budgeting (a shortened name for Planning-
Programming-Budgeting Systems, or PPBS) has three distinct but related aspects. The first is the structural reorientation of the budget expenditure format
from a focus on the inputs purchased to a focus on
the government outputs produced. The second is the
use of analysis to evaluate and to help design governmental programs that produce the desired outputs.
The third major aspect, quite different from the
first two, is the study of political and organizational contexts into which the new system is to be
introduced.[6] This political and organizational aspect of program budgeting has been relatively neglected in the primarily economic literature on the
subject. Although this third aspect is not emphasized in this work, there is some discussion, in
Chapters 3 and 5, of the system of organizational
and political incentives involved in the provision
of police services in Los Angeles City and Los
Angeles County.

In the structural part of program budgeting,
governmental activities that contribute to the same
objective are grouped together into separate programs, and the aggregation of these programs

constitutes the program budget format. However, there are many ways to organize activities into programs, each of which would have some appeal for some purposes. Thus, whatever format is chosen is inevitably a compromise among competing uses. Indeed, during the early stages of introducing program budgeting into any government, the particular budget formats chosen should be considered exploratory and subject to alteration. The concept of the most useful program budget format will undoubtedly be affected by subsequent in-depth analyses of the individual programs, and reorganizations will be desired. This is an important point, because allocation of agencies' expenditures according to a program format can be a very expensive and talent-consuming process; if the choice of a particular format is made prematurely and expenditure data are generated to fit it, the sunk cost of developing the budget may serve only to entrench an inappropriate choice. For this reason, in Chapter 2 several budget format alternatives for the Los Angeles Police Department (LAPD) are presented, and program budgets that have been devised for the police departments of Philadelphia and Detroit are reproduced as supplements. Inspection of the differences among them shows how widely conceptions of an appropriate structure of a program budget can vary.

The budget structures of Chapter 2 serve as a framework for the subsequent program analyses of Chapters 3 and 4 by identifying the objectives of a municipal police department and enumerating the activities that contribute to these objectives. These analyses, along with the investigation of intergovernmental relations among the police agencies of Los Angeles County in Chapter 5, form the major part of this study. This emphasis on analysis accords with Selma Mushkin's recommendation that

> whatever the focus in structuring, it is clear that the central core of a PPB system is analysis of cost and effectiveness of alternative ways of satisfying specified city objectives. With analytical talent in short

supply, the energies devoted to re-
finement of structure can detract
from analytical efforts.[7]

The plea for program analysis rather than program
structure is also made eloquently, and more passion-
ately, by Aaron Wildavsky:

> The fixation on program structure is
> the most pernicious aspect of PPBS.
> Once PPBS is adopted, it becomes nec-
> essary to have a program structure
> that provides a complete list of or-
> ganization objectives and supplies in-
> formation on the attainment of each
> one. In the absence of analytic stud-
> ies for all or even a large part of
> an agency's operations, the structure
> turns out to be a sham that piles up
> meaningless data under vague categor-
> ies. It hides rather than clarifies.
> . . . Although the system dredges up
> information under numerous headings,
> it says next to nothing about the im-
> pact of one program on another. There
> is data but no causal analysis. Hence
> the agency head is at once oversup-
> plied with masses of numbers and under-
> supplied with propositions about the
> impact of any action he might under-
> take. He cannot tell, because no one
> knows, what the marginal change he is
> considering would mean for the rest of
> his operation. . . . The program
> structure, therefore, does not embody
> a focus on central policy concerns.
> More likely, it is a haphazard arrange-
> ment that reflects the desire to manip-
> ulate external support and to pursue
> internal power aspirations. Being
> neither program nor budget, program
> structure is useless.[8]

Though Wildavsky's position is extreme, it is
based on his close observation of the actual workings

of PPBS where it has been tried in the federal government. In any case, his plea for program analysis, particularly analysis of the effects of marginal changes, appears highly justified, and this sort of analysis for police programs has been attempted in the research reported here. Chapters 3 and 4 concentrate on the measurement of the marginal costs and benefits of police program changes where a current policy decision was necessary (the traffic law enforcement program of the LAPD) or where there are important longer-term policy questions (methods of general police patrol). In the performance of these analyses, it became apparent immediately that the greatest need for knowledge lay in the typically unknown relationship between inputs and outputs in police work. That is, even if a program structure shows in great detail the objectives of a police department and the expenditures in each program objective category, it says nothing about how the expenditure really affects the program outputs (except that, presumably, but by no means necessarily, greater expenditure means greater output). As Isabel Sawhill observes: "In cost-benefit analysis perhaps the most difficult task is not measuring costs and benefits themselves but showing how they are related to each other--that is, estimating social production functions."[9]

In relating costs to benefits for most policy purposes, it is not necessary to know the full form of the social production function--that is, the resulting output for _every_ level of input. Rather, a more limited and more easily discovered form of the production function will usually suffice: the change in output related to a change (either increase or decrease) in inputs. In the provision of police protection, the concept of "total output" is ambiguous and almost certainly impossible to measure. For instance, if crime prevention is considered a police output, it is difficult to know the total number of crimes prevented by the presence of a police force because it is not known how many crimes would occur in the complete absence of a police force. However, it is certainly feasible to estimate how the number of crimes, or of traffic accidents, changes in response to a change in police manpower in a given

area. Also, in the process of investigating the relationship between inputs and outputs, the analyst
may be able to suggest improvements in the production process so that greater output can be produced
with existing inputs. This is the aim of the program analyses that follow.

In the investigations of police production
functions, the methods of controlled experimentation have been employed to produce new data and
multivariate regression analysis of existing data.
And the investigations have pointed up the value
for police research of more, and more scientific,
efforts in controlled experiments to provide necessary quantitative knowledge of police production
relationships.

Police departments, of all local government
agencies, are particularly well situated to carry
out such research because they typically have relatively great departmental discretion to undertake
temporary experimental allocations of their resources. Also, the input-output relationship is
relatively easy to observe because for many police
services there is no long time lag between the application of inputs and the ultimate output such as
occurs with other important governmental services,
for example, education or welfare services. This
belief in the great potential of scientifically
controlled experimentation to discover input-output
relationships in the public sector is shared by
Russell Ackoff, who has recommended that "planners
should develop a considerable experimental capabil-
ity. Drawing boards and social surveys are not
enough. If planning is to become scientific it has
no alternative but to become experimental."[10]

Despite the obvious value of measuring output
and estimating social production functions in areas
in which such attempts have been notably lacking,
there is a clear danger that enthusiasm for the
techniques of quantitative analysis of governmental
programs can lead analysts too far in the right
direction. Overreliance on what will for many
years inevitably be only tentative and partial
analyses should be avoided. As Amitai Etzioni
warns:

Most organizations under pressure to
be rational are eager to measure
their efficiency. Curiously, the
very effort--the desire to establish
how we are doing and to find ways of
improving if we are not doing as well
as we ought to do--often has quite
undesired effects from the point of
view of the organizational goals.
Frequent measuring can distort the
organizational efforts because, as a
rule, some aspects of its output are
more measurable than the others. Frequent measuring tends to encourage
over-production of highly measurable
items and neglect of the less measurable ones. . . . The distortion consequences of over-measuring are larger
when it is impossible or impractical
to quantify the more central, substan-
tive output of an organization, and
when at the same time some exterior
aspects of the product, which are
superficially related to its sub-
stance, are readily measurable.[11]

Throughout the following analyses an effort is
made to call attention to the unmeasurable aspects
of both costs and benefits of police services and
to emphasize that intangibles must be accorded as
much consideration as measured values.

The program analyses deal mainly with the
question of police service production relationships.
In Chapter 5 an examination of the distribution of
police service inputs and outputs among recipients
is made. Information is developed on the geographical distribution of services among units of local
governments in Los Angeles County, and this information is used to analyze an important and recurring
question of local and intergovernmental relations--
the legality and equity of police service finance in
California. Attention is focused on the particular
question whether some city residents are in fact
paying twice for police service, first for their

own municipal police department and again for a similar service provided to other residents of the same county by the sheriff's department. The investigation shows that, quite aside from the goal of greater efficiency in producing governmental services, an important contribution of program budgeting can be to help answer the questions, Who gets what? and Who pays for it?

2

POLICE GOALS
AND THE
PROGRAM BUDGET
STRUCTURE

The goals of organizations serve many
functions. They provide orientation
by depicting a future state of affairs
which the organization strives to re-
alize. Thus they set down guide lines
for organizational activity. Goals
also constitute a source of legitimacy
which justifies the activities of an
organization and, indeed, its very existence. Moreover goals serve as
standards by which members of an organization and outsiders can assess
the success of the organization--i.e.,
its effectiveness and efficiency.
Goals also serve in a similar fashion
as measuring rods for the student of
organizations who tries to determine
how well the organization is doing.
                          Amitai Etzioni[1]

Another function of goals can be added to
Etzioni's list. Organizational goals also provide
the basis for developing an output-oriented program
budget structure. In this chapter, alternative
formulations of a municipal police department's
goals will be examined, and recommendations for a
police program budget structure will then be made.
    Despite many statements of students of police
problems concerning the police purpose, the goals

(or missions or objectives) of urban police agencies
remain ill-defined.[2] Many of the statements that
pass as goal oriented are merely lists or descrip-
tions of the functions or activities (that is, means)
of an agency rather than of ends. A search of the
literature reveals no consistent idea of the ultimate objectives of the police. Indeed, O. W.
Wilson's standard text repeatedly stresses that the
purpose of a police agency is to provide a service
to the general public,[3] but at numerous points the
text contradicts this assertion.[4] Other investigators have found that the missions of the police
agency are (1) prevention of crime, (2) repression
of crime, (3) apprehension of criminals, and (4)
traffic control.[5] On the other hand, at least one
author, Gordon Misner, has correctly viewed these
as a functional breakdown that conforms well to the
actual activities of police departments; that is,
they are means, not ends. He has designated the
goals of the police to be made up of providing a
public service and maintaining peace and security.[6]

Just as no consistent, single statement can be
found among academic or other outside observers,
the agencies themselves also seem unable to provide
consistent statements of their own goals. Besides
eliminating crime and eliminating factors leading
to antisocial tendencies in persons, one agency also
sees one of its goals as being the development and
maintenance of "a favorable relationship with all
segments of the community."[7] Finally, the Los Angeles Police Department seems to feel that its own
goals are to protect persons and property and to
preserve the peace of the community.[8]

Clearly, there is no agreed-upon, well-defined
objective or output measure for police agencies
(for reasons that will be presented below). Perhaps, however, one is not needed. That is, a precise _abstract_ statement of the goals of an agency
may serve no purpose if the goals are unmeasurable
and one cannot be sure they are being met. And as
a practical matter, it is probably more valuable to
spend time defining operational goals that can be
communicated through the law enforcement system by
means of incentives to decision makers at all levels,
for ultimately the degree of success in meeting the

goals rests with these decision makers. At the
least, however, a consistent statement of police
goals will serve as a unifying force for organizing
programs and as a reference point for the more specific and quantitative operational objectives of
each program.

At the most abstract level the difficulty of
arriving at well-defined police objectives stems
from the unique relationship of the police and the
state. It is obvious that, realistically, without
public enforcement of the laws enacted by official
bodies (regardless of whether they are democrati-
cally elected or autocratic in nature) the state
would find it a difficult task to maintain its control and, perhaps, existence. It follows that the
most fundamental goals of the police are synonymous
with those of the laws that they are required to
enforce.

Criminologists tend to characterize the body
of law of a state as the expression of norms based
on accepted social values, deviations from which
cause harm that is countered by the imposition of
sanctions.[9] Thus law enforcement can be thought of
as the imposition of sanctions in order to maintain
the accepted values of society. In accordance with
this line of thinking, its mission would be con-
ceived of as the preservation of the existing order
as presented in the body of law.

Since definitions amenable to precise specification and measurement are needed for this study--
and since social values in economic analysis are
generally accepted as given--these general definitions are not immediately helpful. They merely
serve to emphasize the intimate relationship between
the laws of the state and the enforcement agencies
that seek to ensure compliance in order to meet the
accepted goals of the laws. An attempt to formulate
meaningful objectives for police agencies becomes,
in effect, a somewhat narrow effort to define the
goals of all law. In this sense the criminologists'
definition of law is useful. To the extent that
"acceptable social values" are those that define
the "proper" relationships between the various
decision-making units in society, order in all social, economic, and political relationships is

implied. The broadest objectives of law might be
to promote justice and to maintain an ordered en-
vironment (economic, social, and political). But
while the overall goals of the legal system are to
promote justice and social order, the goal of the
police within this system is a much more limited
one: to ensure the public peace and security envisioned by the law. Operationally, the more quantifiable half of this goal, security, may be stated
thus: The police should seek to minimize the cost
of illegal actions to society, with this cost interpreted as being both the harm done by criminals and
the cost of both police and private efforts to prevent it. This statement does not mean that the objective of the police is to reduce the level of
crime to zero; rather, the true objective is to reduce the amount of crime to some "optimal" level
below which the cost (in terms of additional police
resources) of reducing crime further is greater
than the resulting benefit (in terms of a reduction
in the harm caused by crime). Naturally, in pursuing this objective, the police must function as
only one part within the context of the whole criminal justice system, which also includes the courts
and correctional institutions.

This police objective is illustrated in Figure
2.1. In the graph both the cost to the community
of police resources and the social cost of illegal
acts are assumed to be functions of the total police
resources employed. It is assumed that the total
amount spent on police is a positively sloped linear
function of the amount of police resources employed
and that the social cost of illegal acts is a negatively sloped function. In such a situation the
best that can be done is to minimize the sum of
these two costs, which occurs at P police resources
employed and a total cost to society of C. This
"optimum" is obviously making the best of a bad situation. Naturally, these concepts need further re-
finement and the functional relationships must be
quantified before the objective as stated takes on
an operational meaning; the program analyses of
Chapters 3 and 4 attempt such quantification for two
important police programs--traffic law enforcement
and crime deterrent general patrol.

FIGURE 2.1

Minimizing Cost of Illegal Activities

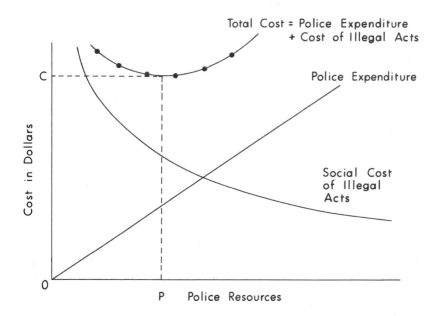

In addition to, and quite aside from, the basic police missions of dealing with crime and preserving public peace, the police have also been assigned a number of public service tasks only loosely related to the primary law enforcement task--and the role of the police in performing these tasks will be taken up subsequently.

MINIMIZING THE COST OF ILLEGAL ACTIVITIES

Since a main goal of the public police agency has been defined as a reduction in the social cost of illegal activities to a minimum level, it is necessary to examine the exact nature of the violations whose social costs are to be minimized. In

carrying out its primary mission, the public police
agency attempts to prevent violations and to apprehend violators of the laws that delineate individual
and property rights and that regulate public conduct.
However, only certain types of violations of the law
are customarily dealt with by the police, at least
at the local level. For instance, the police play a
relatively small part in preventing "white-collar"
crimes, such as tax evasion and antitrust violations.
Rather, the police deal in general with crimes that
are directly harmful to either persons or property;
by logical extension, or perhaps by default, the
police are also responsible for regulating automobile traffic.

Most broadly, violations dealt with by the police may be defined as actions, either individual
or collective, that impose prohibited consequences
on persons or property. But it is necessary to
recognize the wide diversity of illegal acts that
fall under this broad definition, and so for purposes of analysis violations, as they are dealt
with by a local police force, are divided here into
the following five violation categories: (1) violations of property rights, (2) violations of individuals' rights, (3) violations of regulations relating to moral conduct, (4) collective civil violations, and (5) traffic violations. Violations in
each of these categories, and their social costs,
are explored below.

Violations of Property Rights

Violations of property rights are crimes in
which property is either destroyed or transferred.
A net wealth loss to society occurs when property
is destroyed by such crimes as arson or vandalism;
an involuntary wealth transfer within society occurs when property is illegally taken from the owner,
as in burglary or embezzlement. The loss to the
victim of the crime is, of course, the same from
either type of crime, but in the case of transfer
the stolen property at least continues to be of use
to someone within the society, and there is also

the possibility of its restoration to the original
owner. The President's Commission on Law Enforcement estimated that in 1965 crimes against property
(both transfers and losses) amounted to almost $4
billion, of which about 8 percent represented net
losses to society through arson and vandalism and
the rest represented illegal transfers.[10] This
cost estimate, and others mentioned below, are inevitably very rough and intentionally conservative
but do provide useful ideas about relative magnitudes.

This neat distinction between net loss to society and pure transfer within society should be
qualified by the observation that theft of property
is often a very inefficient method of transferring
wealth and that an illegal transfer may be accompanied by significant net losses to society as a
whole, even when the gain to the criminals is included. If stolen property is more valuable to the
original owner than to the thief, the simple transfer from owner to thief results in a net reduction
in wealth for society.[11] The most familiar example
of such a loss is the loss that occurs when items
of significant personal value to the owner but of
small market value, such as heirlooms, are stolen;
the dollar value of the loss to the owner is greater
than the dollar value of the gain to the thief.
Measured in dollar terms, the net loss associated
with the transfer is the difference between the
value of the stolen article to the owner and its
value to the thief. Many stolen items fall within
the category of those that may be more valuable to
the original owner than to the thief, if only because many items have been chosen with some effort
to fit the tastes and requirements of the owner
(for example, clothes that fit the owner) and have
a small probability of being equally serviceable to
a thief.

Quite aside from the case of goods of particular use to a particular owner, a similar sort of
wealth loss may occur whenever goods rather than
money are stolen, because the market value of hot
merchandise is usually below the market value of
identical merchandise legally acquired. This low
value has two causes: First, hot goods have a

cloudy title, and if it is known to the purchaser
that they are stolen, he will be reluctant to pay
the full market price for them; this is especially
true for items that are readily identifiable, as by
a serial number. Second, a price must be paid for
fencing stolen goods; so an additional cost is incurred to transfer stolen merchandise to a point at
which it can be used again. This cost is probably
higher in cases in which the stolen goods possess
some means of identification, as automobiles do,
for then there is the difficulty of disguising,
modifying, or transporting the stolen goods before
they can be used or resold.

It has been argued that when property is transferred by criminal means the simple wealth transfer
aspect may often be accompanied by a net wealth loss
to society. But there is also a further reason to
believe that a net loss to society is associated
with criminal transfers. This further loss occurs
because criminals devote resources--labor time (including possible time spent in prison as a consequence of criminal activity) and their own capital--
to the criminal enterprise. If these resources were
instead devoted to legitimate activity, the total
output of society would be higher. The output that
is lost by having these resources devoted to criminal pursuits is another aspect of the social cost
of criminal property transfers distinct from and
additional to the transfer-associated wealth loss
previously described.[12]

If the value of real resources devoted to
achieving criminal transfers is equal to the value
of property transferred, then the entire transfer
represents a net loss to society. But it may be
that the typical thief's highest alternative earnings in legitimate activities are below those he
can earn in crime. As some observers have pointed
out, there is a strong empirical relationship between low income and the propensity to commit property crimes.[13] Thus, it is necessary to examine
the conditions under which average earnings in
crime would be found or not found to exceed foregone legitimate earnings. (Those to whom this may
seem an unnecessarily narrow economic analysis of

criminal earnings may wish to proceed directly to
the conclusions at the end of this discussion of
violations of property rights.)

The analysis applies only to property crime.
It assumes that a rational individual will choose
to devote his labor to alternative uses on the basis
of monetary returns plus the nonmonetary aspects of
the jobs.[14] Crime, of course, involves high risk as
well as other social disadvantages to the criminal,
and these aspects must be taken into account. Figure 2.2 illustrates the model. In this case an individual compares entering crime with his highest-
valued alternative legal job. Given the distribution of attitudes toward crime, it can be observed
how many persons would be willing to enter crime at
any given expected differential, E(d), between the
expected wages in crime, E(Wage$_C$), and the expected
wages in legal activity E(Wage$_L$).

A possible distribution is shown in Figure 2.2.
Note that some individuals might be willing to engage in crime even at negative expected differentials, whereas most individuals would require positive differentials. This variation could stem from
the higher risk associated with crime and the possible moral qualms on the part of many entrants,
particularly first offenders. From the distribution
of potential entrants to crime a cumulative supply
curve can be derived showing the total number of
persons in crime at each expected wage differential.
In this case the "typical" thief requires a positive
differential. Depending on the position and (or)
variance of the distribution, the differential
could be positive, negative, or zero. The equilibrium differential to be observed in the market would
be determined by curves reflecting the individual's
earning capabilities in crime.

As additional offenders enter crime, the average and marginal product curves decline (the ARP
and MRP curves in Figure 2.2). Although neither
curve reflects the usual sort of demand curve for a
factor, criminals can reasonably be expected to observe the diminishing marginal returns from additional crimes. Hence, the equilibrium earnings differential, $\hat{E}$(d), and equilibrium number of criminals,

FIGURE 2.2

Supply and Demand for Entrance into Crime

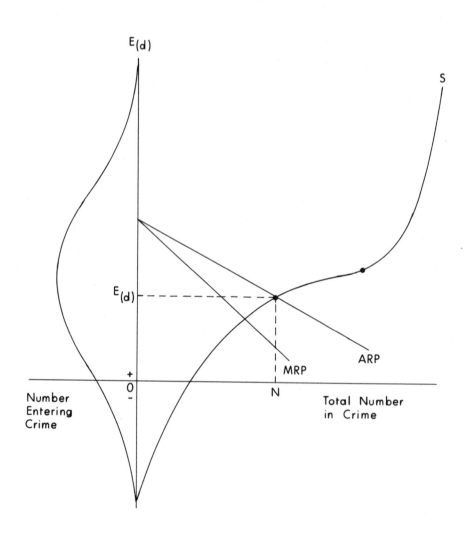

$\hat{N}$, will be determined by these curves. The equilibrium differential may be either positive or negative, depending on the positions of ARP and MRP.
If the equilibrium differential is positive, on
average, criminals will receive greater earnings in
crime than in legal activities. If the equilibrium
differential is negative, thieves on average can
earn more by entering legal activities.

At the intersection of the "demand" and "supply" curves the last thief who enters crime is in-
different between crime and legal activities. Thus,
the real opportunity cost of his activities at the
margin is the full value of his foregone legitimate
income. However, intramarginal criminals have a
lower supply "price" (that is, their $E(d)$ required
to enter this activity is lower), which is also below the ARP curve. These individuals will earn
"rents" by entering crime. For these criminals the
alternative foregone earnings in legal employment
would be less than their income from crime, and
thus the social cost of property crimes, in terms
of reduced legitimate output, would be less than
their criminal income.

Three reasons have emerged for believing that
the loss to victims from violations of property
rights are real costs to society. (1) In some cases
property is directly destroyed (arson or vandalism),
and the loss is obvious. (2) When property is
stolen, there is a net loss in wealth if the stolen
property has a higher value to the victim than to
the thief. (3) Criminals forego alternative legitimate activities, and the legitimate output thus
foregone (including the foregone earnings of incarcerated criminals) may in some cases approach the
full value to the criminals of the involuntary
transfers they effect. Thus, the cost of crimes
involving destruction of property is measured by
the full value of the property destroyed.[15] For
property crimes that involve transfers rather than
complete destruction, the net loss to society may
be below, equal to, or greater than the value of
property stolen (depending on the significance of
the second and third factors mentioned above), even
if the value to criminals of property stolen is

deducted from the cost of crime. If criminals are
excluded from the concept of society and transfer
gains to criminals are thus neglected, the cost of
criminal transfers is the full value to the owners
of the property stolen. As mentioned, the total of
transfers and losses amounted to approximately $4
billion in 1965.

Aside from the value of illegal transfers that
occur, property crimes also involve other important
costs that directly or indirectly affect the quality
of life, especially in urban areas. One far-reaching
aspect of high property crime rates is the disincentive effect that potential theft or vandalism has on
the ownership of certain kinds of property that are
particularly susceptible to criminal loss. If there
is a significant likelihood that property will be
stolen or destroyed, the expected value of such
property to its owner is reduced in proportion to
the likelihood of such loss. And this circumstance
tends to shift consumption in the legitimate sector
of society away from easily stolen or vandalized
goods and into relatively secure goods or locations.
This phenomenon may have far-reaching effects, even,
for instance, influencing the choice of residence in
a suburban rather than a central city location because of a fear of greater central city crime. Of
course, the cost to society of the distortions in
consumption caused by potential loss of property by
crime is very difficult to estimate. It depends on
the loss to consumers caused by a shift from the op-
tional no-crime consumption pattern to the less-
desirable pattern associated with the existing or
expected level of crime. If the shift is large, as
in the case of choice of residential location already mentioned, the reduction in welfare may also
be large. Further, this sort of loss to the legitimate sector does not result in any corresponding
gain to criminals; so the entire loss is a net social cost.

In addition to the loss in welfare caused by a
crime-induced shift in consumption patterns, ineffi-
ciencies may result from crime-induced shifts in
production patterns. Certain firms within an industry may, for a variety of reasons, be more "theft-
susceptible" than others. The firms that are

affected by a greater incidence of crime incur
higher operating costs becuase of (1) the actual
loss of goods and destruction of property, (2) the
need to pay higher wages to employees to compensate
for personal risk of injury,[16] (3) increased insurance rates, and (4) the need for greater outlays on
private protection. These higher costs lead to
higher prices and to lower output of goods and services of which the production is most affected by
crime. An especially important reason that an individual firm may incur relatively high crime-
related costs is simply geographical location in a
high-crime area. If the cost of doing business in
high-crime areas is not reflected in relatively low
rents, firms may be reasonably expected to charge
relatively high prices in the high-crime areas, or
perhaps to relocate to safer jurisdictions. The
cost of such a distortion of prices from what they
would be in a no-crime situation is, of course,
borne by the residents of the high-crime (and often
low-income) area.

Finally, in addition to the welfare loss caused
by a crime-induced shift in consumption and production patterns, there is also the direct cost of public and private expenditures to protect property
from crime. An enumeration of these cost elements
will clarify the concept. Public resource costs include expenditures by police agencies on property
crime prevention and deterrence and on investigation and apprehension. Also, the expenditures of
the criminal justice system on prosecution, incarceration, and rehabilitation are important elements.
For the state of California these costs are shown,
on the basis of criminal justice system expenditures
per crime, in Table 4.12. That table shows that for
most types of crime the average governmental expenditure subsequent to the commission of a crime exceeds
the average dollar loss to the victim.

Private costs about which there is little question are expenditures for crime prevention goods
and services, such as burglar alarms, safes, locks,
and guard services, and the overhead cost of providing property insurance. Also included in this category should be part of the cost of street lighting,
apartment house doormen, financial auditing, and

other measures that are to some extent provided to
counter possible crimes against property. The President's Commission estimated that in 1965, $1.35
billion was spent for private crime preventive service wages, and at least $200 million more was
spent for the purchase of protective equipment,
such as burglar alarms, bullet-proof glass, and so
forth.[17] Of course, most of these expenses are incurred to prevent crimes against persons (discussed
below) as well as against property, and it is impossible to make separate estimates of expenditures
devoted to property violation prevention and those
devoted to other types of crime prevention.

Actual crimes included in the violation of
property rights category are robbery, burglary,
grand theft, auto theft, larceny, and fraud.

Violations of Individuals' Rights

Violations against an individual include such
crimes of personal injury as homicide, manslaughter,
aggravated assault, and rape. A problem involved
in analyzing these crimes, especially homicide, is
that the act is often not carried out to benefit
the offender. Fairly frequent are judicial pleas
of innocence "by reason of insanity" and such
phrases as "crimes of passion," both of which imply
irrational behavior on the part of the violator.
What these phrases seem to mean is that carrying
out the crime did, at the time, benefit the offender but that the subsequent costs of the act, for
both the victim and the criminal, were ignored or
miscalculated by the criminal. That is, the severe
potential punishment did not enter as a constraint.

Also, some of these crimes are often committed
in order to carry out a property violation. To
that extent, the two types of crimes are jointly
produced by criminals, and police activities to
prevent one type will result in reduction of both.

Crimes against persons do not involve the possible transfer factors associated with property
violations; the full cost to the victims of such
crimes can be considered a cost to society.

Naturally, such costs are difficult to measure, and even the concept of an appropriate measurement is unclear. However, one concept of the loss to society when an individual is injured by crime is the present discounted value of his foregone earnings plus any medical expenditures required; in the case of death the cost according to this concept would amount to the full discounted value of all future earnings at the time of death. The President's Commission on Law Enforcement estimated the discounted earnings loss of homicide victims alone at $750 million in 1965.[18] Of course, it is impossible to make any accurate assessment of the economic value of human suffering occasioned by death and injury, but this further cost could substantially increase the cost calculated above.

In addition to the direct cost of crimes against persons just described, there are also additional costs similar to the ones associated with property crimes. Large public and private expenditures are made to prevent crimes against persons, and there is also the private cost related to the "fear of crime." Just as the possibility of theft or vandalism affects decisions about property ownership, the possibility of being the victim of a violation against one's person strongly affects behavior, in some instances extending to decisions about whether or not to venture out in certain areas, where to live, what form of transportation to use, and so forth. The magnitude of the cost associated with this kind of crime-induced alteration in behavior is, of course, extremely difficult to measure, but it must be very large in some areas. One aspect of the cost is the partial shift into safer alternatives, such as the use of taxis instead of subways at night. If individuals cannot shift into safer alternatives, they may be reasonably expected to ask for compensating increases in money wages or, possibly, decreases in money prices to compensate them for the additional risk. As an example, some portion of the higher wage differential for night work is clearly attributable to the risk of criminal victimization.

In general, the potential of crime against individuals raises the expected cost[19] to individuals

of any activity that involves exposure to such
crime. This change in relative costs shifts the
consumption pattern away from the no-crime pattern
to a less preferred pattern that takes into account
the possibility of being a victim of crime. The
shift in consumption patterns is, of course, no benefit to the criminal sector of society (indeed, it is
designed to make crime more difficult), and the cost
involved is wholly a cost to society. This sort of
loss to society does not necessarily involve additional expenditures on the part of potential victims
of crime; the loss may result merely from individuals' refraining from activities they would otherwise
undertake.

Violations of Regulations Relating
to Moral Conduct

In contrast to the crimes against individuals
described above, the crimes in violation of regulations relating to moral conduct are called (sometimes inappropriately) crimes without victims. They
constitute actions by individuals that, while not
being violations of another individual's rights, are
deemed by a majority of society to merit prohibition.
The reasons for forbidding such actions are of two
kinds: (1) the action will have a damaging effect
on the individual agent himself, of which he is un-
aware, and (2) the action will have a damaging effect on others.

Economically, these crimes represent neither
pure redistributions nor complete losses. Instead,
they appear to resemble transactions in which voluntary exchanges between buyers and sellers satisfy
both parties. That is, these "vices" reflect individual wants, and a price is paid to satisfy them.
Thus, gambling, prostitution, trafficking in narcotics, and so forth involve goods and services
that are made available by profit-making entrepre-
neurs.

Although the propensity to participate in "sin-
ful" activities of this sort is perhaps irrepres-
sible, society has agreed that such vices should be

restricted (one cannot but feel that the true goal
is merely to control rather than to eliminate the
activities). Hence, mores forbid the open expression of the wants involved and condemn the profitability incentives that exist for vendors of the
goods and services involved. There is, of course,
no unanimity of opinion about the sort of activities in this category that should be prohibited.
The legal concept of vice changes through time, and
it varies from state to state. For instance, laws
prohibiting the advertising and sale of birth control devices have been eliminated over time, and
laws governing gambling vary from state to state.
Thus, it is difficult to classify expenditures on
these and similar activities either as losses or as
criminal transfers, and it is also difficult to measure the benefit of efforts to prevent violations
or apprehend violators of such laws. Inevitably,
there is a certain amount of selective enforcement.

Nevertheless, it is clear that by prohibiting
gambling, abortion, and so forth, the law creates
black markets for the exchange of the goods and services involved. An unfortunate consequence is that
underworld elements generally become the main sup-
pliers of the goods because of their specialized
skills in avoiding detection, and they may even impose damages in excess of those that might result
if there were legalized but well-regulated sellers.
Indeed, the very illegality of the activities sometimes allows well-organized, large-scale criminal
monopolists to exploit further the profit incentives
that exist. Such monopolists are able to restrict
the market effectively because of the illegality of
the activity, which prohibits potential legal entry,
and by their own violent methods.

In light of the ambiguity surrounding the concept of damages done by these "crimes without victims," no single estimate of their cost can be satisfactory. One useful concept, however, is that the
cost to society of these violations is the value of
the resources used in the production of illegal
goods and services. This includes all wages, other
expenses, and profits, plus the value of foregone
earnings of incarcerated violators. As mentioned

in the discussion of criminal property transfers,
this value is an approximation of the value of
legal goods and services these resources <u>could</u> have
produced in legitimate activities. In contrast to
the situation in which resources are used to produce
criminal property transfers, in this case most of
the resources are used actually to produce an output
that is desired by at least some consumers. This is
the reason the value of the resources devoted to
these crimes must be used cautiously as a measure of
cost; by this measure, the President's Commission on
Law Enforcement estimated the cost of crime involving illegal goods and services to be about $8 bil-
lion, of which from $6 to $7 billion represents the
cost of gambling.[20]

In addition to the cost of producing illegal
goods and services, the cost of other crimes associated with crimes of vice is also to be considered;
an important example is the cost of property crimes
committed to support narcotics addiction. Failure
to control the sale of narcotics undoubtedly leads
to the commission by addicts of many property crimes
that would otherwise not have occurred. Thus, police efforts to reduce narcotics violations would
also reduce property violations, and costs-benefits
analysis of police narcotics programs must account
for this interrelationship.

In contrast to efforts to prevent crimes
against unwilling victims, efforts to prevent these
"crimes without victims" probably involve very little <u>private</u> cost; that is, almost no private expenditure on protective goods and services is attributable to defense against the occurrence of a violation in this category. Rather, the full cost of
combating these crimes is borne by the public police
agency.

Collective Civil Violations

Mass disorders should be treated as a distinct
kind of violation, or as a distinct kind of damage,
even though such group action is a combination of
individual violations. Riots, or macroviolations,

regardless of cause, require a police response that
is much different from that required by individual
crimes, or microviolations. Furthermore, the police
role prior to the occurrence of mass violations is
very different from that prior to individual violations. The National Advisory Commission on Civil
Disorders found that incidents involving the police
precipitated one-half of the riots examined by them
in 1967 and that most of these incidents began as
routine and proper police actions, such as stopping
a traffic-law violator.[21] Although the incidents
in no way "caused" the riots, the finding illustrates the fact that specialized police programs designed to cope with macroviolations must also encom-
pass riot-prevention measures. Of course, there
are police programs, such as youth recreation and
school visitation, of which the goal is to improve
the general conditions that are likely to lead to
mass violations, though they do not have the prevention of riots as a main goal; riot prevention remains a secondary goal of most activities designed
to deal with general conditions that create individual propensities to commit crime. This characteristic of police programs is shared by most urban programs dealing with low incomes, unemployment, racial
discrimination, and so forth. Even so, the police,
unlike other social agencies, do have specific programs devoted to controlling a riot once it has be-
gun. Such programs involve special training for
patrolmen, special weapons, strategic operations,
and so forth. They often involve outside police
agencies (state police, national guard, sheriff),
but the urban police still assume primary and initial responsibility for limiting the damage from
such disorders and arresting their progress. Again,
it is impossible to measure the number of riots prevented or to assess easily the contribution of the
police to prevention. But it is possible to assess
the social costs of mass disorders and thus the
benefits of preventing riots or limiting their
spread. For instance, in the Los Angeles riot of
1965, 34 persons were killed, 1,032 were injured,
and total property loss was estimated to be $40 mil-
lion.[22] The main task of a program budget in this

area would be to demonstrate the possible tradeoffs
between police programs dealing with micro- and
macroviolations and the losses resulting from each.

Traffic Violations

The majority of traffic violations (especially
moving violations) are different from other criminal violations in that when violators are detected,
potential damages are prevented. Or, at least,
this seems to be the assumption behind most traffic
laws. By contrast, most other criminal violations
are detected only after the damage or loss has been
incurred. The traffic violator is assumed to be a
person who, by carrying out the prohibited activity, say of speeding, will impose damages upon him-
self or others.[23] At the very least, the assumption is that there is a high probability that this
will occur.[24] In short, the act of speeding itself
may be harmless, imposing no costs upon society and
yielding a time saving to the motorist, but the
probability of an accident caused by speeding is
judged to warrant its regulation. Indeed, most
traffic enforcement policies clearly recognize that
a tradeoff exists between the twin objectives of
safety (prevent damages to persons and property)
and speed (prevent unnecessary time costs to motorists).

The relationships between types of violations
and traffic accidents and between violations and
deaths or injuries need to be scientifically studied
and measured more precisely than they have been to
date. It may be that the incidence of traffic accidents is difficult or impossible to affect by the
preventive or enforcement efforts of the police.
Scant evidence exists on which to base analytical
studies of the relative effectiveness of different
traffic law enforcement programs; the traffic law
enforcement experiment reported in Chapter 3 is an
attempt to relate the benefits of various types of
enforcement to their costs in order to determine
the most efficient allocation of resources to enforcement of traffic laws.

In evaluating the social costs of traffic accidents, distinction only between violator and victim is not always appropriate, since quite often those at fault suffer the damages and injuries. Thus, an estimate of the economic cost of traffic accidents should include (1) the reduction in output resulting from injuries and deaths from traffic accidents, (2) the medical expenditures caused by traffic accidents, (3) damages to property, and (4) the private and public agency costs associated with traffic accidents, including the police, safety equipment on automobiles, and administrative costs of automobile insurance companies. Of course, some estimate of the human suffering occasioned by traffic accidents is required for a true valuation of loss, but an economic measure of these costs has yet to be devised, even though they conceivably constitute the greatest source of loss.

The National Safety Council estimates that the national cost of traffic accidents in 1967, in terms of wages lost because of deaths and injuries, medical expense, administrative costs of insurance companies, and property damage, was between $10 and $11 billion.[25] While all this cost is not, of course, attributable simply to the violation of traffic laws, the figure does indicate that considerable benefits could be achieved by traffic law enforcement programs that reduce the number of motor vehicle accidents.

GENERAL COMMUNITY SERVICES

In addition to, or in conjunction with, the performance of law enforcement duties, the police have come to perform a significant number of secondary activities that in some cases take more of a police officer's time than do strictly criminal matters. The justifications for this circumstance fall into two broad categories.

First, the police force is a governmental agency that is available around the clock to respond to calls for service on very short notice. Policemen are therefore called on in many noncriminal

emergencies in which they render what are essentially general public services. The tendency to call on
the police in many emergencies is strengthened by
the fact that patrol officers are much of the time
not actually responding to crime calls, but engaged
in preventive patrol; thus, the apparent cost of
having patrol officers respond to general service
calls in their free patrol time is quite low, although time spent in responding to general, noncriminal service calls does, of course, reduce the probability that a patrol officer will be available to
respond to a crime call and that he will observe a
crime in progress. Also, the cost of having an additional governmental agency to respond at all hours
to the wide variety of emergency matters that the
police now deal with would probably be much larger
than the cost of having the police perform such
tasks.

The second reason for the police to provide
general, noncriminal services to the public is the
effect of this function on police-community relations. Quite aside from the value to the public of
the noncriminal services provided by the police,
these services often have the implicit goal of crime
prevention and are thus inputs contributing to protection. For example, many of the programs of an
urban police department are designed to improve the
relations between the police and lower income or
minority group citizens. While this is the espoused
goal, the ultimate aim of these programs is to improve the ability of the police to protect the public by increasing voluntary compliance with the law
by all citizens, thereby decreasing the probability
of a given citizen's becoming an offender. Voluntary compliance with the law is also a generalized
objective of many different social programs, such
as education and training, recreation, welfare, urban renewal, and so forth. Indeed, there seems to
be an implicit tradeoff between preventive programs
aimed at increased voluntary compliance and deterrent and other programs that enter later in the protective system. Also, the police rely on citizens
as the principal source of information about crimes
and suspicious behavior. Finally, close citizen-
police cooperation and support is required for

complainants and witnesses in prosecution efforts.
Naturally, in order for police provision of general
community services to contribute to the police protection goal, the police should not undertake noncriminal activities that cast them in adversary
roles. For instance, one of the costs of having
the police enforce traffic laws is the reduction in
public good will that may accompany citation by a
policeman for a traffic violation.

Later it will be desirable to classify police
programs not directly related to crime as either
directed toward improving police-community relations
or as providing a separate public service; but in
many cases these two objectives are served by the
same activity, and the joint nature of the production should be recognized.

POLICE PROGRAM BUDGET STRUCTURES

Now that both the goals of police departments
and the various police outputs that are produced
have been briefly discussed, the discussion can be
made use of in structuring existing police activities in terms of output-oriented categories. But,
before the alternative organizations of police activities into program budget structures are treated,
it is necessary to describe briefly the main activities that the police carry out. The activities can
be organized into three broad, functional groups:

1. The police attempt to _prevent_ future criminal activity by altering the conditions that lead
to crime. While they cannot very well change the
socioeconomic characteristics of persons or neighborhoods, they do attempt to provide information
and to affect attitudes.

2. The police seek to _deter_ potential criminals by maintaining a conspicuous and continuous
presence in the community and by being able to respond quickly to a reported crime. They do this
mainly through patrol activities, either on foot or
in cars.

3. Finally, when prevention and deterrence
fail, the police must _investigate_ crimes that do
occur and attempt to _apprehend_ individuals who have

committed them. Patrol officers initiate investigations because of their ability to respond quickly,
and detectives carry on the investigations if patrol
officers fail to apprehend the offenders.

As suggested earlier, all three activities are
directed toward the same goal: minimizing the cost
of crime to society. Thus, possible tradeoffs among
these three methods of attaining the same goal are
suggested. For example, given the existing mix of
preventive, deterrent, and investigative efforts,
would additional police resources devoted to preventive efforts (a school visitation program, for example) reduce the cost of crime--in terms of individuals injured or killed and property stolen or de-
stroyed--more or less than the same resources devoted to investigation of crime (new equipment for
a crime laboratory, for example). A police program
budget not only suggests such a question but also
is very useful in structuring the information necessary for an answer.

Though these three basic activities carried on
by the police have been distinguished, there is admittedly some overlapping among them. For instance,
investigation and apprehension serve both to prevent and to deter crime: when a professional burglar is apprehended and imprisoned, he is prevented
from committing additional offenses (at least for
some time), and the possibility that investigation
will lead to apprehension presumably deters a potential offender. However, these activities are very
dissimilar in their methods and target groups, and
the corresponding breakdown implied suggests a reasonable categorization of much police work.

In addition to the three traditional activities of prevention, deterrence, and investigation
of criminal law violations, the police force, as
mentioned before, also deals with traffic law violations and collective violations (public disorders
or riots) and provides noncrime public services of
various sorts. These activities must also be reflected in the program budget in a way that relates
agency cost information to basic objectives.

One possible organization of cost information
is presented in Table 2.1. The scope of this particular structure is quite broad, and some illustra-
tive programs have been included. Clearly this

structure is closely related to the existing organizational structures of most large city police departments. The primary deviation from traditional
organizational frameworks is that all traffic activities are disaggregated into programs of prevention, deterrence, and apprehension instead of being
classified as a separate "traffic" program. An advantage of this structure is that existing police
programs can be costed-out and allocated according
to major objectives.

TABLE 2.1

Major Police Program Categories

I. Protection of persons and property from
       illegal behavior
    A. Prevention of crimes to persons and
           property
        1. Community relations programs
        2. Traffic safety programs
    B. Crime deterrence and response
        1. Motorized patrol programs
        2. Foot patrol programs
        3. Traffic enforcement programs
    C. Apprehension of criminals
        1. General investigative programs
            a. Burglary-robbery-theft
            b. Fraud
            c. Homicide and assault
            d. Narcotics
            e. Juvenile
        2. Scientific investigation
        3. Accident investigation
        4. Incarceration and conviction

II. Provision of public services
    A. General community service programs
    B. Provision of emergency services
    C. Regulation of noncriminal behavior

Source: Prepared by the authors.

One problem arises, however, when an attempt
is made to measure the output of preventive and deterrent programs. It cannot be known how many
crimes are prevented by programs in category IA or
deterred by programs in IB (Table 2.1). That is,
it is impossible to predict the number of violations
that would have occurred in the absence of most of
these programs. Only carefully controlled field experiments can yield such information, and, at best,
the data would be merely approximations.

A second observation to be made about Table 2.1
is that its organization treats all prohibited activities as equally criminal types of violations and
does not differentiate among efforts to reduce the
three or four commonly accepted types of violations
(and the consequences imposed by them). This is not
the case with the structure presented in Table 2.2.
In it programs are organized to conform to the outputs of police agencies in the form of protecting
persons and property from three types of crimes and
of providing traffic control and general public services. This structure has the advantage of permitting a focus on the broad programs of prevention,
deterrence, and apprehension. Also, measuring the
amount and value of protection afforded to individuals from the various types of crime is easier, because of the greater availability of statistics by
types of crime and because not all law violations
are equally important in terms of the costs they
impose.

Though no delineation has yet been made of the
many programs that exist in a large urban police department, it appears obvious that some programs contribute both to protection and to general public
service. For example, many juvenile service programs dealing with recreation are clearly designed
to prevent delinquency. The recreational activities
provided to youths are a valuable output in themselves but also serve as an input in the police effort to prevent juvenile, and subsequent adult, delinquency. Some community relations programs to improve the police image in the ghetto are other examples.

Although published material on police program budgeting is not voluminous, an interesting program budget structure was presented by the President's Commission on Law Enforcement and Administration of Justice, also known as the Crime Commission.[26] The commission's urban police program budget is presented in Table 2.3 in abbreviated form, primarily to reveal what has been done and to compare it with the program structures presented in this study.

A comparison of the Crime Commission Program Budget (CCPB) arrangement with Table 2.1, the first budget of this study, reveals that they both treat all legally prohibited activities as "crime." However, Table 2.1 is less detailed in that it does not break out traffic or collective violations, whereas the CCPB does. A major goal expressed in the CCPB is to control and reduce crime, whereas that of Table 2.1 is to protect persons and property or minimize the damages from illegal behavior. Second, the CCPB does not differentiate between "community type" preventive programs and efforts at deterrence or suppression.

The CCPB and Table 2.2 are more similar. However, the goals or missions of Table 2.2 have been expressed in more quantifiable terms and less generally, even though protection is still the implied goal.

As another alternative it may be valuable to organize information about police programs in terms of recipient groups in order to elucidate particular policy decisions. For the distribution of police services among citizens is an important--though difficult and often underemphasized--public policy consideration. Local police protection, unlike national defense, is not necessarily provided in equal amounts to all citizens of a police jurisdiction. In the case of national defense, essentially the same protection from foreign aggression is provided to all citizens of the nation, and although different persons may value differently the protection thus afforded, they all receive the same amount of protection (that is, national defense is an example of a "pure" public good). However, even within the

TABLE 2.2

Police Program Structure: Major Goals Expressed in Quantifiable Terms

I. Minimize injuries, deaths, and property loss caused by criminal behavior
   A. Preventive programs
      1. General community relations
      2. Special target group community relations
      3. Community relations
   B. Deterrent programs
      1. Patrol
      2. Crime task force
   C. Investigation and apprehension
      1. Personal injury violations
      2. Property violations
      3. Pretrial incarceration and conviction

II. Minimize damages caused by violations of the moral code
   A. Preventive programs
      1. Narcotics information
      2. School visitation
   B. Deterrent programs
   C. Investigation and apprehension
      1. Narcotics violations
      2. Gambling violations
      3. Pretrial incarceration and conviction

III. Minimize damages to persons and property caused by collective violations
   A. Riot prevention programs
      1. Community relations programs
      2. Minority youth programs

B. Riot control programs
   1. Special equipment and training
   2. Advance planning
C. Control of minor disorders
   1. Public events
   2. Family disputes
   3. Other disorderly conduct

IV. Minimize cost of traffic movement and traffic accidents
A. Accident prevention programs
   1. Information analysis
   2. Community education
   3. Assistance to citizens (community relations)
B. Accident deterrence programs
   1. General patrol
   2. Selective traffic law enforcement patrol
   3. Apprehension and conviction
C. Reduction in traffic congestion
   1. Traffic direction
   2. Parking regulation enforcement
   3. Control of conditions

V. Provide general public services
A. Emergency services
B. Informational services
C. Missing persons
D. Others

Source: Prepared by the authors.

39

TABLE 2.3

Crime Commission Police Program Budget

I. Control and reduction of crime program
   A. Prevention and/or suppression
      1. General-purpose patrol
      2. Special-purpose patrol
      3. Intelligence
      4. Community relations
   B. Investigation and/or apprehension
      1. Crimes involving major risk of personal injury
      2. Crimes not involving major risk of personal injury
      3. Vice
   C. Prosecution
      1. Interrogation
      2. Preparation for trial
      3. Trial
   D. Recovery of property
      1. Autos
      2. Other personal property
      3. Commercial property
   E. General Support
      1. Communications
      2. Records and data processing
      3. Technical services

Movement and control of traffic program
   A. Traffic movement
      1. Direction of traffic
      2. Enforcement of traffic-oriented parking rules
      3. Emergency road services
      4. Identification and reporting of congestion points

B. Traffic safety
   1. Enforcement of regulations
   2. Driver training
   3. Educational programs
   4. Vehicle inspections
C. Accident investigation

III. Maintenance of public order program
   A. Public events
      1. Sporting events
      2. Public ceremonies
   B. Minor disturbances
      1. Private quarrels
      2. Parties
      3. Drunkenness
      4. Dereliction
      5. Miscellaneous nuisances
   C. Civil disorder
      1. Prevention
      2. Suppression

IV. Provision of public services program
   A. Emergency services
      1. Fire
      2. Medical
      3. Power failure
      4. Flood
      5. Civil defense
      6. Miscellaneous
   B. Missing persons
   C. Lost property
   D. Miscellaneous

Source: Task Force Report: Science and Technology, President's Commission on Law Enforcement and the Administration of Justice (Washington: Government Printing Office, 1967), pp. 83-87.

jurisdiction of a single local police department
the level of police service (which can be defined
in several different ways) that is afforded to different groups may vary significantly. The distribution of police services is necessarily organized
according to geographical areas instead of by specific types of recipients (income class, race, etc.),
but in many cases geographical location is a good
proxy for the socioeconomic categorization, and in
such cases a geographical breakdown of information
can be very illuminating. When police cost figures
and output (service) indicators are examined in a
geographical breakdown, it is possible to see in a
rough way who is receiving how much service at what
cost. For instance, in 1967 Los Angeles was divided
into 16 police divisions (subsequently into 17 divisions) for purposes of administration. If police
expenditure per capita in each division is taken as
a measure of service to residents, one ranking of
service levels in the divisions is arrived at, and
(excluding the Central Division, which has a very
small residential population) the highest expenditure per capita is 3.4 times the lowest expenditure
per capita.[27] An alternative measure of police
protective service level is the crime rate reported
in each division. The division crime rate, in terms
of reported offenses per 1,000 residents per year,
is an indicator of the likelihood that a division
resident will be a victim of crime. Since reduction
in crime is an output of the police department, a
low crime rate corresponds to a high level of service, and a high crime rate corresponds to a low
level of service. If the crime rate in terms of
Part One offenses[28] per 1,000 residents in each division is taken as the measure of police service,
the ranking is almost a perfect inverse of the previous ranking: those divisions that score high in
terms of police expenditure per capita also have
the highest crime rates (that is, lowest service);
again excluding the Central Division, the highest
reported crime rate is 2.8 times the lowest.[29] The
full divisional ranking of input and output indicators is shown in Table 2.4. The strong inverse
correlation between inputs and outputs does not, of

TABLE 2.4

Example of Divisional Breakdown of Distribution of Police Services in Los Angeles

Division	Input Indicator: Rank Order of Input (1 is high)	Input Indicator: Police Expenditures per Capita (in dollars)	Output Indicator: Rank Order of Output (1 is high)	Output Indicator: Crime Victimization Rate per 1,000, for Part One Offenses
Central	1	210	16	333
Newton	2	45	15	116
77th Street	3	36	14	107
University	4	33	13	89
Hollywood	5	29	12	82
Rampart	6	28	11	68
Hollenbeck	7	28	9	59
Harbor	8	26	10	66
Wilshire	9	25	8	70
Highland Park	10	20	3	44
Van Nuys	11	20	6	54
North Hollywood	12	18	5	51
West Los Angeles	13	18	2	41
Venice	14	17	7	57
Foothill	15	15	1	41
West Valley	16	13	4	47

Source: Statistical Digest, Los Angeles Police Department (Los Angeles, 1967).

course, indicate that a larger force of policemen
causes more crime, but rather that the number of
police officers per capita in each division is only
one among many factors that affect the crime rate.

Naturally, the population of each division is
the most important factor affecting the crime rate,
and the basic crime-inducing characteristics of our
society are largely beyond the control of the police.[30] It is even questionable that the police
can have much influence on certain kinds of crime,
such as homicide committed by a member of the victim's own family, and thus a crime rate purporting
to indicate the level of protective service achieved
by the police should exclude those crimes found
least susceptible to police control. Further, not
all crimes are of equal importance, and a crime rate
obtained by simply adding together different types
of crimes will obviously give a misleading picture
(except in the unlikely event that the division's
patterns of crime are identical, and that the only
variation among divisions is in the total number of
crimes). Thus, although the number of Part One offenses per 1,000 residents is a rough indicator of
the level of exposure to crime in each division, it
is defective as a measure of the relative service,
protection from crime, that each division receives
for at least four reasons: (1) The police can have
relatively little effect on the commission of some
Part One crimes (such as homicide within a family)--
which implies that such crimes should not be included
in a crime rate that is intended to measure police
protection.[31] (2) Not all Part One crimes are of
equal seriousness--which implies that each type of
crime should be weighted according to its importance.
(3) Crimes other than Part One offenses should also
be considered. (4) The proportion of total crimes
reported to the police may vary among divisions,
whereas the total, not just the reported, crime
rate[32] is the appropriate indicator of the level of
protection from crime afforded to residents of each
division.

It is very difficult to construct an ideal
measure of the crime rate, one that would indicate
the level of protection afforded to residents of

each division--which problem will be dealt with
later in connection with the discussion of alternative output measures for police patrol forces. It
should be noted here, however, that, in addition to
the crime rate in each area, there are several other
reasonable measures of police service; for instance,
average response time to a crime call is another
measure of the service level provided by the police
in each division.

Even if it was possible to devise an ideal
measure of the crime rate, one that accurately measured the probability of a resident's becoming a
victim of crime, weighted by the importance of the
crime, in each division, there would remain a very
important problem in the distribution of police
protective services. This problem is that the goal
of providing equal protection from crime to all
groups, in the sense of an equal crime rate in each
division of the city, may conflict with the alternative desirable goal of minimizing the total number
of crimes in the city as a whole.[33] The basis of
this conflict is illustrated in Figure 2.3.

Consider two police divisions within a city,
divisions 1 and 2. Assume that because of complicated social forces, including lack of employment
opportunities in division 1, for any given number
of policemen per capita the crime rate would be
higher in 1 than in 2. Given the total police resources (including policemen and equipment) available, an allocation of police officers that would
result in an equal crime rate per capita in divisions 1 and 2 would necessarily involve a much
higher ratio of policemen per capita in 1 than in 2.
Such a situation is illustrated in the figure, where
both divisions have the same crime rate, A, while
division 1 has D (point C) and division 2 has E
(point B) policemen per capita. If instead both divisions were allocated the same number of policemen
per capita (equality in an input rather than an output sense), division 1 would have a much higher
crime rate than would division 2.

The police cost per capita and crime rate data
mentioned earlier imply that Los Angeles police
forces are allocated to produce a compromise between
the two concepts (input and output) of equality:

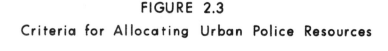

FIGURE 2.3

Criteria for Allocating Urban Police Resources

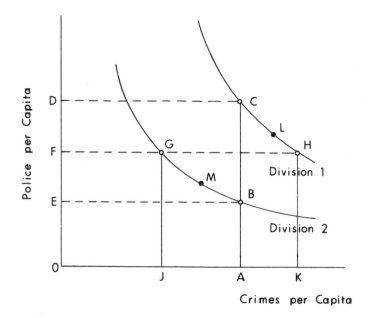

many more policemen per capita are allocated to
high-crime areas than to low-crime areas, but the
concentration of police in the higher-crime areas
is not carried so far as to produce an equal crime
rate in all divisions.

The conflict between the goal of equality in
crime rate among divisions and the goal of minimizing the total number of crimes in the city occurs when, given an allocation of the police force
that produces equality among all divisions in terms
of the crime rate, the marginal product of a police
officer is higher in one area than in another. In
terms of Figure 2.3, suppose police resources are
allocated so that the crime rate in each division
is A (that is, there are D police per capita in

division 1, and E police per capita in division 2);
suppose also that an additional police officer in
division 1 reduces the number of crimes per year by
5 and that an additional policeman in division 2
reduces the number of crimes per year by 10: in
this situation the total number of crimes in the
city would be reduced by 5 if one officer were removed from division 1 (increasing the number of
crimes there by 5) and assigned to division 2 (decreasing the number of crimes there by 10). In
general, the total number of crimes in the city
will be minimized only when the marginal effect of
an additional policeman on the number of crimes is
the same in each division; otherwise, it would always be possible to reallocate police resources
from a division in which the marginal product of
police resources is lower to one in which the marginal product is higher and thereby reduce the total number of crimes in the city. Assuming that
diminishing returns (in terms of the number of
crimes prevented) are associated with increasing
the number of police in any division, such transfers
of police, if carried far enough, would eventually
lead to an equal marginal productivity of police
resources in all areas (and thus a minimization of
the total number of crimes). In graphical terms,
this situation would occur where the slopes of the
two curves in Figure 2.3 are equal (points L and M).

The purpose of emphasizing here the important
geographical aspect of the distribution of police
services is not to advocate any one particular criterion for deciding the optimal allocation of police resources (assuming, in the first place, that
they can be adequately measured), but rather to
point out that an important function of police program budgeting is to provide data with which to
make an informed decision. Since many police services must necessarily be provided on a geographically oriented basis and since there is considerable
ambiguity in measuring the level of services that
any area is actually receiving, it should be very
useful to display cost and performance data with a
geographical breakdown corresponding to the geographical organization of the police department.

Such a structure is presented in Table 2.5, which
is a reiteration of Table 2.2 for each police division within the city.

In addition to providing a rationale for making decisions about the allocation of police services among the different police divisions, Table
2.5 has the advantage of suggesting the possibility
of having a different mix of police programs within
each division. The results of a tradeoff between,
say, a preventive program (community relations) and
a deterrent program (more patrol units) in a high-
crime-rate area may be very different from the results of the same tradeoff in a low-crime-rate area,
and the divisional breakdown of programs and outputs
encourages specific attention to the optimal combination of programs in each area.

A detailed allocation of expenditures of the
Los Angeles County Sheriff's Department according
to geographical and jurisdictional location of service recipients is undertaken in Chapter 5. It is
used there to examine possible inequities in the
distribution of sheriff's department services between city residents and residents of unincorporated
areas in Los Angeles County. That study clearly
demonstrates the usefulness of geographical service
distribution data that could be provided by a program budget.

ESTIMATES OF PROGRAM EXPENDITURES

Following a general examination of law enforcement objectives, the next step might reasonably be a complete cost analysis of program expenditures for the five major programs suggested in
Table 2.2; this would require detailed examination
of all current police activities to determine which
of the program categories each activity contributed
to and a subsequent allocation (or "crosswalking")
of the expenditures for these activities from the
line-item expenditure budget to the program budget
accordingly. To obtain precise program cost figures, however, a strenuous reformulation of data
collection techniques is required, and this is one

of the too infrequently mentioned costs of constructing and presenting a program budget. Such an
estimation of program cost figures is especially
difficult because most police activities contribute
to more than one program goal, and there is no completely satisfactory way to allocate the joint
costs of such activities among programs. For instance, traffic law enforcement patrol contributes
to some extent to crime deterrence, because traffic
officers can make criminal violation arrests; conversely, officers assigned to crime deterrent patrol
also issue traffic violation citations. In such
situations it is very difficult to say confidently
how much is spent on each program.

In light of these difficulties the Los Angeles
Police Department (cooperating with the authors)
chose to construct an unusually detailed program
cost analysis for less than the full department,
rather than attempt a less detailed and less accurate estimation of all police programs--the results
of which are described below. As illustrations of
the results of broader and less detailed cost analyses of complete program budget structures, program
budgets, with expenditure data, developed for the
police departments of Detroit and Philadelphia, are
reproduced as supplements to this chapter and discussed following the presentation of the Los Angeles
Police Department's traffic program budget.

Expenditure Estimate for the Traffic
Program Structure

A detailed program structure for the Traffic
Bureau of the Los Angeles Police Department is presented in Table 2.6. It suggests the inclusion of
information on output and performance indicators as
well as the conventional expenditure data for programs. The program structure is an expansion of
the traffic program component of the full program
budget structure presented in Table 2.2 and uses
the terminology adopted by the authors to describe
the various programs and subprograms that contribute
to police control of traffic.

TABLE 2.5

Police Program Structured on a Geographical Basis

I. Minimize injuries, deaths, and property loss caused by criminal behavior in
   A. Area One
      1. Prevention
      2. Deterrence
      3. Investigation and apprehension
   B. Area Two
      1. Prevention
      2. Deterrence
      3. Investigation and apprehension

II. Minimize damages caused by violations of the moral code
   A. Area One
      1. Prevention
      2. Deterrence
      3. Investigation and apprehension
   B. Area Two
      1. Prevention
      2. Deterrence
      3. Investigation and apprehension

III. Minimize damages to persons and property caused by collective violations
   A. Area One
      1. Riot prevention
      2. Riot control
      3. Control of minor disorders

B. Area Two
   1. Riot prevention
   2. Riot control
   3. Control of minor disorders

IV. Minimize cost of traffic movement and traffic accidents
   A. Area One
      1. Accident prevention
      2. Accident deterrence
      3. Reduction in traffic congestion
   B. Area Two
      1. Accident prevention
      2. Accident deterrence
      3. Reduction in traffic congestion

V. Provision of general services
   A. Area One
      1. Emergency services
      2. Informational services
      3. Missing persons
      4. Others
   B. Area Two
      1. Emergency services
      2. Informational services
      3. Missing persons
      4. Others

<u>Source</u>: Prepared by the authors.

51

TABLE 2.6

Traffic Bureau Program Structure

Program: Traffic control and enforcement

    Objective: To minimize costs of traffic accidents and traffic movement

    Output Indicator: Number of traffic accidents and incidence of congestion

A. Subprogram: Accident prevention

    Objective: Reduce citywide or divisional traffic accident rate by informing and educating public

    Output Indicator: Number of traffic accidents in city or division

    1. Program element: Assistance to governmental agencies

        Objective: Provide traffic accident information to courts and other governmental units

        Performance Indicator: Number of reports requested

    2. Program element: Community education

        Objective: Provide traffic education to individual drivers

        Performance Indicator: Number of drivers receiving information

    3. Program element: Community relations

        Objective: Provide general assistance to individual motorists

        Performance Indicator: Number of assistance calls answered

B. Subprogram: Accident deterrence

    Objective: Reduce accident rate through traffic law enforcement

    Output Indicator: Number of traffic accidents in city, division, or beat

    1. Program element: Patrol

        Objective: Reduce number of traffic accidents through deterrent patrol

        Output Indicator: Number of traffic accidents by patrol beat

        Performance Indicator: Number of blocks provided with a standard level of surveillance

52

2. Program element: Apprehension and conviction
   Objective: Cite violators of traffic laws
   Output Indicator: Number of traffic accidents by patrol beat
   Performance Indicator: Number of citations per officer or per beat

C. Subprogram: Reduction of traffic congestion
   Objective: Reduce obstructions to optimal rate of traffic flow
   Output Indicator: Time of specified trip or time of trip on specified beat
   1. Program element: Traffic direction
      Objective: Maintain or increase flow of traffic at specific locations
      Performance Objective: Number of vehicles passing specific point per unit
      of time (in peak hour)

   2. Program element: Parking regulation
      Objective: Regulate time and duration of use of on-street parking
      Output Indicator: Reduction in congestion at peak hours
      Performance Indicator: Number of parking citations

   3. Program element: Control of conditions
      Objective: Minimize congestion by engineering changes
      Output Indicator: Reduction in congestion resulting from changes effected
      Performance Indicator: Number of engineering changes effected

<u>Source</u>: Prepared by the authors.

53

For each program package an objective is specified, and, when possible, a quantitative indicator
of the output and (or) performance level is suggested. The performance indicators are included to
suggest possible criteria for work measurement by
lower level administrators (often at the task or
activity level rather than at the subprogram or
element level). Within the three principal subpro-
grams--accident prevention, accident deterrence,
and congestion reduction--a number of program elements are proposed. The latter could be reduced
further to the common denominator of all program
structures, the activity or task level.

Output measures for the accident prevention
program elements have been omitted, not because they
cannot be specified but because it is difficult in
this case to link program input with output. The
relationship, if any, between inputs and the reduction of traffic accidents is less direct for accident prevention programs than for the others; that
is, it is difficult to relate traffic accidents to
the number of accident reports distributed or the
number of persons reached by educational efforts
(performance measures).

The structure proposed for the traffic bureau
should constitute a framework for accounting for
both the monetary value of inputs (cost) and the
physical level of output and (or) performance. Cost
and effectiveness measures are presented in a single
document (this is discussed in Chapter 4) and can
be compared on an annual basis. Of course, it still
remains for administrators to assign value weights
to the incommensurate physical indicators in the
table.

Actual 1967/68 budgetary figures from the LAPD
are presented for the traffic bureau in Table 2.7.[34]
The total expenditure for each program and subprogram is shown in column 5, and for each program and
subprogram the breakdown of total expenditure according to expenditures by the existing organizational subunits of the traffic bureau is given in
columns 1 through 4. The bureau's operating divisions closely parallel the program structure in
that each of the four divisions accounts for at

TABLE 2.7

Cost Data for Proposed Traffic Bureau Program Structure
(thousands of dollars)

Programs and Subprograms	Traffic Services Section (1)	Traffic Enforcement Division (2)	Accident Investigation Division (3)	Parking and Intersection Control (4)	Total Program Expenditures (5)
Accident prevention	58	163	564	6	793
Accident information (Assistance to governmental agencies)	35	8	326	0	370
Community relations (Education)	4	3	0	0	7
Assistance to citizens (Acceptance)	19	152	238	6	416
Accident deterrence	38	3,471	1,731	273	5,514
Patrol	16	2,556	1,110	268	3,950
Apprehension of violators	22	915	621	5	1,564
Reduction of traffic congestion	27	79	112	1,396	1,613
Control of conditions	19	44	108	12	182
Traffic directing	4	31	3	1,211	1,249
Parking regulation	4	4	1	173	182
Total Bureau Expenditures	123	3,713	2,407	1,675	7,919

Source: Prepared by the authors; derived from data supplied by the Advance Planning Group, Los Angeles Police Department, for 1968.

least 60 percent of the total outlays associated
with its primary program. For example, 70 percent
of accident prevention program costs are incurred
by the Accident Investigation Division; the Traffic
Enforcement Division accounts for 63 percent of the
accident deterrence program; the Parking and Intersection Control Division is responsible for 87 percent of traffic congestion program expenditures.

Note that the table could have been organized
quite differently. Subprograms could have been
further broken down into the activities performed
by line officers within the operating divisions.
In fact, the program elements of this table are
composed of groupings of even more finely defined
activities, which form the basis for crosswalking
from the existing bureau budget to the program budget. (See Supplement 1 of this chapter for derivation of the data.) A slight departure from normal
crosswalking procedure--which refers to the derivation of program expenditures from the regular line
items of the administrative budget--this budget
crosswalks from operating bureaus to programs. This
approach was taken partly for convenience; but it
also seems to be a more informative statement than
the usual crosswalk. For instance, since it reveals
the sources of the estimates for the programs, the
same data can be used even if a different framework
is to be estimated. Also, it avoids losing sight of
the operating divisions in the drive to build the
program structure; since existing operating division
management processes are inevitably very important
to the success of the fully implemented program budget structure, a program budget structure should not
be constructed without recognition of them.

How is the police administrator aided by this
structure? First, the structure cuts across existing operating divisions--and, indeed, the table
highlights the fact that each division contributes
to several subprograms and program elements. These
organizational entities should be used principally
for data collection purposes rather than for program
analysis.

A second advantage of the program structure is
that separate program elements can be evaluated, to
some extent, in terms of annual costs and output

levels. Thus, an administrator can observe the resulting effect on output of an alteration in the
allocation of resources in one program element or
from one to another. Such expenditure data, being
annual, may be too crude to provide a basis for
lower-level decisions although they will probably
suffice for higher-level tradeoff decisions. Also,
annual comparisons can be made within the same program element. Thus, whether or not input alterations are made, the effectiveness of the resource
allocation can be reviewed over time. Moreover,
when the same output or performance indicators are
used for different program elements, the program
elements can be directly compared. It should be
noted, however, that output indicators for different programs may not be directly comparable, and a
scheme of output weights may be necessary; for
example, to compare the effectiveness of police resources in the traffic and criminal programs, it
may be necessary to assume that the social cost of
one injury traffic accident equals that of five
burglaries. Ideally, the physical measures of output for different programs can be converted into a
common unit, such as dollars, but this method requires estimates of social benefits for each physical output. (These problems of output measurement
and interprogram comparison are discussed in detail
in the program analyses of traffic law enforcement
in Chapter 3 and deterrent patrol in Chapter 4.)
    It should be pointed out that some differences
in the traffic program structure would occur if a
complete program budget structure for Los Angeles
City or Los Angeles County was being constructed.
In fact, the organization of major programs by common purpose and across agency lines has been ignored in this discussion of budget structure. The
police have been discussed in isolation from other
programs even though their activities interact with
programs of other municipal departments--welfare,
recreation, and transportation being some examples.
As a case in point, a portion of the traffic control subprogram proposed above may fit more accurately within a transportation program than a police
(protection) program. The function of traffic

control is to reduce traffic accidents and congestion, both of which impose economic costs on individuals. However, congestion involves factors beyond safety and violations of traffic regulations;
expenditures of the traffic police aimed at reducing
congestion contribute to the rapid movement of goods
and people, serving, in effect, the same purpose as
expenditures by the urban transportation system.
Police decisions that affect congestion and traffic
volume on streets certainly affect these variables
on freeways and within the mass transit system.
This is not to say that allocating police traffic
expenditures to a transportation program will always
be a better procedure.[35] The preferred procedure
would be to allocate only the congestion portion of
traffic outlays to transportation and the safety
portions to the protection program.

Expenditure Estimates for Total
Police Program Structure

The supplements to this chapter include two program statements, for the police departments of Detroit (Supplement 2) and Philadelphia (Supplement 3),
each including program expenditure estimates. The
Detroit budget reveals a lack of a general, agency-
wide, long-run point of view; merely knowing the
relative magnitudes of the programs is not very
useful. The Philadelphia budget is organized across
agency lines and takes a longer-run view; it ar-
ranges a great deal of important information into a
single structure. Still, neither of these estimated
structures reveals all the conventionally stated
advantages of a program budget. Accordingly, it
may be useful to review briefly the claims often
made for a program structure and to examine these
in the context of an example from the Los Angeles
Police Department.
     As a revised budgetary exhibit the program
budget is said to be a link between economic efficiency and the political aspects of public production of goods and services. This link is enhanced
by the two principal characteristics of a program

budget different from the conventional, line-item budget: (1) it is output oriented, and (2) it takes a longer-run view of programs. The output orientation is the source of most of a program budget's advantage. It focuses on what is produced instead of what is purchased, and so the budget becomes a technique for improving resource allocation rather than an administrative device to control expenditures. In addition, explicit consideration of the social goals of urban government and its subsidiary agencies is forced. Lower level administrators are forced to reveal, or at least to consider, "what they are doing" by selecting output measures. The latter are used to gauge "how well they are doing" their perceived tasks. Thus the effectiveness and cost of various programs can be expressed with respect to identified goals and output measures.

The second characteristic, a longer time horizon, is necessary because many new programs (or additional allocations to existing programs) imply an obligation for future outlay. The program budget should reveal all the time-phased stages at which costs will be incurred if a program alteration is adopted. Through this, long-run financial planning is aided and integrated with the allocation and budgeting process.

The two budgets in the supplements of this chapter incorporate both these characteristics in some measure but still do not convey the advantages envisioned by PPBS enthusiasts. Even the inclusion of output statements and measures in the structure in Supplement 3 does not seem to support the claim that cost-effectiveness analysis is facilitated by the budget alone. In fact, as mentioned above, it is unlikely to do so because most analyses should examine the relationship between marginal, rather than average or total, costs and benefits; and, in addition, output measures in an annual budget document ignore many nonagency social costs, agency spillovers, and, often, social benefits.

The program classifications presented above and in the supplements represent some of the dimensions of police production and distribution

activities. Any given level of police output can
ideally be described by a vector of physical quantity and quality measures. At the same time, these
components are likely to be determined by the major
policy issues associated with police production and
distribution. That is, activities performed can be
arranged into different program packages so as to
highlight important budgetary (resource) allocation
decisions, and the choice of packages necessarily
depends on the policy questions involved. As examples, the program structure presented in Table
2.1 was arranged along functional operating department lines, that in Table 2.2 by type of violation,
and that in Table 2.5 along geographical lines.
Clearly, no one of these structures is preferred
over the others. The program budget is intended to
aid decision makers in allocating scarce resources
among competing programs so as best to achieve governmental goals; no single program budget structure
will achieve this aim perfectly. For example, in
the structures proposed here, nowhere is community
relations treated as a separate major program. Expenditures on community relations are included
within the preventive program for each major type
of violation, but it may often be desirable for the
mayor, city council, or police chief to know the
dimensions of the entire police community relations
program. The mayor and (or) city council may wish
to evaluate it in terms of the total city expenditures on community relations; the police chief may
wish to evaluate it as he would any other major police program. Thus, the subprograms in the patrol,
traffic, vice, and juvenile bureaus that contribute
to the goal of improved community relations would
be gathered together and treated under this classification in order to aid in the evaluation of them.
     In short, no single arrangement of programs
can throw light on the multiple potential issues or
decisions that arise in municipal government. Analysts should seek to build several structures so
that flexibility will be integrated into both the
program structure and the accompanying analytical
efforts.

INTEGRATING PROGRAM BUDGET STRUCTURE
AND PROGRAM ANALYSIS

It is often stated that in the ideal program budget statement structure and analysis will somehow be combined. Combining the two explicitly in the budget should be carried out as far as possible so as to avoid the use of ad hoc analyses issued as separate program memorandums. However, it should be recognized that the possibilities for incorporating program analysis into the budget document itself are limited. Since the program budget tends to be most useful to higher level administrators for comparing the costs and outputs of major programs, the structure is most useful for such decision makers as the police chief and major police program administrators (that is, the heads of patrol and detective bureaus). Lower level police administrators, on the other hand, are more concerned with production efficiency, achieving maximum output from a given quantity of inputs. Thus, for instance, they are concerned not with tradeoffs between the patrol and detective divisions but with tradeoffs between vehicle and labor inputs among given patrol beats or divisions, or between two-man and one-man patrol units. This lower level process can also be encouraged by the structure of the budget. For instance, the structure in Table 2.5 illustrates major programs subdivided by geographical divisions. They could easily be further subdivided by beats. However, analysis of the effectiveness of additions to programs or input substitutions within programs normally requires separate memorandums.

The program structure does not by itself suggest the areas or issues for analysis; it merely points out the dollar magnitudes and goals of the programs that will be important if policy analysis is undertaken. Moreover, detailed analysis of the broad program expenditure levels contained in the budget structure would be very difficult to carry out. It is analytically more feasible to take as a starting point the size of an existing program; then the objective is to analyze the effect on program

output of marginal changes (either increases or decreases) in a program's size.[36] This distinction
is represented by the debate between comprehensive
and incremental budgeting. Comprehensive budgeting, often called zero-base budgeting, is based on
the notion that every major program must justify
(through analysis) the expected level of expenditure
requested for each year. The lack of support for
this approach seems justifiable, since tradeoff
analyses (of policies or political decisions) proposed under this approach would be unrealistic and
since the demand for wholesale rather than selective analysis is liable to arouse a defensive rather
than an inquiring attitude among personnel of operating agencies. In addition, the holistic procedure
is very costly.

One weakness of the program structures (and
PPBS generally) occurs at the highest level of policy analysis, where the major goals of a political
jurisdiction (say, a municipality) are formulated.
At that level economic growth, economic stability,
an equitable distribution or provision of a municipal service, safety, culture, recreation, environmental amenities, and so on are all included in the
mix of competing goals that governmental policy
attempts to achieve in order to attain maximum social welfare. Allocative efficiency is achieved
only when the fixed resources available to the jurisdiction are distributed among the city's major
social programs (that is, goals) so that no reallocation can effect an increase in the residents'
welfare. Only an integrated program structure for
all city activities can begin to deal with this
highest level of policy considerations.

But the analytic techniques of program budgeting do not easily handle tradeoffs among these major
social objectives because of the difficulty of
quantifying outputs and comparing effectiveness at
the highest policy-making levels. William Gorham
has commented on this particular aspect of the
problem well:

>   Let me hasten to point out that we
>   have not attempted any grandiose

cost-benefit analysis designed to reveal whether the total benefits from
an additional million dollars spent
on health programs would be higher or
lower than that from an additional
million dollars spent on education or
welfare. If I was ever naive enough
to think this sort of analysis possible, I no longer am. The benefits
of health, education, and welfare
programs are diverse and often intangible. . . . The "grand" decisions--
how much health, how much education,
how much welfare, and which groups in
the population shall benefit--are
questions of value judgments and pol-
itics. The analyst cannot make much
contribution to their resolution.[37]

An obvious question in the face of such pessimism
is how program budgeting improves the situation at
this level of public decision making--and, moreover,
although many writings in the PPBS literature as-
sert that this is the area in which much of the
technique's contribution lies, convincing quantitative proof is not available. As proposed and prac-
ticed at state and local levels PPBS is focused
more on operating agencies than on grand social
program packages that cut across agencies and jurisdictions. An important reason is that there are
rarely any local decision makers who can effectively act on recommendations stemming from interjurisdictional program packages. State and municipal
governments often share responsibility for various
services at different levels (that is, state, regional district, county, special district, city,
borough). Thus, an ideal, general PPBS framework
would have to cut not only across agency lines but
also across political boundaries to account both
for the multiple levels of responsibility and for
any jurisdictional externalities that might occur
and otherwise be unreflected in the program budget.
This interjurisdictional aspect of program budgeting is less serious for municipal police services

than for most other local governmental services,
but even for police services difficult interjurisdictional problems arise.

Merely devising a governmentwide program budget
that cuts across existing agency and jurisdictional
borders does not mean that any decisions can or will
be made on the basis of the information revealed by
the budget. And even within a single governmental
jurisdiction the highest-level political decisions
may not be greatly affected by any reformulation of
budget data or program analysis. But even if these
areas of decision making remain immune to change by
PPBS, a wide range of governmental activities still
remains for which the management techniques associated with a program budget can increase the efficiency of public service.

The objective of the next three chapters is to
show how analytic studies conducted within the
framework of a program budget can help achieve just
this goal. Chapter 3 is an analysis of an important
Los Angeles Police Department program, traffic law
enforcement, and Chapter 4 is a study of perhaps the
single most important activity in all police departments, general crime deterrent patrol. In both
these chapters the analytic techniques of production
function analysis and benefit-cost analysis are
used to evaluate and suggest improvement in current
police practice. Finally, in Chapter 5, program
budget information on the geographical distribution
of services in Los Angeles County is used in an
examination of intergovernmental equity in respect
to the provision and finance of police services by
city and county governments.

SUPPLEMENT 1:   METHOD FOR CROSSWALKING FROM
LINE-ITEM TO TRAFFIC PROGRAM STRUCTURE

The procedure for estimating the traffic program costs in Table 2.8 was as follows: (1) Interviews were conducted with a number of traffic bureau
line and staff officers to determine the goals and
programs of the bureau and the activities and tasks
contributing to programs and goals.   (2) A sample

of Daily Field Activities Reports (DFARs) for the
traffic bureau was taken in selected months in 1967
for the Metro Division of the city, which includes
10 of the 17 total LAPD divisions. The activities
performed by the officers and listed on their DFARs
were used to check the interview statements so that
a complete classification of all tasks could be
made. Distinction was drawn between primary and
miscellaneous activities, the latter including such
items as time spent at lunch and on uniform check
and so forth. The following 21 primary activities
emerged:

1. Supervise operations
2. Perform nontraffic police activities
3. Assist motorists
4. Answer complaints
5. Remove hazards
6. Recover vehicles
7. Direct traffic
8. Perform patrol
9. Cite violators
10. Cite drunk drivers
11. Cite parking violators
12. Investigate accidents (includes report
    writing)
13. Issue warnings
14. Arrest on traffic warrant
15. Participate in training, roll call, ser-
    vicing of equipment
16. Participate in community relations
17. Participate in traffic services (statis-
    tical reports)
18. Follow up traffic accident information
19. Follow up warrants
20. Appear in court
21. Process abandoned vehicles.

From the DFARs information was obtained on the
number of minutes each officer spent performing each
activity in each program. Using average cost per
hour of motorized units (officer and vehicle) in
each operating division, plus the overhead costs of
supervisory and auxiliary personnel and fringe benefits, the total cost of each activity in each program was calculated. When possible, joint costs

TABLE 2.8

Los Angeles Police Department Traffic Bureau Budget Crosswalk, 1967/68

Activity or Task Performed	I. Maximize Public Acceptance		
	Assist Govern-mental Agencies (1)	Participate in P.R. (CR) Programs (2)	Assist Citizens (3)
Traffic Services Section			
Supervise operations	7,028	786	3,710
Answer complaints			11,199
Furnish public relations data		2,685	
Plan special event deployment			
Maintain a special events file			
Provide assistance to special events sponsors			
Provide liaison with special services (fire dept., etc.) for events			139
Provide information or statistics for legislation	10,009		
Processing T.A. information for deployment and enforcement			
Provide information for special enforcement campaigns			
Provide engineering reports on structural defects	13,345		
Provide information for statistical studies (e.g., arrest index)		417	
Perform radar checks			556
Attend Traffic Comm. meeting-- inform Traffic Bureau			556
Prepare statistical studies	4,721		2,361
Total	35,103	3,888	18,521
Traffic Enforcement Division			
Supervise operations	1,405	468	19,205
Perform non-traffic police activities	438	146	5,987
Answer complaints			21,665
Participate in school programs		171	
Investigate commercial vehicle complaints			
Assist motorists			76,244
Remove hazard (eng. defect)	1,721		
Train personnel	200	67	2,733
Receive training (roll call)	1,013	338	13,836
Recover vehicles			
Initiate sigalerts			
Perform patrol activity			
Cite violators			
Cite drunk drivers			
Investigate accidents	3,407		3,407
Service equipment and repairs	255	85	3,485
Appear in court	289	96	3,953
Perform in nonpolice activities	60	20	814
Issue warnings			
Direct traffic			
Arrest on traffic warrants			
Cite parking violations			
Rain (Code B)	32	11	441
Perform special survey	72	24	988
Perform helicopter surveillance			
Participate in community relations		1,465	
Helicopter flights			
Total	8,892	2,891	152,758

Patrol (4)	Apprehend Violators (5)	Control Conditions (6)	Control Conditions (7)	Direct Traffic (8)	Regulate Parking (9)
3,096	4,423	1,475	2,334	860	860
			2,964	2,965	2,965
			186	185	185
			186	185	185
			139	139	139
10,048	10,048				
	1,668				
	1,251				
		556	556		
		556	556		
2,361	4,722	4,721	4,721		
15,505	22,112	7,308	11,642	4,334	4,334
322,272	115,231	1,874	3,747	3,747	468
100,462	35,921	584	1,168	1,168	146
	27,342				
		1,721			
45,865	16,399	267	533	533	67
232,179	83,018	1,350	2,700	2,700	338
			14,418		
			359		
1,671,308					
	356,364				
	146,982				
3,407	3,406	1,514			
58,481	20,910	340	680	680	85
66,332	23,718	386	771	771	96
13,659	4,884	79	159	159	20
	3,441				
				20,958	
	69,221				2,407
7,405	2,648	43	86	86	11
16,574	5,926	96	193	193	24
		5,328	5,328		
18,409					
2,556,353	915,411	13,582	30,142	30,995	3,662

(continued)

TABLE 2.8 (continued)

| Activity or Task Performed | I. Maximize Public Acceptance | | |
	Assist Govern- mental Agencies (1)	Participate in P.R. (CR) Programs (2)	Assist Citizens (3)
Accident Investigation Division			
Supervise operations	46,607	104	34,179
Perform nontraffic police activities	8,319	18	6,100
Assist motorists			11,061
Remove hazard (eng. defect)	1,078		
Follow-up required for T.A. information	70,614		
Follow-up warrants			
Recover vehicles			
Direct traffic			
Perform patrol activity			
Cite violators			
Cite drunk drivers			
Train personnel	6,516	14	4,779
Receive training (roll call)	26,103	58	19,142
Investigate accidents	82,299		82,299
Write accident reports	71,901		71,901
Service equipment and repairs	7,670	17	5,625
Perform special survey	842	2	618
Appear in court	3,224	7	2,364
Cite parking violations			
Recreation	20		15
Perform nonpolice activities	456	1	334
Arrest on traffic warrants			
Issue warnings			
Participate in community relations		275	
Total	325,649	496	238,417
Parking and Intersection **Control Division**			
Supervise operations	30	15	558
Perform nontraffic police activities	2	1	35
Assist motorists			561
Remove hazard (eng. defect)	125		
Recover vehicles			
Direct traffic			
Perform patrol activity			
Train personnel	4	2	76
Receive training (roll call)	10	5	181
Investigate accidents	56	56	56
Service equipment and repairs	2	2	42
Perform special survey			2
Cite parking violations			
Perform nonpolice activities	1		13
Arrest on traffic warrants			
Attend abandoned vehicles			3,596
Issue warnings			
Answer complaints			936
Total	230	81	6,054

II. Minimize Traffic Accidents			III. Minimize Traffic Congestion		
Patrol (4)	Apprehend Violators (5)	Control Conditions (6)	Control Conditions (7)	Direct Traffic (8)	Regulate Parking (9)
159,155	89,072	14,845	690	345	242
28,407	15,898	2,650	123	62	43
		1,078			
	14,808				
		2,905	2,905		
				1,963	
614,751					
	107,838				
	137,408				
22,252	12,454	2,076	97	48	34
89,135	49,885	8,314	387	193	135
82,299	82,299	36,577			
71,901	71,901	31,956			
26,193	14,659	2,443	114	57	40
2,876	1,610	268	12	6	4
11,009	6,161	1,027	48	26	17
					684
70	39	7	303		
1,557	871	145	7	4	
	16,531				
	51				
1,109,605	621,485	104,291	4,383	2,704	1,199
24,140	422	332	693	108,960	15,536
1,456	26	20	42	6,573	937
		124			
		2,838	2,838		
				1,034,252	
229,071					
3,292	58	45	95	14,858	2,118
7,828	136	108	225	35,334	5,038
	56	25			
1,830	32	25	52	8,261	1,178
90	1	2	2	406	58
					147,318
544	10	7	16	2,456	350
	125				
			3,596		
	3,680				
268,251	4,546	3,526	7,559	1,211,100	172,533

Source: Prepared by the Advance Planning Group, Los Angeles Police Department, 1968.

were allocated to each program according to the
percentage of an officer's time devoted to particular programs and subprograms. However, in a few
cases in which activities contributed jointly to
several programs the costs were divided equally
among them. For example, the cost of investigating
accidents (mainly performed by the Accident Investigation Division officers) was divided equally among
the governmental agency and citizen acceptance, patrol, and apprehension subprograms. The final figures are approximate, and although they reflect
fairly reasonable assumptions, they are not very
useful in some instances, since some activities
(which are input-oriented) reappear as subprograms
(which should be output-oriented). For example,
performing patrol (activity 8) contributes only to
the patrol subprogram; directing traffic (activity
7) contributes only to the direction subprogram;
participating in community relations (activity 16)
contributes mainly to the community relations sub-
program. However, many other activities also contribute to all three subprograms, with the result
that the subprograms are not simply synonyms for
the activities of the same name.

SUPPLEMENT 2: AN ESTIMATED PROGRAM BUDGET FOR THE DETROIT POLICE DEPARTMENT

In Table 2.9 the two chief program packages are
criminal and noncriminal; they are further subdivided into 12 subprograms and numerous program elements. The categories are similar to but not the
same as those in Table 2.1.

The intention is not to recommend this particular budget organization nor, in fact, the numerical
estimates. Attention is called to it as one effort
in the literature that, as do many others, involves
a fairly detailed classification and cost estimation
of urban police activities. The procedures used to
estimate the figures are not presented; if an identical structure was to be estimated for another city,
the assumptions and computations would vary according
to the responsibilities and institutional organization of the police department in that city.

TABLE 2.9

Detroit Police Department Resources Allocated
toward the Control of Specific Criminal
and Noncriminal Activities

Part 1: Criminal Activities		
Category	Allocation	Percent Criminal
1. Protecting citizens from personal violence	$2,118,200	10.90
2. Protecting citizens' property	3,770,200	19.41
3. Maintaining the established social order by suppressing:		
Vice	1,351,000	
Rackets	404,600	
Total	1,755,600	9.03
4. Preventing crime by Suppressing intent through fear of apprehension:		
Patrol	9,090,700	
Suppressing desire by educating youth	1,507,000	
Reducing capability	n.a.	
Total	10,597,700	54.56
5. Administration and support	1,184,900	6.10
Grand total	13,538,200	100.00

Note: n.a.=not available.

(continued)

TABLE 2.9 (continued)

Part 2: Noncriminal Activities		
Category	Allocation	Allocation
1. Emergency medical services		$830,700
Sick, transporting	n.a.	
Injury, transporting	n.a.	
2. Security in public buildings		1,723,404
Prevention	$1,159,659	
Detention	563,745	
3. Traffic		5,103,100
Facilitating movement	n.a.	
Safety	n.a.	
4. Crowd control		3,320,000
Profit-making ventures	n.a.	
Public-social	n.a.	
5. Inspection and license		631,800
6. Control and support		3,036,625
Administration	1,930,241	
Communications	1,106,384	
7. Miscellaneous	2,355,000	2,355,000
Total		17,001,000

Note: n.a.=not available.

Source: Robert J. Rigg, "A Conceptual Framework for Program Budgeting by Cities" (Ph.D. diss., Wayne State University, 1968). By permission.

SUPPLEMENT 3:   JUDICIARY AND LAW ENFORCEMENT
ASPECTS OF THE PROGRAM BUDGET OF
PHILADELPHIA, 1970/71

Although the following excerpts from the mayor's
operating budget and programs for Philadelphia for
1970/71 do not attempt the detail suggested by many
proposed budget structures (including the authors'),
they present an attractive and appealing arrangement of the needed information. More information
is included than in any other similar structure the
authors have observed to date. The following items
are included: (1) Statements of objectives and outputs, (2) output measures with annual values, (3)
cost allocations by program level and by regular input categories (materials, equipment, and so forth),
(4) capital outlays by program level, (5) future
obligations by program level, (6) the agencies involved at each program level, and (7) the source of
funding for each level. Much of this information
is helpful on an annual basis. However, unless objectives or output measures change, elaborate de-
scriptions of these items need not be included in
each annual budget.

The entire Philadelphia budget is well organized and can be recommended as an excellent guide
to organizing a program structure.

The framework and style of the fiscal 1971
Washington, D.C., budget are similar to those of
the Philadelphia budget, though there are numerous
differences.

PROGRAM	NO.
JUDICIARY AND LAW ENFORCEMENT	C

PROGRAM OBJECTIVES

To prevent and suppress crime; to apprehend criminals; to
investigate and prosecute crime; to support a complete Court
System; and to confine, control, and rehabilitate all persons
committed to Prisons and Detention Centers.

PROGRAM OUTPUTS

This program includes the full range of law enforcement and
adjudication services in the City and County of Philadelphia,
involving the operations of 16 separate City and County agencies.
These activities involve all phases of law enforcement from
crime prevention, patrol and apprehension, through investigation,
prosecution, trial and adjudication, and detention and
rehabilitation.

These activities are brought together in one program to provide
a foundation for carrying out the recommendation of the President's
Commission on Law Enforcement and Administration of Justice to
develop a comprehensive plan for the long-range improvement of
the quality of law enforcement.

COST SUMMARY BY SUB-PROGRAM

SUB PROGRAM (1)	1967 OBLIGATION (2)	FISCAL 1968-69 ANNUAL LEVEL (3)	FISCAL 1970 OPERATING BUDGET (4)	FISCAL 1970 CAPITAL PROGRAM (5)
Crime Prevention	3,448,113	3,743,572	3,618,886	–
Patrol and Apprehension	55,843,345	56,735,222	58,215,997	189,000
Criminal Prosecution	1,453,657	1,795,980	1,853,061	–
Judiciary and Court Administration	14,842,706	16,759,404	18,133,944	–
Detention and Rehabilitation	16,062,978	15,543,258	15,496,701	2,423,000
PROGRAM TOTAL	91,650,799	94,577,436	97,318,589	2,612,000

PROGRAM	NO.	SUB-PROGRAM	NO.
JUDICIARY AND LAW ENFORCEMENT	C	PATROL AND APPREHENSION	2

SUB-PROGRAM OBJECTIVES

To deter and suppress criminal activities; to apprehend criminals; and to investigate causes of deaths.

SUB-PROGRAM OUTPUTS

Three City agencies are involved in this subprogram. The Police Department conducts foot and motorized patrols, canine patrols, surveillance, stake outs, and similar patrol activities; and brings criminals to justice by investigation of crimes, apprehension of criminals, and assistance in prosecution. The Fairmount Park Guards conduct the same activities throughout the City's park system.

The Office of the Medical Examiner of the Department of Public Health is responsible for investigating sudden, unexpected, violent or suspicious deaths, to determine the cause and manner of death so that proper police action can be taken if warranted.

COST BY PROGRAM ELEMENT

AGENCY (1)	PROGRAM ELEMENT (2)	1967 OBLIGATION (3)	FISCAL 1968-69 ANNUAL LEVEL (4)	FISCAL 1970 OPERATING BUDGET (5)	FISCAL 1970 CAPITAL PROGRAM (6)
Police	Community Protection and Police Services	44,320,549	43,221,663	44,037,830	80,000
Police	General Support	6,612,186	8,246,454	8,747,606	88,000
Fairmount Park	Park Patrol	4,335,116	4,629,934	4,734,567	21,000
Public Health	Investigation of Deaths	575,494	637,171	695,994	–
SUB-PROGRAM TOTAL		55,843,345	56,735,222	58,215,997	189,000

CITY OF PHILADELPHIA FISCAL 1970 OPERATING BUDGET		PROGRAM ELEMENT	

PROGRAM	NO.	PROGRAM ELEMENT	NO.
Judiciary and Law Enforcement	C	Community Protection and Police Services	03
		DEPARTMENT	NO.
SUB-PROGRAM	NO.	Police	11
Crime Patrol and Criminal Apprehension	2	FUND General	NO. 0170

STATEMENT OF OBJECTIVES

1. PRIMARY PROGRAM ELEMENT OBJECTIVE:

   To deter and suppress criminal activities and to apprehend criminals.

2. RELATIONSHIP OF PROGRAM ELEMENT OBJECTIVE TO SUB-PROGRAM AND PROGRAM OBJECTIVES:

   Provides for the investigation of crimes, preparation of cases for
   court, and the prosecution of such cases. It also provides for preventive measures in conjunction with the efforts of the Crime
   Prevention elements.

OUTPUT STATEMENT	UNIT	ACTUAL 1967	ESTIMATED ANNUAL LEVEL FISCAL 1968-69	ESTIMATED FISCAL 1970
1. PRIMARY PROGRAM ELEMENT OUTPUT:	Offenses—Major	30,371	31,879	33,472
	Offenses—Minor	179,052	155,963	135,843
	Arrests	95,373	94,888	93,939
	Police Services	729,848	797,027	870,353
	Investigations	56,856	66,712	78,253

2. RELATIONSHIP OF OUTPUT TO PROGRAM ELEMENT OBJECTIVE:

   The outputs indicate the activity, and the efficacy of such activity,
   of the patrol and the investigative functions of the Department.

3. RELATIONSHIP OF PROGRAM ELEMENT OUTPUT TO OTHER PROGRAM ELEMENT OUTPUTS IN SAME
   SUB-PROGRAM AND PROGRAM:

   The arrests, investigations, and Police services are directly related
   to the prosecutive function of the District Attorney's Office and to
   the administration of justice by the Philadelphia Court System.

4. CONTRIBUTION OF PROGRAM ELEMENT OUTPUT TO ACHIEVING CITY-WIDE PROGRAM OBJECTIVES:

   By analyzing the nature and scope of crime problem, the Department
   is better able to direct the total departmental effort toward reducing
   crime by better patrol methods and increasing the quality and quantity
   of investigations and arrests.

COST SUMMARY BY CLASS

CLASS (1)	DESCRIPTION (2)	1967 OBLIGATION (3)	FISCAL 1968-69 APPROPRIATION (4)	FISCAL 1968-69 ANNUAL LEVEL (5)	FISCAL 1970 REQUEST (6)	INCREASE (DECREASE) (7)
100	Personal Services	41,863,320	63,551,256	41,232,929	41,041,828	(191,101)
200	Purchase of Services	166,352	254,882	160,004	339,355	179,351
300	Materials and Supplies	1,418,799	1,628,236	1,004,504	1,827,013	822,509
400	Equipment	872,078	1,738,800	824,174	829,582	5,408
500	Contributions, Indemnities, Refunds and Taxes		52	52	52	
	Other					
OPERATING BUDGET		44,320,549	67,173,226	43,221,663	44,037,830	816,167
FISCAL 1970 CAPITAL PROGRAM					80,000	

CITY OF PHILADELPHIA		PROGRAM ELEMENT	
FISCAL 1970 OPERATING BUDGET			

PROGRAM	NO.	PROGRAM ELEMENT	NO.
JUDICIARY AND LAW ENFORCEMENT	C	GENERAL SUPPORT	04
		DEPARTMENT	NO.
SUB-PROGRAM	NO.	POLICE	11
CRIME PATROL AND CRIMINAL APPREHENSION	2	FUND	NO.
		GENERAL	0170

OBJECTIVES

To provide the central leadership and department-wide supportive
services essential to the smooth execution of police functions by
the various divisions and units of the department.

DESCRIPTION

Consists of the Executive Officers of the Police Department,
along with their immediate staffs, the Director of Central
Services and his staff, and those functions of a department-wide
supportive or administrative nature. Included are the management
of personnel and fiscal matters, data processing, communications,
identification, detention, the maintenance of criminal records,
research and planning, building maintenance, motor vehicle
maintenance, management of materials and supplies, training,
safety, and a number of small-scale, supportive activities not
readily assignable to other program elements within the department.

COST SUMMARY BY CLASS

CLASS (1)	DESCRIPTION (2)	1967 OBLIGATION (3)	FISCAL 1968-69 APPROPRIATION (4)	FISCAL 1968-69 ANNUAL LEVEL (5)	FISCAL 1970 REQUEST (6)	INCREASE (DECREASE) (7)
100	Personal Services	5,628,045	9,040,395	7,131,609	7,221,379	89,770
200	Purchase of Services	225,527	377,560	255,342	370,442	115,100
300	Materials and Supplies	465,151	809,565	539,375	328,027	(211,348)
400	Equipment	291,364	347,243	320,028	827,658	507,630
500	Contributions, Indemnities, Refunds and Taxes	99	150	100	100	−
	Other	2,000				
	OPERATING BUDGET	6,612,186	10,583,913	8,246,454	8,747,606	501,152
	FISCAL 1970 CAPITAL PROGRAM				88,000	

PROGRAM ELEMENT

PROGRAM	NO.	PROGRAM ELEMENT	NO.
Judiciary and Law Enforcement	C	Park Patrol	07

		DEPARTMENT	NO.
SUB-PROGRAM	NO.	Recreation-Fairmount Park Commission	17
		FUND	NO.
Crime Patrol and Criminal Apprehension	2	General	0170

STATEMENT OF OBJECTIVES

1. PRIMARY PROGRAM ELEMENT OBJECTIVE:

To provide patrol service, to apprehend persons committing illegal acts, to provide the citizens of Philadelphia with a sense of security and safety when using the 8,000+ acres of Fairmount Park, and to enforce all federal, state, local and Park laws, rules, and regulations.

2. RELATIONSHIP OF PROGRAM ELEMENT OBJECTIVE TO SUB-PROGRAM AND PROGRAM OBJECTIVES:

To provide services faster and more efficiently through various types of patrol (foot, motor, horse, boat and canine). A professional approach maintained at all times, constantly changing, reorganizing and training according to changing conditions.

OUTPUT STATEMENT	UNIT	ACTUAL 1967	ESTIMATED ANNUAL LEVEL FISCAL 1968-69	ESTIMATED FISCAL 1970
1. PRIMARY PROGRAM ELEMENT OUTPUT: More efficient professional police services and patrol.	Acres patrolled	8,000+	8,000+	8,000+

2. RELATIONSHIP OF OUTPUT TO PROGRAM ELEMENT OBJECTIVE:

Police services are sometimes impossible to measure; one can only assume that when a patrol is efficient a crime or incident did not occur.

3. RELATIONSHIP OF PROGRAM ELEMENT OUTPUT TO OTHER PROGRAM ELEMENT OUTPUTS IN SAME SUB-PROGRAM AND PROGRAM:

The output is tied to recreation. Other program element outputs require our services to be effective--e.g., programs involving large crowds require proper crowd controls. All subprograms aimed at improving overall patrol function and service.

4. CONTRIBUTION OF PROGRAM ELEMENT OUTPUT TO ACHIEVING CITY-WIDE PROGRAM OBJECTIVES:

Ensuring that citizenry can safely enjoy recreation and services, to maintain the national reputation that Fairmount Park is the safest large municipal park in the United States.

COST SUMMARY BY CLASS

CLASS (1)	DESCRIPTION (2)	1967 OBLIGATION (3)	FISCAL 1968-69 APPROPRIATION (4)	FISCAL 1968-69 ANNUAL LEVEL (5)	FISCAL 1970 REQUEST (6)	INCREASE (DECREASE) (7)
100	Personal Services	4,198,115	6,363,963	4,421,903	4,551,605	129,702
200	Purchase of Services	12,100	23,768	15,845	15,845	–
300	Materials and Supplies	77,481	117,515	79,010	87,191	8,181
400	Equipment	47,420	169,763	113,176	79,926	(33,250)
500	Contributions, Indemnities, Refunds and Taxes	–	–	–	–	–
	Other					
	OPERATING BUDGET	4,335,116	6,675,009	4,629,934	4,734,567	104,633
	FISCAL 1970 CAPITAL PROGRAM				21,000	

<table>
<tr><td colspan="2">CITY OF PHILADELPHIA
FISCAL 1970 OPERATING BUDGET</td><td colspan="2">PROGRAM ELEMENT</td></tr>
</table>

PROGRAM	NO.	PROGRAM ELEMENT	NO.
LAW ENFORCEMENT	C	INVESTIGATION OF DEATHS	08
		DEPARTMENT	NO.
SUB-PROGRAM	NO.	PUBLIC HEALTH	14
CRIME PATROL AND CRIMINAL APPREHENSION	2	FUND GENERAL	NO. 0170

STATEMENT OF OBJECTIVES

1. PRIMARY PROGRAM ELEMENT OBJECTIVE:

To investigate sudden, unexpected, violent, or suspicious deaths, and to determine cause and manner of death.

2. RELATIONSHIP OF PROGRAM ELEMENT OBJECTIVE TO SUB-PROGRAM AND PROGRAM OBJECTIVES:

Facilitates proper action of Police, District Attorney, and Courts, when investigation has determined that death was caused by, or related to, criminal activity.

OUTPUT STATEMENT	UNIT	ACTUAL 1967	ESTIMATED ANNUAL LEVEL FISCAL 1968-69	ESTIMATED FISCAL 1970
1. PRIMARY PROGRAM ELEMENT OUTPUT:	Deaths Examined	5,993	6,335	6,400

2. RELATIONSHIP OF OUTPUT TO PROGRAM ELEMENT OBJECTIVE:

The circumstances of every death reported are evaluated by our staff. If warranted, a complete investigation is undertaken.

3. RELATIONSHIP OF PROGRAM ELEMENT OUTPUT TO OTHER PROGRAM ELEMENT OUTPUTS IN SAME SUB-PROGRAM AND PROGRAM:

Provides expert information serving as a basis for action by other agencies participating in subprogram and program.

4. CONTRIBUTION OF PROGRAM ELEMENT OUTPUT TO ACHIEVING CITY-WIDE PROGRAM OBJECTIVES:

Provides expert information regarding cause and manner of certain deaths. This information may serve as the basis for, or a measure of, activities undertaken by Health, Welfare, Services to Property, and Judiciary and Law Enforcement agencies.

COST SUMMARY BY CLASS

CLASS (1)	DESCRIPTION (2)	1967 OBLIGATION (3)	FISCAL 1968-69 APPROPRIATION (4)	FISCAL 1968-69 ANNUAL LEVEL (5)	FISCAL 1970 REQUEST (6)	INCREASE (DECREASE) (7)
100	Personal Services	528,107	880,438	580,691	621,849	41,158
200	Purchase of Services	12,204	18,945	12,630	21,675	9,045
300	Materials and Supplies	19,224	30,225	20,150	27,080	6,930
400	Equipment	15,933	27,005	23,670	25,360	1,690
500	Contributions, Indemnities, Refunds and Taxes	26	45	30	30	
	Other					
	OPERATING BUDGET	575,494	956,658	637,171	695,994	58,823
	FISCAL 1970 CAPITAL PROGRAM					

3

**PROGRAM ANALYSIS
FOR TRAFFIC
LAW ENFORCEMENT**

As mentioned in the preceding chapter, the setting out of measurable agency goals can be very useful in forcing attention to the question, What are we really trying to do? Organizing agency activities into separate programs that make identifiable the responsibility for accomplishing specific aims leads to the question, Who is doing what? Allocating agency expenditures according to program categories requires an answer to the question, What is our money actually being spent on? If these three questions have been answered satisfactorily, a program budget is in hand, but the process of program budgeting is by no means finished, for there is still the important step (perhaps the most important in the process) of analyzing each program to determine (1) whether the resources devoted to each program category are being used to produce the program output as efficiently as possible (that is, at least cost) and (2) whether, given that the program output is efficiently produced, the amount of resources devoted to the program is the optimum (or anywhere near it) in terms of marginal benefits related to marginal costs. A program budget that provides full details on expenditures in all program categories really gives no information whatever on these two questions, although it is a prerequisite to a well-considered attempt to answer (or even to ask usefully) these two important questions. The answer to the question whether resources

are allocated in a way that will best achieve an
agency's objectives must come from policy analysis
of each program. Such analyses run the gamut from
carefully detailed comparisons of benefits and costs
to informal listings of vague and uncertain advantages and disadvantages, but in either case a decision to maintain an existing allocation of resources
as displayed in a program budget, or to reallocate
resources among programs, implies a judgment about
each program. Program analysis makes the bases of
these judgments more explicit and, it is hoped,
better.

Before going into a detailed analysis of a law
enforcement program, it is useful to list the ways
in which the program budget structure alone, even
in the absence of program analyses, can aid in decision making. Then a sample analysis of an important police program, traffic law enforcement, can
be used to show how a well-designed budget structure
should suggest areas for program analysis and how
the analyses can assist in decisions about the allocation of resources among and within programs.
The program budget structure itself gives information on a number of points:

1. What the general goals of the agency are
and how these are expressed in terms of specific
objectives, preferably objectives expressed in
quantifiable terms

2. Who is responsible, in program terms, for
achieving the specific agency objectives that have
been set, that is, the <u>accountability</u> of individuals or groups for the results of their activities

3. What alternatives are being pursued to attain the goals set for the agency and how much is
being spent on each of the alternative methods of
achieving desired results

4. If one or more output indicators are included in the program budget structure, some idea
also of the output level that each program is
achieving as a result of its expenditures. Output
indicators are used to compare output levels among
different areas and to record the direction and
size of any changes of output. The output indicators need not, however, correspond to the traditional economic concept of <u>total</u> output of a firm.

For instance, when the crime rate is used as an output indicator, showing the probability of the occurrence of crime in an area, it does not represent
"total output" in terms of crime reduction achieved
by the police department in that area; nevertheless,
by this measure, areas can be compared in terms of
safety, and the effectiveness of variations in police inputs in an area can be measured in terms of
the resulting variations of the output indicator.

Even if all this information has been provided
by a completed program budget, it alone does not
provide a sufficient basis for making decisions
about the use of resources within, and allocation
of resources among, the various programs to meet
agency objectives most effectively. Tables 2.6 and
2.7 in Chapter 2 illustrate the problem: The cost
data show that there were expenditures of $3,950,000
for traffic law enforcement patrol and of $1,613,000
for reduction of traffic congestion. But there is
no way of knowing whether (1) existing resources
were used so as to produce the greatest output within
each program or (2) whether the benefits of an increase in traffic law enforcement patrol activity
would exceed, equal, or fall short of the costs of
the increased patrol. An answer to the first question requires knowledge of what happens to the program output indicator when the program inputs are
used in different ways. Often it seems to be simply
assumed that, within programs, outputs are being
produced as efficiently as possible and that the
main contribution of the program budget is to focus
attention on possible tradeoffs among various outputs that can be produced with available resources.
However, a more significant contribution of program
budgeting may very well be to focus attention on
the various processes by which agency inputs are
converted into desired outputs. That is, agencies
should be prodded by program analysis into examining
their methods of production in order to produce
each output most efficiently. Such attention to
production functions (relating inputs to outputs)
is illustrated in detail below in an examination of
a major Los Angeles Police Department program--
traffic law enforcement by specially assigned motorcycle officers.

Examination of production functions for public services is particularly important because there is much disagreement about public services, often not so much about whether the services are socially valuable as about what sort of results, if any, will follow from any particular allocation of resources intended to produce results. This is unfortunate, because as a consequence much time is wasted arguing over the form of production relationships that are not known--though they could be known. For instance, in the field of traffic law enforcement there has long been disagreement about whether officers on motorcycles ("two-wheel" enforcement) or officers in patrol cars ("four-wheel" enforcement) are more effective in terms of reducing auto accidents under urban traffic conditions. Various reasonable advantages have been claimed for each technique of enforcement by proponents on both sides of the issue--for instance, that four-wheel units can operate under all weather conditions and that two-wheel units are more mobile under congested traffic conditions. Most of the arguments seem to center on assumed qualitative advantages of each method rather than on any clearly observed differences between the two in cost per unit of output, and more effort appears to be put into discussion of the possible merits of two-wheel versus four-wheel enforcement than into any scientific attempt to test the actual performance results of alternative deployments of traffic law enforcement units.

It is clear that without more information about the actual production function for agency outputs, decisions about resource allocation within the agency must be made largely on the basis of "judgment" and "feel" rather than on the basis of explicit calculations of the costs and benefits of alternatives. However, such judgments often turn out to be decisions based on ancient rules of thumb, on myths, or simply on extensions of past policies. Such is the case as much for law enforcement as it is for other public service agencies--and it has been said that it is especially so in respect to traffic law enforcement. The report on a recent and quite comprehensive survey of police traffic services states:

"Our summary conclusion is that there is no quantitative and objective evidence currently available
that enables us to recommend any 'optimal' or 'desirable' levels of traffic law enforcement or standards for police performance based on the material
collected and analyzed in the course of this
study."[1] In particular, it was found that research
is particularly deficient in respect to some of the
most important questions: "Two problem areas are
conspicuous by their absence; one is the effectiveness of police activities in urban areas, and the
other is a justification of the concept of 'selective enforcement.' There are no direct studies of
the effects of police activities in urban areas. . . .
Nowhere is an attempt made to compare selective and
nonselective enforcement."[2]

Another survey of traffic safety literature
concludes:

> At present, there is no firm evidence
> to indicate the degree to which en-
> forcement contributes to traffic ac-
> cident prevention. The objective
> investigation of optimum methods of
> police supervision of traffic is just
> beginning. In view of the high cost
> of this activity and of the possible
> contribution that expansion and im-
> provement of police supervision could
> make to traffic safety, further studies
> of tactics as applied to specific
> situations should prove to be reward-
> ing. The limited amount of investi-
> gation now under way concerns prin-
> cipally rural roads and particularly
> the Interstate system. Specific study
> of the quite different problems of
> urban traffic supervision would seem
> to be in order.[3]

Thus, information is almost entirely absent on
relationships that are central to much metropolitan
traffic law enforcement activity: (1) the overall
effect the police have on the important traffic

variables safety and speed in urban areas and (2)
the localized effect of selectively higher enforcement levels in particular areas (a very common enforcement technique).

Perhaps because of the lack of hard facts concerning the effects of police resources allocated
to traffic law enforcement, there is enormous variation among police departments in the attention devoted to traffic. For instance, the police departments of Boston and Dallas, which have approximately
equal populations, wrote 11,242 and 273,626 moving
violation tickets, respectively, in 1965--a twenty-
four-fold fifference.[4] And from a series of case
studies of traffic law enforcement in Massachusetts
towns, John Gardiner concludes that

> variations in traffic-enforcement
> policies can be explained only to a
> limited extent by such environmental
> variables as political pressures,
> demographic characteristics, or court
> conviction and accident rates. Al-
> though a high degree of population
> instability may increase the reliance
> on formal sanctions, the evidence
> presented in the case studies suggests
> that the most significant variables
> are within the departments--specializa-
> tion of the traffic enforcement func-
> tion, demands by the chief and command-
> ing officers that ticket writing or
> courtesy to motorists be stressed,
> and so forth. Where the norms of the
> department reward active ticket
> writers, the police will respond with
> tickets; where norms are neutral or
> openly hostile toward traffic enforce-
> ment ticketing will be low and only
> serious offenders will be cited.[5]

Obviously, police departments have great discretion in enforcing traffic laws, but an empirical
basis for choosing the optimal level of enforcement
does not exist. Because of the fact vacuum in which

enforcement levels are chosen, the opinions of police administrators concerning the importance of
traffic services determine what polices are followed; this has led to a wide divergence among police departments in policies actually followed, a
divergence certainly wider than can be explained by
differences in traffic conditions among cities.

The analytic processes of program budgeting
seem particularly well-suited for application to
problems of traffic law enforcement. For this
reason, examination of the interaction of program
analysis with the program budget structure will begin with a traffic problem. Moreover, traffic law
enforcement appears to be a good starting place because the policy issues involved in police traffic
work are, as police matters go, not controversial
or likely to divide the community along racial or
class lines. Thus the examination of police department outputs in this field can proceed with a
somewhat less heavy load of value judgments concerning distributional questions within a community
than can examination of the outputs of some other
police programs. For another thing, output is
somewhat more easily quantified in the traffic field
than in most other fields of police work, and there
is less question concerning the reliability of the
traffic data that is collected than there is regarding most crime data. Traffic accidents are
less susceptible to variations in reporting than
are most crimes, and the accident rate is the most
important output indicator for traffic law enforcement (although not the only one). Finally, despite
the seeming advantages of traffic law enforcement
as a topic of research in the area of public service
production, a review of the literature indicates
that there has been no conclusive evidence concerning the effectiveness of police traffic work, especially on surface streets in urban areas. Thus,
if program budgeting techniques are capable of making a significant contribution to the improvement
of decisions about the allocation of police resources, this should be demonstrable in the area of
traffic law enforcement, where the program analysis
involved is of reasonable proportions and clear
practical value.

TRAFFIC LAW ENFORCEMENT
PRODUCTION FUNCTIONS

Ideally the police traffic administrator should
have complete knowledge of the effects on traffic
variables of any particular level or method of
traffic law enforcement, under all conditions.
Such knowledge is usually viewed as a production
function, the desired effects on traffic safety and
flow (reduced accident rates and increased speed of
travel) being the outputs and police resources employed (officers, motorcycles, automobiles) being
the inputs. The relationship between inputs and
outputs depends heavily on the service conditions
(weather, type of road) and on the technology of
enforcement used (motorcycle patrol, unmarked cars,
radar).[6] In its mathematical form, the production
function can be expressed as

$$O = f(I, S, T)$$

where

    O = output, the effects of traffic law enforce-
        ment

    I = inputs, the police resources

    S = service conditions under which enforcement
        takes place

    T = technology or method of enforcement.

In this formulation, both inputs and outputs are
measured per unit of time.

It is obvious that police administrators have
some relationship of this sort in mind when they
make decisions concerning how traffic laws are to
be enforced, but it seems fair to say that the em-
priical basis for asserting any _specific_ form of
the relationship is weak. That is, it is usually
expected that greater expenditure for traffic law
enforcement, I, will produce more of the desired
results, O, and that the degree to which these desired results are produced for any given expenditure
depends on both the particular conditions under
which the services are rendered, S, and the enforcement technology employed, T. But just what the
quantitative relationship is has remained a mystery,
despite its obvious usefulness in making an efficient allocation of police resources in traffic

duties. Further, the lack of knowledge concerning
traffic enforcement effectiveness does not appear
to stem from the fact that the basic production relationships are unknowable; it is rather explained
by the limited amount of research that has been
done on the subject. Given the current level of
knowledge, it is almost certainly true that the
rewards of research on traffic law enforcement production functions will be greater than the rewards
of equal expenditure directly on enforcement itself.
This assertion gains force when it is realized that
much knowledge is potentially available by simply
making a greater attempt to collect and interpret
data on output indicators when reallocations of
police resource inputs are made. Numerous before-
and-after experimental situations occur in the
course of police manpower reassignments that are
made from time to time. With some extra effort the
results of these reassignments could be routinely
monitored to determine what the actual effects have
been. Far too often, changes in police resource
uses are made without follow-up investigations to
determine just what the results of the changes were.
In traffic law enforcement, for instance, manpower
is occasionally strengthened in specific areas in
response to high accident rates, but the results in
terms of the effect of the additional officers on
accident rates is typically not examined. Of course,
police departments are not unusual in this regard,
for the situation is the same for other municipal
services, and also frequently for private industry.[7]

Quite aside from attempts to evaluate the results of the routine changes in operating procedures
that occur from time to time, police departments
are in an unusually favorable position to undertake
specially designed, controlled experiments to estimate the relationships between inputs and outputs
under varying service conditions and technologies.
But before going into the details of procedures for
estimating police production functions, it will be
useful to discuss briefly the general uses to which
public service production functions may be put.

First, it must be remembered that although
ideally the production function describes the output

that results from every possible combination of inputs, public service outputs are usually impossible
to describe fully or measure accurately, with the
result that output in the production function is
usually represented by one or more output indicators.
Thus, basically, the production function should show,
for a given police program, the relation between the
resources used in the program and the corresponding
magnitude of the output indicator that results.
Perhaps more important for decision making, the
production function also shows how output varies in
response to input changes. This point is important
because most questions of resource allocation actually deal with marginal changes: How much additional output will result from an additional expenditure on a program? Or how much reduction in
output will result from a reduction in program expenditure? For many purposes it is necessary to
have only such limited information to make intelligent decisions about resource allocation. That is,
it is typically much more useful to know the effect
on output of marginal variations in inputs than it
is to know the size of total output. And in many
cases the measurement of changes in output may be
possible even though measurement of total output is
impossible or too difficult to be feasible. An
example from the field of traffic law enforcement
can be used to illustrate this aspect of output
measurement.

First, although traffic accident reduction is
not the sole goal of enforcement, let it be assumed
for simplicity that this is the single goal. In
the absence of any traffic law enforcement on a
stretch of street or highway, the traffic accident
rate would presumably be higher than if traffic
laws were strictly enforced. Suppose that the
accident rate in the absence of enforcement would
be 400 injury-accidents per 100 million miles driven
and that every additional unit of police resources
devoted to enforcement would lower the accident
rate. This situation is displayed in Figure 3.1.

Although the curve shows the accident rate as
a function of the enforcement level, it does not
indicate the total output related to enforcement

FIGURE 3.1

Accident Rate as a Function of the Level of Enforcement

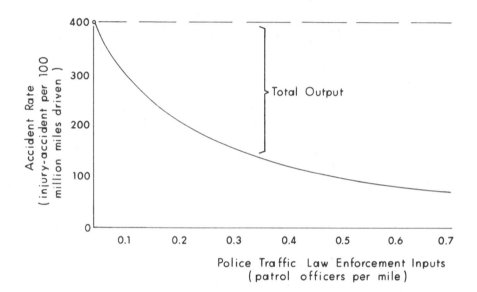

inputs. If the total output is traffic accident
prevention, the total output is the difference between the "no enforcement" accident rate (the dashed
horizontal line at the 400 level) and the accident
rate actually observed at each level of enforcement.
This total output (accident rate reduction) curve
is shown in Figure 3.2, which is found simply by
subtracting the lower curve from the horizontal,
dashed line in Figure 3.1. Thus, although the accident rate itself cannot be directly interpreted
as a total output measure, changes in the accident
rate can be interpreted as equal changes in the total output measure, but of the opposite sign (an
increase in the accident rate signifies a decrease
of the same magnitude in accident prevention, and

FIGURE 3.2

Accident Rate Reduction as a Function of the Level of Enforcement

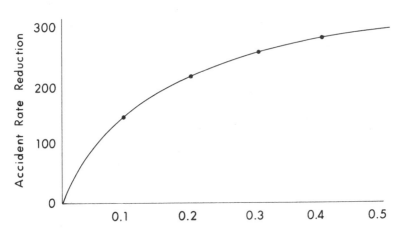

Police Traffic Law Enforcement Inputs
(patrol officers per mile)

vice versa) when the basic "no enforcement" accident
level remains unchanged. Use of the accident rate
as an output indicator for traffic law enforcement
is similar to the use of the crime rate as an output
indicator for criminal law enforcement. However,
for criminal laws it seems less conceivable that
one would ever know the "no enforcement" rate because under normal circumstances it never occurs.
Despite the difficulty or impossibility of estimating the "no enforcement" level of traffic accidents
or criminal law violations, and thus of estimating
the total number of traffic accidents or criminal
violations prevented by the police, traffic accident rates and crime rates are extremely useful for
indicating a change in output in response to a

change in input; and if a dollar value can be placed
on the output measure, the value of the increased
output can be compared with the cost of the increased input to see whether it is worthwhile to
expand a program or contract it.

Even without the difficult step of valuing
program output, examination of public service production functions focuses attention on whether program output is produced as efficiently as possible.
When both inputs and outputs are valued in dollar
terms, the investigation is usually called cost-
benefit analysis; when the inputs are valued in
dollar terms but the outputs are described in physical terms, it is called cost-effectiveness analysis.
There are many situations in which formal cost-
benefit analysis is so expensive or uncertain that
the results are not worth the cost of making the
analysis but in which simpler cost-effectiveness
studies can still contribute to significant improvements.

The basic goal of a cost-effectiveness study
is to ensure that a given level of output is produced at least cost or, equivalently stated, that
for a given expenditure the maximum possible output
is produced. It should be noted that even though
a given level of output may be produced at least
cost, it may still not be worth producing (in the
sense that the benefits lost by reducing output may
be less than the costs saved thereby). Cost-
effectiveness analysis tells nothing about the appropriate level of output to be produced or of inputs to be devoted to a program, but rather concentrates on efficient production techniques. However,
useful program analysis can often start with a
cost-effectiveness study of production techniques
and only subsequently undertake an evaluation in
dollar terms of benefits produced; indeed, too often
it is simply assumed in cost-benefit analysis that
benefits are being produced in the most efficient
manner possible while in reality the same output
might be produced by a different and less costly
set of inputs. In diagrammatic terms cost-
effectiveness research is intended to put production
on the highest possible total output curve.

Figure 3.2 shows total output as a single function of inputs, given a particular set of service conditions; an implied assumption is that each point on the curve represents the maximum output obtainable for the given expenditure on inputs. Of course, it is also possible to produce a much lower output for the same expenditure on inputs, by using improper production techniques or poor management. For instance, if two-wheel motorcycle traffic law enforcement was more efficient than four-wheel traffic law enforcement and if the only output of enforcement was reduction in traffic accidents, the two total output curves could look as shown in Figure 3.3. It is apparent that if both methods cost

FIGURE 3.3

Accident Rate Reduction as a Function of the Level of Two-Wheel and Four-Wheel Enforcement

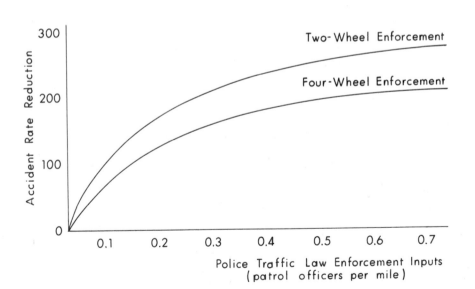

the same, it would be worthwhile to shift to two-
wheel enforcement in all situations for which this
sort of total output relationship held. The difficulty lies, of course, in discovering the true shape
of the two output curves shown in the figure and in
discovering whether one curve really is above the
other, by how much, and under what conditions.
Rainfall furnishes one example of the conditions
that must be specified for a production function of
this sort: frequency, duration, and heaviness of
rainfall certainly affect the relative operating
efficiency of motorcycles and patrol cars, and thus
the relative effectiveness of the two sorts of enforcement depends on the rainfall experienced.

     An output-oriented program budget invites both
cost-effectiveness and cost-benefit analysis of public service production—-and so the program analysis
of traffic law enforcement described below will contain both elements, investigation of efficient
methods of production and an attempt to ascertain
the optimum level of enforcement on a traffic beat.
An estimate of the optimum level of enforcement
does, of course, require valuation of the output of
enforcement in dollar terms; however, it is worth
noting that even when output cannot be valued by
any generally agreed method, analysis of the production process alone may be sufficient to demonstrate that too many resources are being devoted to
a particular program. Such a statement can be made
if it is discovered that enforcement has been carried to a point at which the marginal product of
police resources is zero or negative in any particular activity. This situation is illustrated by
the horizontal portion of the curves in Figure 3.3:
above approdimately 0.5 officers per mile, additional police inputs produce no increase in output.
Given the present lack of knowledge of actual production relationships in so many governmental programs,
it is not certain that such a situation does not
occasionally occur.

     For estimating a production function there are
three basic methods that relate output to input
under specified service conditions: (1) Statistical
examination of cross-sectional or time-series data

on inputs, outputs, and service conditions, (2) use
of engineering data that, for particular technical
processes, give information on designed productions,
and (3) controlled experiments in which the public
agency deliberately alters the inputs or the technology with which the inputs are used and observes
what happens to output as a result.

Statistical Data

The first method of production function estimation, multivariate statistical investigation, has
been used in several instances, mainly in the field
of education.[8] According to this method data on
output and the variables that are assumed to affect
it are used to show the effects that each public
agency input and each of the various service condition variables have on output when all the other
factors are held constant. Numerous difficulties,
most of which are connected with availability of
accurate data, are involved in the statistical estimation of production functions. Both the method
and its difficulties are discussed later, in Chapter 4, where an attempt is made to estimate a statistical production function that relates crime
rates to the quantity of police patrol service.

Engineering Data

The second method of relating inputs to outputs
is to rely on engineering data that describe the
designed operation of certain clearly defined processes. Where the production process requires relatively fixed proportions of labor and capital
equipment and fixed methods of operation, the designed methods of operation can give information
about the input requirements for each level of output. Application of this sort of production function is usually confined to rather narrowly defined
processes, and the output produced is often intermediate rather than final. For instance, engineering data for a communications system can tell how

quickly a patrol car can be contacted for assignment, but they cannot tell what effect the speed of
communication will have on arrest rates or crime
rates. Thus, production functions derived from engineering data are generally most useful in finding
the least-cost method of obtaining intermediate
outputs, but the relationship between inputs and
the desired final output must be estimated by other
means.[9]

Experimental Data

The third method of estimating production functions, and the one to be emphasized here as being
particularly useful for law enforcement, is controlled experimentation. By controlled experimentation is meant the comparison of alternative situations that are, as far as practically convenient,
alike in all respects except the one under test.
In the field of law enforcement comparison would
normally be made of alternative situations that
were alike except for some input under the control
of police (for example, the number of patrol officers per capita) in order to discover what difference that police input would make.

At an informal level experimentation goes on
all the time, and the process of learning by experience can be called experimentation of a very
crude (and sometimes unreliable) sort; that is, men
try something, see what happens, and form an opinion from the experience about the relationship between the action and the result. However, the circumstances surrounding such casual empirical investigation are frequently not carefully controlled,
and so the experience is not really a reliable
guide to action; rather, other factors not considered may in fact account for differences in results
observed, and in such cases the effects of the inputs will be misinterpreted.

"Experimental observations are only experience
carefully planned in advance, and designed to form
a secure basis of new knowledge."[10] But careful
planning is essential before the results can be

interpreted usefully. And there seem to be many
more opportunities for carefully planned experiments
in law enforcement than in most other local public
services because police departments have considerable discretion in allocating resources, whether by
geographical area, time of day, or method of enforcement used.[11] There are relatively few legal
constraints on how police resources may be allocated
within a city, and thus administrators are free to
make quite significant experimental reassignments
of manpower or changes in enforcement techniques
without violating city, state, or federal regulations. Their circumstances contrast sharply with
the circumstances of administrators in the fields
of education or welfare, for example, in which procedures of operation are often explicitly mandated
in federal or state legislation. Such mandates
from a higher level of government are usually a con-
comitant of financial aid to the local government,
but such mandates (and aid) for law enforcement are
relatively few. There are also relatively few labor
union restrictions on manpower allocation within
police departments that would hamper reassignment
for experimental purposes.[12]

Experimentally derived police production functions have several distinct advantages. First, by
careful choice of the test location it is often
possible to keep all important factors other than
the police variable very nearly the same. In the
traffic law enforcement experiment described below,
motorcycle beats were chosen so as to be as nearly
similar in all respects as possible, so that any
changes in accident experience could be primarily
related to changes made in enforcement. By contrast,
in the attempt described in Chapter 4 to estimate a
production function for police patrol by statistical
regression techniques it was possible to control
only for those variables for which census data were
available, and even then some of the data were
available only for differing periods.

Another advantage of controlled experimentation
is that the results apply directly to the areas in
which the experiments are conducted--providing a
basis for substantial confidence that the research

results are valid policy guides for the specific
local circumstances under which the research is
done. Many resource allocation questions are of a
specific nature, requiring information concerning
the effects of police manpower or enforcement techniques in a variety of situations. To answer these
questions it is necessary to assess the effectiveness of enforcement <u>in each situation</u>, rather than
to rely on some overall relationship that is presumed to hold in an aggregate sense.[13] When such
detailed information is required, controlled experiments appear to be the only feasible method of
investigation.

     Still another advantage of deliberate experi-
mentation in police research is that it is possible
to investigate the effect on output of great variations in police inputs. In contrast, when a statistical examination of existing data is used, only
the variations in police inputs that happen to occur
over time or among areas are observable. Often
these variations are small, and the effect of variations in other important variables swamps the effect of the police variable under investigation.
The ability to investigate the impact of wide variations in police inputs is particularly important
for the purpose of validating possible negative
findings of effectiveness. That is, if no change
in output indicators is found to result from relatively small input variations, it may be argued
that this negative finding is to be explained by an
inability to measure output finely enough or by a
simultaneous, offsetting variation in other important causal factors; but if little or no change in
output indicators is found to result from a large
input alteration, the evidence is more conclusive
that the particular method of input used may be inefficient in producing the desired result. Knowledge in this form becomes especially useful when a
value estimate in dollar terms can be put on the
output, so that some minimum increase in the output
indicator must be demonstrated before dollar benefits of the increased input allocation exceed additional input costs (or before the decrease in
benefits exceeds the decrease in costs for an

experimental reduction of inputs). For instance, if it is estimated that the average loss per traffic accident is $1,000 and that a motorcycle traffic officer costs $12,000 per year, then it would be necessary to demonstrate that adding a motorcycle officer reduced the number of accidents by at least 12 per year before benefits would exceed costs of the increased enforcement (assuming there are no other costs or benefits). Or, alternatively, if it is shown that an additional motorcycle traffic officer does reduce accidents by 12 per year, then it must be agreed that the average loss per accident is $1,000 before the allocation of the additional officer is justified in cost-benefit terms.

Of course, for this procedure to serve its purpose one must have confidence that the output indicator used is appropriate, that all forms of output are considered, that the possible effect of time-lag between inputs and resulting output is not neglected, and so forth.

To sum up this discussion, decision making in regard to traffic law enforcement resource allocation requires (1) estimates of the value of outputs and the cost of inputs and (2) an estimate of the effect of alternative input allocations on output, particularly the effect of small variations in input on output. It has been argued that controlled experiments on the part of police departments are a promising way of gaining knowledge of the production relationship between inputs and outputs. In the next section a report is made of an experiment intended to estimate such a relationship for motorcycle traffic law enforcement, and estimation of the value of outputs and cost of inputs in dollar terms is also attempted.

AN EXPERIMENTAL INVESTIGATION OF TRAFFIC LAW ENFORCEMENT PRODUCTION FUNCTIONS

During 1968 and 1969 the Los Angeles Police Department conducted a controlled experiment to assess the effects of traffic law enforcement activity on city streets. This experiment was an exploratory

part of the Los Angeles Police Department's effort
to introduce a planning-programming-budgeting system
into its operations and was valuable not only in
terms of its empirical results but also as a demon-
stration of the ways in which the methods of program
budgeting can increase the efficiency of police department operation. Since the Los Angeles Police
Department spends approximately one-sixth of its
budget on traffic regulation (which is defined to
include both accident investigation and traffic law
enforcement), the problem of efficiency in this
operation is a sizable one.[14] And despite the considerable expenditures for traffic law enforcement
by municipal police departments, almost no empirical
studies have appeared in the literature on the effectiveness of police for urban traffic supervision.[15] A further practical reason for making this
study of input-output relationships in traffic law
enforcement was that in late 1969 the California
State Highway Patrol assumed responsibility for
patrolling freeways in Los Angeles City and the Los
Angeles Police Department traffic officers who had
until then been assigned to that duty were available
for reassignment, either to surface street traffic
duties or to other, nontraffic duties elsewhere in
the department. Thus, research on effectiveness of
police officers in traffic law enforcement had the
heightened importance of being directly relevant to
a key policy decision on manpower reassignment that
had to be made by the Los Angeles Police Department.

Background of the Experiment

Traffic laws are enforced throughout Los Angeles by units of the patrol bureau; but to those
surface streets that have the greatest number of
automobile accidents the traffic bureau assigns
special motorcycle traffic law enforcement officers.
This assignment procedure is known as "selective
enforcement" and is based on the assumption that a
concentration of enforcement effort at the times
and places at which most accidents occur will produce the greatest output in terms of accident reduction.

Each motorcycle patrolman is assigned a patrol route (beat) of from three to six miles in length. These beats, assigned for six-month duration (winter and summer), are semiannually reviewed to ensure that traffic enforcement officers are assigned to areas that have experienced the greatest number of traffic accidents. However, the specific allocation of beats among possible street segments is performed intuitively by a clerk who works with large maps pinned to show the number of accidents that have occurred over the previous six-month interval and the type of accident. Unfortunately the allocation process operates without any real knowledge of the quantitative effect of traffic law enforcement on traffic accident rates; also, it neglects the effect that enforcement may have on the traffic volume and on the average speed at which traffic flows; that is, if stricter enforcement reduces accidents along a beat by reducing average speed and/or volume, this negative output of enforcement is not taken into account. Furthermore, there is no empirically established criterion of what the _overall_ level of traffic law enforcement activity should be. The method used to measure the need for enforcement is the enforcement index, which is the ratio of traffic convictions to injury-accidents occurring in the city, but there has been no explicit analysis of what would be a desirable level of the enforcement. For instance, O. W. Wilson suggests that the arrest index[16] should not be less than 10 but bases this recommendation only on "the fact that violations, and consequently accidents caused by them, are decreased by enforcement. The presence of accidents is evidence of a need for enforcement, and their frequency is a measure of the amount of enforcement needed."[17]

In an attempt to obtain information on the effect produced by motorcycle patrol enforcement, the Los Angeles Police Department with the cooperation of the Institute of Government and Public Affairs at UCLA conducted a controlled traffic law enforcement experiment. Briefly, the experiment was designed to relate different levels of enforcement effort to the resulting effect on accident rates

and other variables of interest. If there is a
definite relationship between the level of enforcement and the frequency of traffic accidents, comparison of similar traffic beats that have different
numbers of motorcycle officers should reveal the
successive reductions in accidents achieved by the
successive additions of motorcycle patrol officers;
then, ignoring for the moment other benefits and
costs of enforcement, by estimating the benefit of
reducing accidents (in terms of lives saved and of
injuries and property damage avoided) and the cost
of enforcement (in terms of the cost of motorcycle
patrol), it should be possible to tell at what
level of enforcement the marginal cost of enforcement is equal to the marginal benefit (that is,
what the optimal level of enforcemment is). Such
controlled experimentation and analysis is at the
heart of any attempt to improve the efficiency of
police resource allocation, and it is a fundamental
building block of program evaluation.

The Experiment Design

The experiment was designed to discover the
effect (1) of the method of patrol enforcement and
(2) of the number of motorcycle patrol officers on
such variables as traffic accident rates and average speed and volume of traffic--and also on one
nontraffic variable, the reported crime rate--on
the patrolled street segments. Eight experimental
beats were selected, as similar as possible in
length, width, previous accident experience, volume
of traffic, and other relevant characteristics.
However, to make the data for the experimental period comparable to the data for previous years on
each beat, it was necessary to employ beats of
slightly different lengths. This was taken into
account by expressing enforcement levels in terms
of officers per mile on each beat. The beats were
as isolated as possible from parallel or intersect-
ing beats.

On the eight beats the following methods of
patrol were employed during the experiment:

1. Visibility only (on one beat): The motor-cycle patrol officer refrained from citing traffic law violators (except for flagrant offenses).

2. Warning only (on one beat): The officer stopped and warned violators but did not issue ci-tations (except for flagrant offenses).

3. Standard enforcement (on five beats): The officer patrolled the beat and issued citations in the same manner as before the experiment began.

The motive for examining these three alterna-tive methods of patrol was to find whether, with the same level of manpower allocated to each, the output depended on the patrol method used. In terms of Figure 3.3 this part of the experiment was in-tended to indicate which of the three patrol tech-niques produced the highest total output curve for two-wheel enforcement. The experimentation with techniques was undertaken at only one level of man-power input (approximately 0.3 officers per mile)--and if one technique appeared more effective than the others, it could be tried at other levels of manpower input to discover the full production rela-tionship using that technique.

In addition to the examination of patrol tech-niques (visibility only, warning only, and standard enforcement), the experiment was designed to show the effect of varying the level of manpower alloca-tion on each beat when the standard technique of enforcement is employed. The following manpower allocations were employed during the experiment:

1. No change: The manpower allocation re-mained at the preexperiment level.

2. Increased allocation: The manpower allo-cation was increased to a level higher than the pre-experiment level.

3. Stripped allocation: The manpower alloca-tion was reduced to zero.

The manpower allocations and patrol techniques together with the time span of the experimental change are summarized in Table 3.1.

As shown in Table 3.1, beats 3 through 8 were designed to elucidate the effectiveness of the use of the standard patrol technique by motorcycle of-ficers as their number was varied from 0 to 1.7 per

TABLE 3.1

Base Period and Experimental Period Data for Traffic Beats

| Beat Number (1) | Base Period Conditions | | | Experimental Conditions | | |
	Number of Officers (2)	Officers per Mile (3)	Method of Enforcement[a] (4)	Number of Officers (5)	Officers per Mile (6)
1	1	0.28	visibility only	1	0.28
2	1	0.31	warnings only	1	0.31
3	1	0.29	standard	4	1.17
4	0	0	standard	4	0.81
5	1	0.29	standard	1	0.29
6	0	0	standard	1	0.23
7	1	0.26	standard	3	0.79
8	1	0.31	n.e.[b]	0	0

[a]During the base period the standard method of enforcement on all beats that had motorcycle patrol.

[b]n.e.=no enforcement.

Source: Prepared by the authors.

linear mile. (Just how effectiveness is to be measured is discussed below.) As a simplified example
of the use that can be made of such information,
consider a situation in which the successive addition of motorcycle patrol officers decreases the
number of traffic accidents on a beat, but at a decreasing rate. If, for instance, the average cost
of an automobile accident was $2,000 and the exper-
imental accident data were as shown in Table 3.2,
the resultant measure of the marginal product of
traffic enforcement officers would produce the
marginal product curve shown in Figure 3.4 (assuming again that the number of accidents is the only
variable affected). The marginal product of an
officer (plus his motorcycle) at each level of enforcement is the reduction in the cost of traffic
accidents on the beat produced by the allocation of
one additional officer to the beat.

TABLE 3.2

Hypothetical Traffic Enforcement
Experiment Data
(nine-month period)

Number of Officers on Beat	Number of Accidents on Beat	Accidents Prevented on Beat	Reduction in Accident Costs (4) = 3 x $2,000	Marginal Product of One Officer
(1)	(2)	(3)	(4) = 3 x $2,000	(5)
0	100	0	0	n.e.
1	80	20	40,000	40,000
2	70	30	60,000	20,000
3	65	35	70,000	10,000
4	64	36	72,000	2,000

Note: n.e.=no enforcement.

Source: Prepared by the authors.

FIGURE 3.4

Hypothetical Traffic Enforcement
Marginal Product Curve

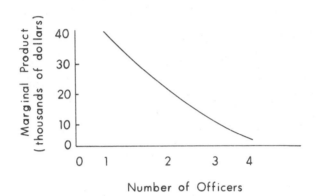

Number of Officers

Such information, combined with data on the cost of motorcycle patrol, makes it possible to say at what level the addition of another traffic enforcement officer would cost more than the resulting reduction in traffic accidents is worth. For instance, if the marginal cost of one motorcycle patrol officer for a nine-month period was $8,000, three officers on a beat would be optimum, based on these rudimentary calculations.[18] The addition of the third officer to the beat reduces the cost of accidents by (that is, produces a benefit of) $10,000, while costing only $8,000. However, a fourth officer would bring a further reduction in accident costs (that is, a benefit) of only $2,000 while adding $8,000 to patrol costs.

Naturally, there are difficulties in the interpretation of the data; most of these difficulties probably work in the direction of showing motorcycle patrol to be less significant than it actually is in influencing accident rate, average speed, volume, and other variables. First, as was mentioned earlier, there may be a significant lag between the increase (or decrease) in enforcement level and the full recognition of this by motorists using the patrolled street; and since driving habits are not quickly changed, there may be a further lag between the recognition of altered enforcement level (or techniques) and reaction (if any) to it in terms of altered driving habits. Thus, if the response lag time is long in comparison to the length of the experiment (nine months), the experimental data will underestimate the long-run effect of traffic law enforcement. Second, there is undoubtedly a large spillover effect associated with traffic law enforcement on any particular beat; the driving behavior of motorists is affected not only on the experimental beats but presumably also on other streets on which the exposed motorists subsequently drive. This presumed spillover is called the halo effect by traffic enforcement officers. There is also a time dimension as well as a spatial dimension to the spillover: motorists' driving behavior may be influenced beyond the nine-month period of the experiment (another lag effect). Third (and related to both the first and second points), motorists enter the experimental beats from areas of normal enforcement and perhaps either travel along them for only a short distance or just cross them. Such motorists have little or no exposure to the experimental patrol levels, and their behavior probably more nearly reflects enforcement conditions off the experimental beats than on them (a reverse halo effect).

For each of these three reasons, the measurable results on the experimental beats themselves probably tend to understate the total influence of enforcement levels on accident rates, speed, volume, or other variables, given additional off-beat effects.

The experiment was conducted during the day watch (10 a.m. to 6 p.m.), Monday through Friday, between October 1, 1968, and June 30, 1969. Data for the experiment were collected on the experimental beats on the following items: (1) total accidents (fatal accidents, injury-accidents, and property damage accidents); (2) traffic citations

issued; (3) traffic violation arrests; (4) traffic
volume; (5) average speed (timed by radar); and
(6) crime (reported crimes and arrests). The data
were compiled separately for the experimental hours
(10 to 6, Monday through Friday) and for the remaining hours of the week. In addition, except for
items 2, 3, and 5, the same data were available for
the previous years on the same basis. Data were
collected for the nonexperimental hours of the week
in the expectation that the hours when enforcement
was not varied would constitute a control with
which to compare the hours when enforcement was
varied from the preexperimental period. During the
nonexperimental hours traffic enforcement patrol
was maintained the same as before the experimental
period, and for both experimental and nonexperimental hours other nontraffic police manpower was continued at its previous level on each beat. The
crime data were collected in an attempt to determine whether the level of visibility of traffic enforcement patrol had any effect on the crime rate
on the experimental beats, for any such traffic effect should be counted among the benefits of manpower allocated to traffic law enforcement; looking
only at the effects on traffic accidents or other
traffic variables would understate the benefits of
traffic officers.

Valuation of Benefits and Costs of Traffic Law Enforcement

In the hypothetical experiment on traffic law
enforcement described, it was simply assumed that a
reduction in the number of traffic accidents was
the only output produced and that each accident
avoided represented a benefit worth $2,000. Admit-
tedly, this assumption is far too simple. Traffic
law enforcement activity involves a much more complex array of inputs and outputs, and attaching
dollar values to these inputs and outputs is usually
difficult and sometimes impossible. Both inputs
and outputs of the traffic law enforcement production process must be valued in dollar terms in order

to be made comparable for a decision about whether
or not benefits exceed costs at the margin. And
since this chapter is intended to show how program
analysis can improve resource allocation decisions,
measures of benefits and costs will be developed in
some detail to illustrate the general principles and
specific techniques involved, even though the empirical results of the experiment are not conclusive
in terms of unambiguously indicating an optimal
level of two-wheel enforcement. (Those more interested in the empirical results of the traffic law
enforcement experiment may wish to turn to the sub-
section in which details of the traffic law enforcement experiment are given, beginning on page 117.

Only when measures (in dollar terms) of the
cost and the associated benefits of the various
levels of motorcycle traffic law enforcement have
been established can the benefit of adding an additional motorcycle officer on a traffic beat be compared with the cost of adding an additional motorcycle officer. Ideally, motorcycle officers should
be added to each beat until the additional benefit
(mainly in terms of accident reduction) is equal to
the cost (in terms of police costs and reduced speed
or volume of traffic); however, some reservations
to this dictum, dealing with the problems of intangibles or imperfect measurements, must be noted.

Cost of Traffic Law Enforcement

Fortunately, the problem of measuring the cost
of traffic law enforcement is reasonably well in
hand. Data supplied by the Los Angeles Police Department show that the average cost of day watch
motorcycle patrol is approximately $8.00 per man-
hour, including salaries, vehicle and equipment
costs, and overhead.[19] Although this is an average
cost, it is probably very close to the actual marginal cost, for it represents mostly wages and vehicle costs for the motorcycle officers (90 percent
of the total). And, of course, the marginal cost
is the crucial figure in an attempt to balance the
cost of an additional patrol unit against the resulting additional benefit. This cost amounts to

approximately $12,000 per motorcycle unit for the
nine-month day watch.

Another possible cost, not borne by the police
department itself, may occur if strictler traffic
law enforcement results in a reduced speed of traffic flow. This must be counted as a cost of enforcement because speed is one of the primary objectives of automobile travel. Conversely, some
aspects of enforcement may very well increase average speed of travel, such as stricter prohibition
against double parking, left turns in heavy traffic,
or other forms of traffic obstruction. Much illegal
traffic behavior, like other forms of illegal behavior, is prohibited because of its possible harmful effects on others. That, enforcing prohibitions
against certain left turns may increase the travel
time for those who would have benefited from an illegal turn but reduce the travel time of other
drivers who might have been delayed while it was
being made. In this case, it is the net effect on
average travel time that should be calculated, and
it may be that enforcement decreases average travel
time rather than increases it.

The net effect of a change in enforcement on
travel time should be valued in dollar terms to
make it comparable to the other costs and benefits.
Depending on whether enforcement decreases or increases travel time, this item could be either a
benefit or a cost.

Naturally, the average value of automobile
travel time is a very difficult figure to estimate
with any precision, for it depends on assumptions
about the alternative earnings opportunities of
drivers and passengers, on the value of leisure
time, on the pleasantness or unpleasantness of time
spent driving or riding, and on the average number
of occupants per passenger car. The California Division of Highways uses the figure of 3¢ per vehicle-
minute,[20] and several other estimates of the value
of travel time cluster around the 3¢ per vehicle-
minute figure.[21]

If an increase in the level of enforcement does
alter average travel speed on the patrolled route,
the cost or benefit (per day) to the motorists of

this reduction in speed is arrived at by multiplying (1) the increase or decrease in time required
to traverse the beat by (2) $0.03 per minute and
this by (3) volume of passenger car traffic tra-
versing the beat per day. (This value would apply
to passenger car traffic only; if there were a significant amount of commercial traffic using the patrolled street, an additional calculation, using a
commercial vehicle travel time value, would also be
required.)

If motorists independently make their own in-
tuitive balancing of the expected cost of reduced
safety against the benefit of increased speed, why
should the police interfere with their preferences
and enforce greater safety? One possible answer,
apparently assumed in many discussions of traffic
safety, is that motorists underestimate the probability that traffic law violations, such as speeding, will lead to accidents and that motorists must
therefore be protected from themselves as well as
prevented from harming others. Whether or not this
is true is difficult to say; however, even if motorists do accurately estimate the danger involved
in traffic violations, there are reasons to believe
that motorists neglect certain important costs of
illegal driving practices. Traffic safety behavior
has considerable external effect not necessarily
taken into account by an individual motorist in his
own benefit-cost decisions; that is, private calculations about the optimal tradeoff between safety
and travel time may partially or entirely leave out
the possible harmful consequences of decreased
safety for other motorists, pedestrians, and property.

Traffic safety laws and their prescribed penal-
ties are designed to provide a framework to take the
external effects into account, and the existence of
liability laws forces motorists to consider the effects on others of their own safety decisions.

However, present liability laws undoubtedly do
not induce motorists to consider fully all the possible consequences for others of their own driving
actions. For example, motorists at fault pay no
compensation to those who lose time in the monumen-
tal traffic tie-ups that sometimes result from

accidents under congested road conditions, and so
this lost time is an external cost that need not be
considered by the individual motorist in his own
private calculation of the benefits and costs of
his driving behavior. Even in the case of directly
injured victims, unless compensation for damage or
injury is set high enough to make it a matter of
indifference to innocent victims whether they are
unharmed or harmed but compensated, the motorist is
not forced to pay the full cost of accidental injury
or damage. If the victim is compensated merely for
the cost of medical treatment or for repairing
property damage, he is certainly not fully compensated. Even for measurable economic losses, according to a recent study by the Department of
Transportation, on the average only about one-half
of total personal and family economic loss (medical
costs, property damage, and future lost earnings)
was recovered by compensation in a sample of police-
reported injury and fatality automobile accidents.[22]

For these reasons, without some enforcement of
traffic laws incentives to motorists to drive safely
do not include all the social costs that can result
from unsafe driving. Reduction of these costs is
the goal of traffic law enforcement.

Benefits of Traffic Law Enforcement

Accident Reduction. Whereas the costs of
traffic law enforcement seem reasonably amenable to
measurement, it is the proper measure of benefit
that is difficult to calculate. The chief benefit
sought is a reduction in the number of traffic accidents. To be sure, measurement of one aspect of
this benefit, property damage avoided, is not a
great problem. When a property-damage-only (PDO)
accident is prevented, the benefit is at least equal
to what it would have cost to repair such damage,
which the California Division of Highways estimated,
for 1964, at an average of $600 per reported acci-
dent.[23] To this figure should undoubtedly be added
an amount to account for the unpleasantness and in-
convenience of being involved in a traffic accident
and the potential (marginal) cost of legal proceedings and/or insurance adjustment.

The measure of benefit becomes more difficult when one moves from a consideration of property damage avoided to a consideration of injuries avoided. The California Division of Highways uses an estimate, based on survey data, of $2,100 as the direct cost of each injury-accident. This direct cost includes "the money value of: Damage to property, ambulance use, hospital and treatment services, doctor and dentist services, loss of use of vehicle, value of work time lost, legal and court fees, damage awards and settlements, and other miscellaneous items. . . ."[24] However, the loss of future earnings of persons permanently injured as a direct result of an injury-accident is excluded—except insofar as damage awards or settlements may have compensated for such loss.[25] In addition, the figure also makes no allowance for the very real personal suffering involved in injuries. These omissions are made, of course, because of the extreme difficulty—or impossibility in the case of personal suffering—of making a meaningful estimate. It is necessary to be mindful, therefore, in using this estimate of $2,100 per injury-accident, that it represents only the measurable portion of a total cost and that it is the total (measurable + intangible) cost that is relevant for decisions about traffic safety.

The measure of benefit becomes most difficult when the issue of avoiding traffic accident fatalities is broached. And while it may seem offensive to place a money valuation on human life, such a valuation is indispensable in assessing the benefit of traffic safety measures. Obviously no wide agreement can be expected on any specific value, but several estimates have been proposed and used in highway work, and it is instructive to examine them.[26] Using the direct-cost method described above, the California Division of Highways places the cost of fatalities per fatal accident in urban areas at $7,700.[27] However, while the direct-cost method may be appropriate for property damage or injuries, it is a questionable guide to public decisions concerning life-saving measures. At best, the direct-cost method provides an irreducible minimum estimate of the cost of a fatal accident.

In an attempt to supply a more inclusive concept of the cost of traffic fatalities, a study by
the U.S. Department of Transportation added to the
medical and property damage losses an estimate of
the present discounted value (at time of death) of
expected lifetime earnings. Using this concept,
the Department of Transportation estimates the
average total loss per fatality at $89,500.[28] This
would imply an average cost of fatalities per fatal
accident of $89,500 times 1.15, or $102,900, based
on the California average for urban areas of 1.15
fatalities per fatal accident. In a similar study,
which assessed the benefits of motor vehicle injury-
prevention programs, the U.S. Department of Health,
Education, and Welfare estimated the average expected lifetime earnings foregone as a result of
traffic fatalities at $93,000, which is very close
to the Department of Transportation figure.[29]

A third concept of the value of preventing a
traffic fatality is the direct cost of the fatal
accident (medical cost and property damage) plus an
amount that represents the difference between the
discounted foregone earnings and the discounted
foregone consumption of the deceased (that is, the
net rather than gross loss of production to society).
D. J. Reynolds has estimated costs on this basis,
using data from the United Kingdom for 1952. His
calculations showed an average loss of $4,800 per
fatality, based only on the difference between discounted earnings and consumption.[30] Jacques Thedie
and Claude Abraham made similar calculations for
France using 1957 data and estimated that average
net production loss (discounted future earnings
less consumption) per traffic fatality was $8,000.
However, they were agnostic on the question whether
net loss or the full gross loss of production should
be counted as the cost of a fatal accident (that is,
whether future consumption should or should not be
deducted from earnings to determine the loss resulting from traffic fatalities).[31] A reservation
worth noting about both of these net loss calculations is that, when they are broken down into age
and sex groups, a negative value results for three
main categories (old males and both young and old

females), so that on this basis the death of some members of society is actually remunerative--which fact merely illustrates the earlier stress on the fact that calculations must take into account more than the measurable costs of traffic accidents.

Although these various measures have been suggested and computed, it is obvious that no single, usable estimate of the cost of a traffic fatality can be made from the available data. Indeed, the estimates that have been offered are really attempts to answer an impossible question, What is the value of a human life? Answers to this question have usually turned out to be, instead, estimates of the value of the victim's livelihood rather than of his life.[32] Rather than one of these figures, both the low estimate of the California Division of Highways and the high estimate of the Department of Transportation of the cost of a traffic fatality will be used to illustrate the benefit of reducing accidents, and the sensitivity of the final benefit-cost results to the varying concepts of the cost of traffic fatalities will be pointed out.

A summary of the estimates to be used for valuing the cost of traffic accidents (and thus of the benefit of reducing traffic accidents) is presented in Table 3.3, the values adopted being tentative estimates. The estimation of each figure properly deserves a separate in-depth investigation, but it does not seem a sensible expenditure to make an independent, full-scale investigation of the cost of injury or death in each benefit-cost analysis that involves a reduction in traffic accidents, especially in the present case, in which the relatively neglected production side of the analysis is being emphasized.

Although traffic safety is, of course, the prime motive for traffic law enforcement patrol, there are additional side benefits that may occur, that is, nontraffic benefits.

Crime Reduction. One possible side benefit of an increased level of traffic law enforcement is a reduction in crimes along the beat. Presumably some criminals would be deterred from committing crimes if they knew that police could respond very quickly

TABLE 3.3

Cost of Traffic Accidents
(in dollars)

Type of Accident	Average Value of Loss per Accident
Property damage only	600
Injury	2,100
Fatality	
California Division of Highways	7,700
Department of Transportation	102,900

Sources: For fatality (Department of Transportation) information, U.S. Department of Transportation, Economic Consequences of Automobile Accident Injuries, Vol. I (Washington: Government Printing Office, 1970), p. 2; for all other figures, California Division of Highways, "Direct Costs of California State Highway Accidents" (1967), p. 2.

to an alarm. But the experiment can throw little light on this factor since it ran only from 10:00 a.m. to 6:00 p.m., Monday through Friday, and thus entirely missed the high-crime-rate hours. Another problem is uncertainty about what area should be considered to be affected, in terms of crime, by the experiment: the data are limited to the area covered along the beat, but surely a larger area was affected since a policeman could respond to calls in adjacent areas as well. Thus, whatever the police-induced change observed in number of crimes along the beat, it is an underestimate of the total change resulting from patrol variation. Nevertheless, the percentage change in crime along the beat in response to change in patrol force should not be an underestimate of the percentage change in total number of crimes in the entire affected area, because the percentage change is presumably greater in the immediate path of patrol. Thus, in nontraffic criminal activity the percentage change in reported

crimes along the beat can be used as an indicator
of effect on crime.

Valuing the benefit of a reduction in crime is
in many ways more difficult than valuing the benefit of a reduction in traffic accidents, although
some of the difficulties are common to both evaluations. Nevertheless, an attempt to ascribe minimum
dollar cost estimates to various crimes is made in
Chapter 4, which focuses on the effect of deterrent
patrol on crime, and the value estimates presented
in Table 4.2 are used to measure the benefit of any
crime reduction that may take place as a result of
traffic law enforcement patrol.

Details of the Traffic Law
Enforcement Experiment

The Control Groups

At the beginning of the experiment it was
thought that on each beat the accident experience
during the nonexperimental hours (in which enforcement was not altered from its previous level) would
form one kind of control with which to compare the
accident experience during the experimental hours.
Insofar as accidents are caused by the environmental
factors of the roadway, it seems that there should
be a positive correlation between accident rates at
different hours of the same day, week, or month.
That is, if the conditions of the roadway worsen so
as to cause more accidents, it seems that accidents
should increase both in the morning and in the evening; they should decrease at those times if the
condition of the roadway is improved. How strong
the correlation would be depends on (1) the degree
to which traffic accidents are caused by the physical aspects of the road and (2) whether these physical aspects act to cause accidents in the same way
at different times of the day. In regard to the
second point, many environmental aspects of a street
appear to affect accident rates in the same way regardless of the time of day--road surface, median
barriers, physical obstructions to visibility,

signposts, traffic signals, lane markings, and so
forth. Other environmental aspects appear to affect accident rates differently at different times
of day--notably the quality of artificial street
lighting. A priori, it is not possible to say how
important the environmental aspects of each of the
eight experimental traffic beats are in influencing
accident rates or whether the influence is in the
same direction during both the experimental and nonexperimental hours. To test the relation, correlation coefficients for each beat were calculated between the following variables for the five-year
period before the experiment began:

   1. Number of accidents per month during the
hours 10:00 a.m. to 6:00 p.m., Monday through Friday
(the hours of the experiment); and

   2. Number of accidents per month during hours
12:00 p.m. to 10:00 a.m. and 6:00 p.m. to 12:00 p.m.,
Monday through Friday (the nonexperimental hours).
The correlation coefficients, which are measures of
the strength of the linear relationship between each
pair of variables, are shown in Table 3.4.

TABLE 3.4

Correlation Coefficients between Number of
Accidents per Month in Experimental and
Nonexperimental Hours, January 1, 1964,
to September 1, 1968

Beat Number	Injury-Accidents r	Total Accidents r
1	− 0.0937	− 0.0046
2	0.0423	0.0547
3	− 0.1598	− 0.2113
4	− 0.0472	− 0.1980
5	− 0.0287	0.1238
6	0.2947	0.1368
7	0.3567	0.2249
8	0.0078	0.1869

Note: Sample size, 58 observations per beat;
r signifies rank correlation coefficient.

Source: Prepared by the authors.

A surprisingly weak correlation occurs between
the number of accidents per month in the experimental and nonexperimental hours in the five years
preceding the initiation of the experiment; a small
negative correlation occurs in some cases. Several
alternative explanations could account for this
weak relationship: (1) The environmental characteristics of the street were unimportant relative
to other elements in the accident-causation process
on these eight beats. (2) Or even though environmental characteristics were important, on these
eight beats any changes in environmental characteristics affected the accident-causation process in
different ways during experimental and nonexperimental hours. (3) Or even though environmental
characteristics were important, there was no significant change in these characteristics during the
period 1964-68 on these eight beats. Which of
these explanations accounts for the results in this
case it is difficult to say, but the third explanation gains some support from the fact that the criteria for selection of the beats included the requirement that no major changes had occurred on the
beats in the recent past. Whatever the cause, the
nonexperimental hours appear to be unsuitable as a
control with which to compare the experimental
hours to predict what would have happened in the
absence of altered traffic law enforcement manpower
or techniques during the period of the experiment.
It is necessary, then, to rely on simpler comparisons of the numbers of accidents during the experimental hours with the average number of accidents
in the previous five years during the same hours,
without the parallel check (which the nonexperimental hours were expected to provide) of what change
would have occurred on the same beats without any
alteration of enforcement. However, the comparison
of accident experience during the experiment with
the average accident experience before the experiment does appear justified in this case, for the
test streets chosen had undergone no significant
changes known to the police and traffic departments
over the period in which the data were collected.
    The test of the validity of the potential con-
trol data shows the danger of assuming that a

seemingly plausible control group really has the
property of showing what would happen in the absence
of the experimental changes. Other studies of the
effects of traffic law enforcement in nonurban areas
have sometimes used similar parallel roads for control purposes, apparently without testing whether
the control road accident experience is sufficiently
correlated with that of the test road to predict
what would have happened on the test road in the
absence of experimental traffic law enforcement
activity.[33]

Traffic Volume

One of the most important determinants of the
number of traffic accidents occurring on a beat is,
of course, the volume of traffic. The number of
traffic accidents may increase or decrease simply
because volume has increased or decreased, without
any change in all the other factors that enter into
the process of accident causation. To make comparisons of traffic safety among areas or over time,
traffic accident rates are used--numbers of traffic
accidents per 1,000 population, per 1,000 automobiles registered, or per 1 million passenger car
miles driven. These rates are meant to account for
the factor of exposure to the accident-causation
process. To estimate the exposure on the eight experimental beats, the volume of traffic, in terms
of the number of cars per day traveling along the
beat, was measured at a point near the middle of
each beat. Admittedly this measure of exposure was
imperfect, but it did serve to show whether any obvious changes in volume of traffic had occurred in
recent years that could account for changes in the
total number of accidents on the beat. For traffic
volume in the years prior to the beginning of the
experiment, it was necessary to rely on volume
counts that happened to have been made at the same
location for other purposes. There were thus fewer
counts for each beat in previous years than for the
experimental period, and there were more ample data
for previous years on some beats than on others.
Table 3.5 shows the volume counts for those beats

TABLE 3.5

Traffic Volume, 1964-69

Intersection	Weekday Average Volume, 1964-68, October-June	Weekday Average Volume, 1968-69, October-June
Pacific Coast Highway at Avalon Boulevard (Beat 4)	29,270 [2,270]	27,810 [1,180]
Avalon Boulevard at Pacific Coast Highway (Beat 4)	18,970 [2,860]	18,370 [1,670]
Van Nuys Boulevard at Magnolia Street (Beat 7)	34,500 [2,890]	36,280 [2,530]
Olympic Boulevard at Normandie Avenue (Beat 8)	28,740 [805]	28,070 [1,890]

Note: Standard deviations of the weekday volume counts are shown in brackets below the averages. Data for other beats (for which fewer volume counts in the years before experiment are available) are shown in Supplement 2 to this chapter.

Source: Prepared by the authors.

on which the largest numbers of counts were available at the same intersection for the test period and for previous years. The volume counts for other beats (where the averages necessarily included counts from different, and therefore less comparable, intersections along the same beat) are shown in Supplement 2 to this chapter.

The data presented in Table 3.5 show that on each beat the average weekday volume during the experimental period was very close to the average weekday volume for the previous years, and in each case it falls within one standard deviation of the

average weekday volume in the previous years. The
data in Supplement 2 to this chapter, although less
accurate for purposes of comparison, also show a
pattern of only slight volume change between the
experimental period and previous years.

Since the traffic-volume measure of exposure
indicates no significant change on any of the beats,
it is not necessary to express accident experience
in terms of accident rates to make a comparison between the test period and previous years. Instead
direct comparisons can be made between the number
of accidents during the test period and during previous years to see whether there was a change in
the underlying accident-causation process at work.

Interpretation of Accident Statistics

A fundamental problem in interpreting traffic
accident statistics is the variability of accident
experience even in the absence of any changes in
all identifiable factors that determine the accident-
causation process, including the factor of traffic
law enforcement by police. Thus, when trying to
analyze the accident experience of an area, one is
confronted by the problem of determining how the
random nature of traffic accidents has interacted
with the basic causation process to bring about a
particular result. For example, assume that past
experience indicates that patrolmen can expect
10 injury-accidents per week along beat A; if, in a
particular year, there were actually 15 per week,
how would this deviation from the expectation be
explained? Was there some unknown change in the
accident-causation process? Was the change merely
random? Did both of these possibilities contribute
to the change? (It should be noted that both changes
might not move in the same direction; that is, the
accident-causation process might have improved, thus
tempering a random change that alone might have resulted in 17 accidents.) As a general rule, large
deviations from the expected value can be attributed
to changes in the accident-causation process, whereas small deviations can be attributed to the random
nature of traffic accidents, but it is possible to
be more precise by the use of alpha and beta errors.

An alpha (or Type I) error is one of commission; in the example, it would be the error resulting from an assumption that the increase to 15 traffic accidents was caused by a change in the accident-causation process when, in fact, the increase was random. A beta (or Type II) error is one of ommission; in the example, a beta error would be one resulting from the assumption that the change in the number of traffic accidents was random when it was actually the result of a change in the causation process. An important feature of alpha and beta errors is that, other things being constant, a decrease in one of them must result in an increase in the other. Because of this tradeoff, it is necessary to determine which of the two errors would have the more serious consequences for the decision-making process. In this experiment it can be argued that because the absolute number of traffic accidents is small, the relative effect of a random variation would be great; thus, to avoid identifying these random fluctuations as being significant changes, a low alpha error (and, consequently, a high beta error) might be desirable. On the other hand, since examination of traffic accidents only would probably result in an underestimate of the benefit of increased patrol (for reasons discussed later), perhaps a low beta (high alpha) error would be appropriate.

The Accident Data

The data used to estimate the effect of the enforcement experiment were reported injury-accidents occurring during the hours of the experiment (10:00 a.m. to 6:00 p.m., Monday through Friday), both during the experiment and during the previous five years. Although data for property-damage-only (PDO) accidents were also collected, the reporting of PDOs is much less reliable than the reporting of injury-accidents. During the comparison period (the period before the experiment) the criterion for required reporting of a PDO was changed from $50 or more in property damage to $200 or more. Furthermore, the number of officers on a traffic beat can easily influence the proportion of PDOs that are

reported to the police; if no officer observes an
accident, the parties involved in a minor PDO may
prefer not to report it. Thus, reported PDOs may
increase when patrol intensity is increased simply
because more accidents that do occur are reported.[34]

Because the inclusion of PDO data might have
been misleading, analysis was restricted to injury-
accidents. The definition of a reportable injury-
accident had not changed during the periods under
study, and, as mentioned above, the reporting of
injury-accidents by the LAPD Accident Investigation
Division is substantially uniform. However, in the
assessmnet of the benefit of any measured reduction
in injury-accidents, an estimate will be required
of the resulting benefit of any accompanying change
in PDO and fatality accidents.

Effect of Traffic Law Enforcement
on Traffic Accidents

The accident experience results of the traffic
law enforcement experiment are summarized in Table
3.6. In column 2 the number of officers on each
beat during the years before the experiment are
shown, and in column 3 the number during the experimental test period. In column 4 are given the
average numbers of injury-accidents during the same
months for the preexperiment years 1964-68, and in
column 5 the number of injury-accidents during the
nine-month test period in 1968-69.

On the first two beats the intention was to
see what effect different methods of enforcement
had on injury-accident experience, manpower remaining the same; only on the warning-only beat was
there a reduction in the number of accidents from
the average of the four preceding years, during
which the enforcement technique had been the standard method of issuing citations for observed violations.

The other six beats were designed to show the
effect an increase or decrease in the number of
officers (employing the standard citation method)
had on observed injury-accident experience. Before

TABLE 3.6

Enforcement and Accidents on the
Experimental Beats

Beat (1)	Number of Officers		Injury-Accidents		Injury-Accident Reduction (-) or Increase (+)
	Before (2)	Test (3)	Before (4)	Test (5)	(6)
1	1	1 (Visibility)	61.25	62	+ 1%
2	1	1 (Warning)	65.50	57	- 13%
3	1	4	74.75	75	0%
4	0	4	49.50	40	- 19%
5	1	1	55.50	59	+ 6%
6	0	1	41.25	39	- 5%
7	1	3	54.00	47	- 13%
8	1	0	50.00	58	+ 16%

Source: Prepared by the authors.

each beat is examined in detail, one interesting overall observation can be made: On each beat on which enforcement patrol was increased (beats 3,4, 6,7), the number of accidents either declined (beats 4,6,7) or remained the same (beat 3) and that on the beats on which enforcement was unchanged (beat 5) or was decreased (beat 8), the number of accidents increased.

More specifically, the six beats on which the number of officers was altered (beats 3,4,5,6,7,8) can be ranked according to the change in the number of accidents. Table 3.7 shows the changes for each beat, and their relative ranks. With this information a correlation coefficient can be calculated for the two ranks. There is an obvious rough negative rank correlation between the two variables; a greater increase in officers is associated with a greater decrease in accidents. The rank correlation

TABLE 3.7

Input-Output Rankings on Six
Experimental Beats

Beat (1)	Change in Officers (2)	Rank of (2) (3)	Percent Change in Accidents (4)	Rank of (4) (5)
8	− 1	1	+ 16	1
5	0	2	+ 6	2
6	+ 1	3	− 5	4
7	+ 2	4	− 13	5
3	+ 3	5	0	3
4	+ 4	6	− 19	6

Source: Prepared by the authors.

coefficient, r, tests the significance of this relationship. In this case $r = 0.829$; it is significant at the 0.05 level of significance.[35] This significant negative rank correlation between the input
and output rankings suggests that an increase in the
number of officers does reduce the number of traffic
injury-accidents, but it shows nothing about the
magnitude of the effect of traffic officers on traffic accidents.

Before these data are interpreted as evidence
that increased manpower decreases accidents, it is
necessary, of course, to examine the possibility
that changes may be the result of random movements
in the number of accidents, such as occur from year
to year even in the absence of any changes in enforcement techniques on manpower. This problem of
statistical inference will be discussed below.
However, assuming for the moment that the observed
changes in accidents are in fact the result of
changes in enforcement and that there are no other
effects (on travel speed, crime rates), how can the
traffic accident results be evaluated in cost-
benefit terms?

Before a cost-benefit analysis can be undertaken, however, some estimate must be made of effects

on fatality and property damage accidents, since
measurements have been made of the effect of enforcement on injury-accidents only. As mentioned
above, the percentage of property damage accidents
reported depends partly on the number of officers
on the beat, and so the reported PDOs are not a reliable indicator of actual PDOs on a beat when manpower is varied. And since fatality accidents are
so rare on any one traffic beat, the sample size is
much too small to make possible any inferences concerning them. In the absence of reliable data on
PDO and fatality accidents, it will be assumed that
enforcement affects the accident-causation process
for fatality and PDO accidents in the same way it
does that for injury-accidents and that these other
two categories of accidents increase or decrease in
the same proportion as do injury-accidents.

Further, it will be assumed that the ratios of
fatal/injury and property-damage/injury-accidents
on each beat are the same as the citywide ratios
for surface streets. These accident figures are
given for 1967 in Table 3.8.

Thus, there were 0.939 property damage accidents per injury-accident, and 0.013 fatal accidents
per injury-accident. Assuming that this relationship between injury-accidents and property damage
and fatal accidents also holds for changes in the
number of accidents, it is possible to construct an

TABLE 3.8

Surface Street Traffic Accidents,
Los Angeles, 1967

	Totals	Ratios
Injury-accidents	27,530	
Property damage accidents	25,810	
Fatal accidents	348	
PDO-injury		0.939
Fatal-injury		0.013

Source: Los Angeles Police Department, Statistical Digest, 1967, pp. 49-54.

injury-accident equivalent cost that includes, for
each injury-accident, the associated cost of 0.939
property damage accidents and 0.013 fatal accidents.
This injury-accident equivalent makes it possible
to represent the total cost of all accidents on a
beat in terms of the number of injury-accidents
only. The construction of the injury-accident
equivalent figure is shown in Table 3.9, together
with data for the cost of each type of accident
taken from Table 3.3.

With the estimates of the total injury-accident
equivalent cost, it is possible to make a preliminary and partial evaluation of the costs and benefits of the enforcement changes, at this point in
terms only of the cost of patrol and the cost of
accidents. This is done in Table 3.10. Column 2
shows the change in the number of motorcycle officers on each beat, and column 3 shows the cost to
the police department of any change, using the cost
figure, developed above, of $12,000 per nine-month
period. Column 4 in Table 3.10 shows the change in
the number of injury-accidents (taken from columns

TABLE 3.9

Injury-Accident Equivalent Cost

Type of Accident (1)	Cost (2)	Number per Injury-Accident (3)	Equivalent Cost (4) = (2) x (3)
Injury	$2,100	1	$2,100
Property damage	600	0.939	560
Fatality: High	102,900	0.013	1,340
Low	7,700	0.013	100
Injury-accident equivalent:		High	4,000
		Low	2,760

Note: Accident costs are taken from Table 3.3.

Source: Prepared by the authors.

TABLE 3.10

Enforcement Costs and Accident Costs on the Experimental Beats
(thousands of dollars)

Beat (1)	Change in Number of Officers (2)	Change in Cost of Patrol (3) = (2) x $12,000	Change in Number of Injury-Accidents (4)	Benefit		Net Benefit	
				High (5) = (4) x $4,000	Low (6) = (4) x $2,760	High (7) = (5) - (3)	Low (8) = (6) - (3)
1	0 (Visibility)	0	+ 0.75	- 3	- 2.1	- 3	- 2.1
2	0 (Warning)	0	- 8.5	+ 34	+ 23.5	+ 34	+ 23.5
3	+ 3	+ 36	0	0	0	- 36	- 36
4	+ 4	+ 48	- 9.5	+ 38	+ 26.2	- 10	- 21.8
5	0 (no change)	0	+ 3.5	- 14	- 9.7	- 14	- 9.7
6	+ 1	+ 12	- 2.25	+ 9	+ 6.2	- 3	- 5.8
7	+ 2	+ 24	- 7	+ 28	+ 19.3	+ 4	- 4.7
8	- 1	- 12	+ 8	- 32	- 22	- 20	- 10.1

Source: Prepared by the authors.

4 and 5 in Table 3.6), and columns 5 and 6 show a
high and a low dollar value of the change in the
number of injury-accidents, with the difference
arising because of the alternative high and low
values for the cost of a fatal traffic accident.
Columns 7 and 8 show the high and low estimates of
the net benefits of the change, obtained by subtracting the cost (column 3) from the benefits
(columns 5 and 6).

The low estimate of net benefit of each enforcement change results from the use of the low
California Division of Highways figure for the average cost of a fatal traffic accident, and the
high estimate results from the use of the high Department of Transportation figure for the loss from
a fatality. As mentioned, neither figure is recommended here as the correct one; however, if the
benefits of traffic accident reduction by means of
traffic law enforcement are to be compared with the
benefits of other methods of accident reduction,
such as highway improvement, a uniform figure for
the value of fatality reduction should be adopted
in the evaluation. Otherwise, those methods of accident reduction would be artificially favored that
were evaluated using the higher value for fatality
reduction.

One interesting aspect of Table 3.10 is that,
on the five beats on which the number of officers
was changed (and restricting the analysis to measured benefits of accident reduction versus public
agency costs only--a narrow point of view often
adopted in traffic safety studies), none of the
changes in manpower from the status quo (either increases or decreases) appears clearly desirable.
Thus, according to this criterion, the initial allocation was better than any of the alternative
manpower allocations proposed. On beat 8, which
had previously had the standard allocation, the
magnitude of the accident cost increase (both high
and low estimates) was greater than the magnitude
of the patrol cost decrease achieved by eliminating
motorcycle enforcement, implying that the previous
level of enforcement was worth the cost. On beat 6,
which previously had no motorcycle allocation, the

introduction of the standard allocation did not reduce accident costs (by either the high or the low
estimate) by as much as the increased cost of patrol, implying that the introduction of a motorcycle on this beat was not worth the cost. On beats
3 and 4, which were treated with saturation-level
enforcement, the cost clearly exceeded the benefit;
and on beat 7, also a saturation beat, the net benefit is negative for the low estimate and positive
only for the high estimate.

Statistical Significance

Before any use can be made of these preliminary
estimated benefits of traffic accident reduction,
it is necessary to decide whether the changes in
the number of accidents that accompanied the changes
in enforcement can reasonably be interpreted as
caused by the enforcement changes or can instead be
easily explained by the year-to-year range of random fluctuation that is ordinarily observed even
without any changes in enforcement. To decide
whether the change in the number of accidents was
random or not, a tradeoff must be made of the probability of an alpha error (concluding that the
change in number of accidents was the result of a
change in the accident-causation process when in
fact there was only a random variation in accidents)
against the probability of a beta error (concluding
that the change in the number of traffic accidents
was random when it was actually the result of a
change in the causation process). Naturally, the
smaller the observed change, the more likely it is
that it is merely random; the problem is to decide
how large a change in the number of injury-accidents
must take place before it can be concluded that it
was not random.

Fortunately, the random aspect of traffic accidents has in numerous instances been found to be
accurately described by the Poisson Distribution,
and it will be assumed that it is here also. The
Poisson Distribution gives, for any expected mean
number of accidents (that is, the mean determined
by the basic traffic accident-causation process),

the probability that any higher or lower number may
occur as a matter of chance during any time period.
Since the highest probability of accident frequency
is centered around the mean of the distribution, an
observed number of accidents far away from the expected mean implies a small probability that the
observation came from the expected distribution and
a high probability that the observation came from a
distribution having a different mean number of accidents. Using the Poisson Distribution, limits
can be calculated above and below the expected mean
number of accidents such that there is a low probability of observing any number of accidents outside
those limits if the mean of the accident distribution is unchanged. The decision rule is, then,
that if the number of accidents during the test period falls outside the limits that have been set up,
it can be concluded that the test period accident
number results from an accident-causation process
with a different mean. Usually the limits are set
such that there is only either a 5 percent or a 1
percent probability that any number of accidents
outside the limits would result from a chance deviation from the expected mean. With limits set at
the 5 percent probability level an experiment rerun
a large number of times would give an accident
number outside the limits in 5 percent of the cases
just as a matter of chance; it would thus have been
concluded in 5 percent of the cases that there was
a changed mean (and changed accident-causation process) when in fact nothing had changed. A low
probability of 5 percent or 1 percent is usually
adopted so as to guard against reporting spurious
findings (the Type 1 or alpha error mentioned
above). But this low probability of reporting a
change when it did not occur may also be associated
with a high probability of failing to detect some
changes that do occur (the Type 2 or beta error).
In most traffic accident studies a low probability
of Type 1 error is specified, on the assumption
that it is very important to avoid false reports of
a change in the accident-causation process, and the
probability of making a Type 2 error is not discussed. But when the problem of Type 2 errors is

not explored, there is an unknown probability that, because of the requirement of a low Type 1 error, there may be a large probability of failing to detect some changes in the accident-causation process that do occur. To take this problem into account, columns 4 through 7 of Table 3.11 show for each beat the probability of failing to detect (beta error) either a 10 percent or a 20 percent change in the mean number of accidents that would result from requiring that the size of the alpha error be no more than either 0.1 or 0.2. Also, in column 3 is shown the size of the alpha error associated with the conclusion that the number of accidents that did occur during the test period indicates a significant change in the accident-causation process as compared to the base period.

As shown, none of the changes is significant if the requirement is made that there be only a 0.05 chance that the change from the base period to the test period could have occurred as a matter of chance. And only on beat 4 is the change significant if alpha is set at 0.1. However, the table also shows that if an alpha of 0.1 is required, there is a large probability (beta) that real changes as great as 20 percent in the mean number of accidents on each beat might not be detected. (The probability of failing to detect a real change of this magnitude would not be lower than 0.3, and on two beats it would be as high as 0.59.) For an alpha of 0.2 the beta error is lower, but still sizable on most beats. There is no easy way to select an appropriate combination of alpha and beta errors; what is appropriate depends on the cost of making each type of decision error. In this regard, it should be noted that, except for beat 4, a decrease in the accident mean of 20 percent would change the net cost to a net benefit (as measured in Table 3.10) on all beats on which enforcement manpower was increased or on which enforcement techniques were altered. Thus, a high beta error probability of failure to detect a change in the accident mean of 20 percent would imply a high probability of rejecting a potential improvement in resource allocation. The cost of making an alpha

TABLE 3.11

Tradeoff between Alpha Error and Beta Error

Beat (1)	Percent Change in Accidents (2)	Percent Change Is Significant for Alpha (3)	Beta Error If Alpha = 0.1 K = 10% (4)	K = 20% (5)	Beta Error If Alpha = 0.2 K = 10% (6)	K = 20% (7)
1	+ 1%	> 0.2	0.82	0.59	0.70	0.42
2	- 13%	= 0.13	0.76	0.45	0.64	0.32
3	0%	> 0.2	0.65	0.30	0.48	0.20
4	- 19%	= 0.08	0.71	0.42	0.56	0.30
5	+ 6%	> .02	0.82	0.59	0.70	0.42
6	- 5%	> .02	0.74	0.48	0.58	0.35
7	- 13%	= 0.15	0.71	0.42	0.56	0.30
8	+ 16%	= 0.14	0.71	0.46	0.56	0.26

Note: K equals the change from the base period to the test period in the mean of the accident frequency distribution.

Source: Prepared by the authors.

type error may, however, be much less. The disadvantage of interpreting a random decrease in accidents as evidence of a change in the accident-causation process (alpha error) may be relatively less important because the measurable benefit of the assumed decrease in accidents may not exceed the additional enforcement costs, and the experimental enforcement allocation would be rejected anyway; for instance, on beat 4, if the measured decrease in injury-accidents was the result of random fluctuation rather than a change in the accident-causation process, according to the preliminary benefit measurement in Table 3.10, the cost of the increased enforcement would exceed even the spurious measured benefit and an erroneous decision would not be made that the enforcement increase was a worthwhile policy (neglecting for the moment other costs and benefits of the experimental change).

Even if accident results of the experimental enforcement policy do lead to the conclusion that there has been a change in the accident-causation process, it cannot be concluded that the particular number of accidents observed in the experimental period is the new mean number of accidents that would occur if the experimental enforcement policy was made permanent. A reliable estimate of the new mean would require a continuation of the enforcement policy for several periods, so that the new mean could be calculated from the repeated observations. Thus, the conclusion on statistical grounds that there had been a change in the accident-causation process on any beat would suggest the necessity of further investigation of those experimental enforcement techniques or enforcement levels that appear most promising. For instance, the results in Table 3.10 indicate that the enforcement methods on beats 2 and 7 are worth further investigation. And this potential for further experimentation with the most promising experimental methods is another reason for tolerating statistical tests of significance with a relatively high alpha error: if the results stemmed only from chance variation in numbers of accidents, further tests should reveal the mistake. Conversely, the size of the beta error would call

for particular attention because acceptance of a
high beta error means a high probability of rejecting from further consideration a potential improvement in enforcement methods.

If these arguments are deemed sufficiently important to warrant acceptance of a change in the
number of accidents as significant if the probability of making a Type 1 error is as high as 0.15,
then four beats show a significant change in the
accident-causation process, and two beats, 2 and 8,
are of particular interest because the preliminary
calculation of costs and benefits shows that the
change in benefits exceeded the change in costs of
enforcement. It should be noted that these preliminary results are insufficient as a basis for judg-
ing the worth of traffic law enforcement because
they refer only to a portion of total costs and
benefits. But before moving on to consideration of
other costs and benefits, it may be useful to question why traffic accident results turned out as
they did on the selection of experimental beats.

First, it can be observed that, so far as the
effect of enforcement on accidents is concerned,
manpower was obviously not misallocated before the
experiment began, because no form of reallocation,
either an increase or decrease, showed a clear increase in benefits. Apparently the previous method
of determining allocation was not grossly in error.

Another observation is prompted by the experience on beat 2, the warnings-only beat. The number
of accidents was reduced on this beat without any
increase in the manpower allocation, and some elementary but important reasons may serve to explain
this fact. Despite widespread silence on the matter, many police departments have informal quotas
for the number of citations that traffic law enforcement officers should write in a day or week.
This quota system is an understandable response to
the difficult problem of defining the duties of officers and ensuring their performance, especially
in a field in which the final output is difficult
to quantify. Because final output is difficult
both to measure and to relate to agency inputs, police administrators tend to rely on work statistics

(intermediate outputs) that appear to be related to
final output. But this use of work statistics as a
proxy for output can lead to unproductive behavior
unless there is a close congruence between the intermediate goal as defined for lower level decisions
and the ultimate goal of the agency. For instance,
if output is defined to the traffic officers as a
certain number of citations issued per day, there
is no particular incentive for an officer to concentrate his citations on violations most likely to result in accidents. In fact, traffic officers are
not always given accident statistics that reveal
the high-accident intersections or the violations
involved in accidents during past periods on the
beat. Rather, officers have an incentive to issue
citations for obvious violations that are difficult
for the violator to contest, because contested violations can lead to lengthy court appearances by
the citing officer. Thus, there is an inappropriate
incentive to concentrate citation issuance at "apple
orchard" locations--locations where the traffic patterns are such that a large number of obvious violations occur and are easy to cite without risk of contest by the violators--even though these citations
may not be at the locations or for the violations
accounting for the greatest numbers of accidents on
the beat.

In the experimental situation on beat 2, where
the traffic officer was assigned to issue warnings
only, he could stop motorists for any potentially
dangerous violations even though the proof of violation was not incontestable. In addition, the warning-
only officer never had to lurk in a concealed location while waiting for an incontestable citation and
was thus able to patrol the beat more visibly. While
this speculation on the possible explanation of the
effectiveness of greater use of warnings would have
to be tested by further experimentation, it illustrates the potential conflict between a lower level
work measure--citations issued--and a higher level
agency goal--reduction in accidents and congestion.
For instance, if 40 percent of the accidents along
a beat are caused by illegal turning and 10 percent
by following too closely, then a patrol procedure

that discerned no difference between issuing tickets
for the former and issuing tickets for the latter
would not be very efficient. The marginal benefit
of a ticket for illegal turning might be far greater
than that of a ticket for following too closely, and
yet the two would be treated as equal by the lowest
level decision makers--those who actually carry out
the policy.

The preceding discussion has somewhat exaggerated the actual situation in the LAPD traffic bureau.
Some attention is given to a beat's previous accident experience, and some violations are considered
more serious than others in light of that experience.
However, the fact remains that the patrolman is to a
large extent judged on the number of tickets he issues, not on the incidence of traffic accidents
along his beat. The intermediate goal of issuing
tickets has become an end unto itself instead of being a means to the goal of accident deterrence.

To see if in fact a shift in the goals of the
patrolman would result in a reduction in accidents,
a further experiment could be undertaken at little
or no cost. It would involve analyzing a particular beat's history with emphasis on the types and
locations of violations that have most often resulted
in accidents. The data would be made available to
the patrolman, who would be instructed that his goal
was to be accident reduction and that the number of
tickets he issued would be considered only insofar
as certain violations had been shown to be likely
to result in accidents. If this were done for several beats over a sufficient period (probably at
least one year), the results should show whether
such a reorientation of output measures at lower
levels to conform to higher level police department
goals would be useful.

Effect of Traffic Law Enforcement
on Crime Rates

So far the effect of traffic law enforcement
patrol has been analyzed only with respect to traffic accidents. That analysis has been somewhat

detailed because traffic safety is the main program objective of the traffic program and because the assumed effect of patrol on safety has in the past been the chief criterion for assignment of traffic officers. Furthermore, most other studies of police traffic law enforcement have concentrated on the relationship between patrol and accidents--and this study was meant to augment that literature, which has largely neglected urban traffic law enforcement research. However, one of the important aspects of program analysis is that it provides a framework for the consideration of costs incurred and benefits produced outside a particular agency as a result of that agency's actions; such nonagency costs and benefits are too frequently neglected, even with respect to different bureaus within the same (police) department. Existing organizational demarcations tend to concentrate the attention of each bureau on its own primary objective--and this is true in the field of traffic as well as in other fields. For instance, traffic law enforcement patrol may achieve some of the crime deterrent effects produced by general patrol, though the traffic bureau is not organizationally charged with responsibility for doing so. And if traffic patrol does have the effect of crime reduction, the net benefit of traffic patrol would be underestimated if all the cost of the patrol was charged to the traffic program and measured only the benefit of any traffic accident reduction. The side effect of crime reduction should be counted as a separate and additional benefit of traffic patrol. (Conversely, any reduction by general patrol of traffic accidents should also be counted as a benefit of general patrol.)

To estimate the effect of the experimental changes in traffic law enforcement patrol on crime, the percentage change in reported crime from the average number during the four previous years to the number during the experimental period was measured for each beat and for each of 11 separate crimes.[36] Then the correlation coefficient for the percentage change in reported crime on each beat and the absolute change in the number of traffic law enforcement officers per mile on each beat was

calculated. The correlation was surprisingly weak
and insignificant for all crimes, except that there
was a negative relation between traffic law enforcement patrol and the number of robberies. For robberies the negative correlation was sufficiently
strong ($r = 0.823$) to indicate less than a 1 percent chance ($\alpha < 0.01$) that it was the result of a
random fluctuation in robberies on the eight beats.
(It should be noted that this result may be untypical of other forms of patrol under other situations--
and an especially important qualification is that
the beats were patrolled during low-crime hours of
the day.)

Although further research would be necessary to
confirm this relationship (for robberies) or lack of
relationship (for other crimes) between traffic patrol and reported crime, for the present preliminary
purpose the reduction in robberies on each beat will
be included as one of the benefits of traffic patrol
in the interest of determining what effect it has on
the previous calculation of net benefit in terms of
accident reduction. This calculation is, however,
even more tentative than was the calculation in the
case of traffic accidents, for there is the possibility that robberies were not really deterred by
the patrol, but rather merely diverted to other locations. If such was the case, the crime reduction
benefits of the traffic patrol would be purely local,
compensated for by an increase in the cost of crime
elsewhere. The extent of such a diversion, if one
occurred at all, is unfortunately unknown; however,
the econometric study in Chapter 4 of the effect of
general patrol on crime indicates that the total
amount of crime in any city is negatively related
to the number of patrol officers per capita, so that
the police are at the very least able to reduce
crime within their own political jurisdiction.

The slope of the straight line correlation between the percentage change in robberies and the
change in officers per mile indicates that, on the
average, a 0.1 increase in officers per mile leads
to a 7.9 percent reduction in the total number of
robberies. Using this result, an estimate of the
benefit of robbery reduction (or increase) associated with the experimental change in traffic officer

allocation is made in Table 3.12. Column 2 of the
table shows the average number of robberies for the
previous four years during the period corresponding
to the experimental period (10 a.m. to 6 p.m., Monday through Friday, October through June). Column 3
shows the change in traffic officers per mile on
each beat as compared to the base period, and column
4 shows the associated percentage reduction in robberies, assuming that a 0.1 change in officers per
mile changes the number of robberies by 7.9 percent
in the same direction. The absolute change in robberies is found in column 5.

Estimating the dollar value of the social cost
is as difficult for a robbery as it is for a traffic
accident; the estimate that will be used here is
that developed in the following chapter and shown in
Table 4.12, which includes the cost of the goods
stolen and the subsequent cost to the criminal justice system of dealing with the robbery. That estimate is $1,600 per robbery. Using this dollar es-
timate, it is possible to translate the change in
the number of robberies on each beat into a change
in the cost of robberies; the result appears in column 6 of Table 3.12. A decrease in the cost of
crime is, of course, a benefit of the traffic patrol,
and for any final evaluation of costs and benefits
it should be added to the previously measured benefits (Table 3.10) of a reduction in the number of
traffic accidents associated with patrol changes.
However, before this is done, another potentially
important effect of traffic law enforcement patrol
will be considered--the effect on the speed of traffic flow.

Effect of Traffic Law Enforcement
on Speed of Travel

One of the chief goals of the traffic program
is to reduce congestion and the travel time of trips
on surface streets. Consequently, an important question is whether motorcycle patrol contributes to
this goal, since the existing method of enforcement
allocation is based almost entirely on an accident
reduction criterion. As discussed earlier, it seems

TABLE 3.12

Effect of Traffic Law Enforcement on Crime

Beat (1)	Robberies, Average 1964-68 (2)	Change in Officers per Mile (3)	% Change in Robberies, 1968-69* (4) = (3) x -79	Absolute Change in Robberies (5) = (4) x (2)	Change in Cost of Robberies (6) = (5) x $1,600
1	3.75	0	0	0	0
2	3.75	0	0	0	0
3	1.00	+ 0.88	- 69	- 0.70	- 1,120
4	2.75	+ 0.81	- 64	- 1.76	- 2,820
5	3.50	0	0	0	0
6	1.50	+ 0.23	- 18	- 0.27	- 432
7	0.75	+ 0.53	- 42	- 0.32	- 510
8	1.50	- 0.31	+ 24	+ 0.36	+ 575

*The correlation of change in robberies and change in traffic patrol indicates that an increase in patrol intensity of 0.1 officer per mile leads to a decrease in robberies by 7.9 percent.

Source: Prepared by the authors.

a priori that enforcement could either increase or
decrease average travel time for motorists traveling
along a patrolled beat.

Increased travel time could come about through
fewer drivers' exceeding the speed limit, making
time-saving but illegal turns, failing to come to a
full halt at stop signs, and so forth. Decreased
travel time could come about through encouraging
drivers to adhere to the "rules of the game," whereby one driver is prohibited from imposing external
costs on other drivers in the form of either increased travel time or reduced safety.

It is, of course, extremely difficult to obtain
data on all aspects of the effect of enforcement on
average travel time; however, during the experiment
data were obtained on perhaps the most important indicator of the effect of enforcement on travel time--
the speed distributions of moving automobiles at
selected points on each beat. These were obtained
by means of radar observations made during the experimental period. Unfortunately, no comparable
body of radar observations was available for the
years preceding the experiment, and so the effect
of enforcement on speed must be inferred from a
cross-sectional comparison of the eight beats on
which enforcement was varied. (The data on speed
distributions are shown in Supplement 2 to this chapter.)

An immediate inference from the radar speed
data is that, regardless of the level of enforcement,
only a very small proportion of drivers exceeded the
speed limit on the selection of beats under study;
on no beat was there an average of more than 5 percent of drivers exceeding the speed limit by more
than 5 mph during the speed observations. This
could have been expected because of the normally
heavy traffic flow conditions on main surface streets
in Los Angeles. There is not even a negative rank
correlation between enforcement levels in terms of
officers per mile and the percentage of drivers exceeding the speed limit (rank correlation between
the two is +0.045), indicating that opportunities
for speeding are determined more by traffic and road
conditions than by enforcement level on these beats.

This situation is, of course, different from that
on rural highways or freeways, where drivers have
more individual discretion with the result that enforcement may be a relatively more significant de-
terminant of speed.

Since so few drivers exceeded the speed limit
on the beats under study at any level of enforcement, it seems unlikely that enforcement would appreciably reduce the steady flow or speed of traffic, especially since such a small proportion of
drivers exceeded the posted speed limit by an amount
likely to lead to a citation for excessive speed
(the average percentage of drivers exceeding the
posted speed limit by more than 5 mph was only 1.3
percent).

Because the limited evidence on speed distributions indicates very little effect of enforcement
level on the (generally small) fraction of drivers
exceeding the speed limit and because other effects
(even the direction of the effects) on traffic delay are almost impossible to measure, no attempt
will be made to arrive at a dollar value estimate
of the effect of enforcement on travel time. Instead, as a second-best solution, an estimate will
be made of what the magnitude of the effect of enforcement on average speed and travel time would
have to be to seriously affect the previous calculation of other costs and benefits. (To anticipate
the results, it is interesting that a very small
change in average speed can greatly affect the calculation.)

To estimate the social cost of a change in
traffic speed, it is necessary first to know the
volume of traffic on each beat during the experiment. Though traffic volumes in Supplement 1 to this
chapter show only the average 24-hour volume counts,
detailed examination of daily traffic volumes shows
that at least one-third and often close to one-half
of total daily volume occurs during the hours of
the experimental patrol, 10 a.m. to 6 p.m. Also,
the average volume on all street lengths of the
eight beats was approximately 27,000. A conservative estimate of average traffic volume on a beat
during the experimental hours would thus be 9,000

vehicles per day. The average traffic beat length
was 3.7 miles. With this information and with the
valuation of the cost of travel time of 3¢ per
vehicle-minute that was discussed earlier, it is
possible to estimate the effect on travel time cost
of a change in average steady-flow speed of traffic.
For instance, at 30 mph it takes 7.40 minutes to
travel 3.7 miles. If speed is reduced to 29 mph,
it takes 7.66 minutes, or 0.26 minutes longer. With
a cost of travel time of 3¢ per vehicle-minute, this
reduction in speed of travel by 1 mph implies an increased cost of travel of 78¢ per vehicle travers-
ing the full beat. This is, of course, an extremely
small cost per vehicle, but for 9,000 vehicles per
day it amounts to a total cost of $70 per day, or
$13,650 during the nine-month period of the experi-
ment (which included 195 weekdays). Conversely, if
the effect of enforcement was to increase the
steady-flow speed of traffic from 30 mph to 31 mph,
it would produce a benefit of the same amount.
Thus, the size of the cost or benefit of even a
seemingly small change in the speed of traffic flow,
relative to the measures of net benefit calculated
in Table 3.10, is surprisingly large.[37] An important implication of this fact is that the traditional concentration of traffic law enforcement patrol on the goal of reducing traffic accidents may
represent a serious overemphasis; the less obvious
and much less easily measured effects on travel
time may very well be of as much quantitative importance.

The traditional tendency of police departments
to consider a low traffic accident rate (or perhaps
a high enforcement index) as the main or sole objective of traffic law enforcement is perhaps a result
of the fact that the number of accidents is relatively easy to measure, and average travel time on
surface streets is not. But if the State Highway
Department values for vehicle travel time are valid,
the effect of enforcement on travel time may be as
worthy of explicit consideration as the effect on
traffic accidents. But the current practice of selective enforcement on patrol assignments is based
only on accident rates, without regard to possible

effects on congestion. Clearly, if motorcycle patrol does have an effect on reducing congestion,
this should also be an explicit factor in beat assignments.

Although the method of speed measurement available for the experiment was, unfortunately, inadequate to detect small changes in average speed of
traffic flow, it is possible to show that the benefit of a small reduction in travel time (or the cost
of a small increase) would appreciably affect the
cost-benefit calculation. This is, of course, an
indication that the traffic bureau's expressed objective of reducing congestion is indeed an important one, deserving more consideration than it currently receives in traffic patrol assignments. If
such a finding is acted upon, it is an example of
the value of program analysis, which should continu-
ally redirect attention to the basic objectives of
each agency and to the relationship between agency
activities and those objectives.

SUMMARY AND CONCLUSION

The results of the traffic law enforcement experiment in terms of benefits and costs that have
been measured are summarized in Table 3.13. The
data come from Tables 3.10 and 3.12, and all quali-
fications pertaining to the earlier development of
these data apply here also. There is an unfortunate
gap in column 7, where data should be given for
benefits of reduced travel time, because of inability to measure the benefits; however, the hypothetical calculation has at least showed the relative importance of this traffic program goal. This benefit would, of course, have a negative value if traffic law enforcement increased average travel time.

The most striking implication of the measured
results is that, with the exception of the warning-
only beat, no experimental change resulted in a
clearly demonstrated net benefit. Where manpower
was increased, the marginal measured cost exceeded
the marginal measured benefit. Where manpower was
reduced, the reduction in measured benefits exceeded

TABLE 3.13

Summary of Costs and Benefits of Experimental Patrol Changes
(thousands of dollars)

Beat (1)	Change in Number of Officers (2)	Change in Cost of Patrol (3)	Benefit of Accident Reduction		Benefit of Crime Reduction (6)	Benefit of Reduced Travel Time (7)	Measured Net Benefit	
			High (4)	Low (5)			High (8)	Low (9)
1	0 (visibility)	0	- 3	- 2.1	0	n.a.	- 3	- 2.1
2	0 (warning)	0	+ 34	+ 23.5	0	n.a.	+ 34	+ 23.5
3	3	36	0	0	+ 1.1	n.a.	- 34.9	- 34.9
4	4	48	+ 38	+ 26.2	+ 2.8	n.a.	- 7.2	- 19
5	0 (no change)	0	- 14	- 9.7	0	n.a.	- 14	- 9.7
6	1	12	+ 9	+ 6.2	+ 0.4	n.a.	- 2.6	- 5.4
7	2	24	+ 28	+ 19.3	+ 0.5	n.a.	+ 4.5	- 4.2
8	- 1	- 12	- 32	- 22	- 0.6	n.a.	- 20.6	- 10.7

Note: n.a. = not available.

Source: Prepared by the authors.

the reduction in measured costs. Such a uniformly
negative net benefit associated with the experimental changes indicates that the existing allocation
of resources to beats was superior to any reallocation that was tried and that the "saturation" technique of concentrated traffic law enforcement resources in a small area is not justified on the
basis of the measured results. In no case was the
value of the marginal product of an additional traffic officer clearly greater than the marginal cost
when there was already one officer on a typical beat.
In terms of motor officers per mile, there was no
net measured benefit from an enforcement level above
approximately 0.3 officers per mile on main surface
streets.

Aside from the findings on patrol intensity,
the results also indicated that a change in patrol
techniques may be desirable. The warning-only beat
showed a large benefit at no cost, and this result
was interpreted as possibly stemming from the inappropriate reward structure imposed on other officers
whose output was, at least partially, measured by
the number of citations written per day. A revision
of work measurement was proposed that would make the
reward structure for traffic officers more consistent with the goals of the traffic bureau.

The benefit and cost figures developed in Table
3.13 refer, of course, only to the items that were
quantified, measured, and evaluated in dollar terms.
There are other intangible aspects of traffic law
enforcement that must also be taken into account before the data are used for decision-making purposes.
For instance, the evaluation of benefits did not
measure off-beat effects of enforcement on accidents,
though some influence almost certainly exists. Thus,
the accident reduction estimates to some extent un-
dervalue the true value of enforcement.

However, if all costs are accurately measured
and if off-beat effects of enforcement bear the same
relationship to on-beat effects for all beats, the
ranking of experimental changes according to measured benefits may be the same as the ranking according to all benefits (measured and unmeasured).
For instance, if the (unmeasured) change in accidents

on each beat is 50 percent of the (measured) change
in accidents on each beat, the ranking of beats according to net benefit is not greatly affected, and
not affected at all at the upper and lower ends of
the ranking.

In addition to the question of unmeasured benefits of traffic law enforcement, there is also the
problem of the significance of statistical inferences made on the basis of the experimental outcomes.
That is, are the results valid indicators of the relationship between cause and effect, or do they represent only random variations in accident and crime
rates that would have occurred even without enforcement changes? This question has to be answered in
terms of probabilities; because of the small sample
size that was necessary, there is an appreciable
chance that the changes in the number of accidents
occurring during the experimental year were actually
random variations (see Table 3.11). Thus, the
benefit-cost calculations based on these results
should not be considered evidence of the proved
worth of any particular method or intensity of patrol, but rather indicators that some allocations
are worth further investigation and that other allocations are distinctly less promising for future research.

Even if further research does validate the
findings that certain patrol techniques and intensi-
ties produce net benefits, other methods of producing the same result at less cost should still be
explored. For instance, this experiment examined
alternatives only within the context of two-wheel
patrol. It may be that four-wheel patrol is more
effective under certain circumstances. Thus, after
the best method of two-wheel patrol is discovered,
it should be tested against four-wheel methods of
accomplishing the same result. If analysis is to
be used for decision makers at a level above that
of the police department, other possibilities also
become feasible; for instance, the effect on safety
of higher fines for traffic violations could be
tested on an experimental basis. This would change
one of the important givens of the problem for the
police department, and thus would change the terms

on which suboptimization takes place. Also, there
are numerous investments in road construction and
engineering that are alternative methods of producing outputs similar to those of traffic law enforcement. Before these higher level comparisons
are attempted, however, it is first necessary to
discover the most efficient techniques among the
lower level programs that are to be compared. It
would be misleading to compare one program operating
well below its potential with another program operating at its highest potential and to interpret the
comparison as final evidence of the relative production possibilities.

Finally, an important finding that emerged during the traffic law enforcement experiment is that
there is a need for and difficulty in obtaining police data for a small area. For example, the experiment required data on traffic accidents aggregated on the basis of the traffic beats--but the
data were available only for the city as a whole or
for individual intersections. A large amount of
data manipulation was required to produce meaningful aggregates of data to test the effect of enforcement on accidents, and the difficulty of this task
is alone adequate explanation of the absence of
other such studies for urban areas. The job of col-
lecting crime data was even more of a problem, because crimes are aggregated only by police division;
to obtain data on the basis of traffic beats required
an examination of all the original records for crimes
that occurred on the specific beats in question.
Such data acquisition is costly, and yet having the
data in usable form is essential for progress in police research. Indeed, it is not an exaggeration to
say that the chief conclusion of this study is that
the highest research priority for police departments
is to put the vast amount of data already collected
into a meaningful and useful form suitable for computer use. When this task is accomplished--and it
is well under way for traffic data in Los Angeles--
further experimentation and evaluation will be possible at a far lower cost.

SUPPLEMENT 1:   DETAILED ANALYSIS OF
THE COSTING EFFORT

Determining Activities

For a program budgeting format, it is necessary
to define activities of programs, which satisfy
goals, and to cost the effort expended in programs.
(Costing for the experiment presented here was based
on data in the Los Angeles Police Department Traffic
Services Section.)

To quantify the effort expended in a program
relating to the goals of the Los Angeles Police Department Traffic Bureau, the amount of time spent
performing various activities had to be specified.
This was accomplished by the following steps:

1.   Interviews were conducted at the various
divisions to determine the various activities being
presently performed by sworn and civilian personnel.
These interviews took place at all levels, to include operations, supervision, and command. The activities surveyed were assembled into categories to
which time allocations could be attached.

2.   Daily Field Activity Reports (DFARs) were
selected on the basis of a two-month sample. After
a discussion with Traffic Enforcement Division personnel, the months of July 1967 and March 1968 were
selected as typical. These months were also sampled
for the other divisions to ensure uniformity.

3.   The DFARs were obtained for the Traffic Enforcement Division, the Accident Investigation Division, and the parking control checkers and S-Units
of the Parking and Intersection Control Division.
A 10 percent sample, by watch, of each division was
selected using a random numbers table. Personnel
assigned to the LAPD Traffic Services Section completed a questionnaire relating to time spent on
various activities.

4.   From the sample DFARs, time spent on each
activity and the miles traveled were recorded.

5.   The total time allocations for each activity were divided by the total time worked (less

code 7 activity time) for each watch to derive a
percentage figure for each activity. The average
mileage per day for each watch was determined.
      6. The monthly averages for each watch were
averaged together to obtain the final percentage of
time spent and miles traveled for each watch throughout the year.

Salary Costs

      After activities and time allocations to each
were defined, the following steps were taken to establish a salary cost per hour worked:
      1. From divisional timebooks for all person-
nel in the traffic bureau from July 1, 1967, to
June 30, 1968, timebook allocations were recorded
(days off, days worked, special days off, sick days,
and so forth).
      2. From this information, a profile of a
year's timebook allocation was made for each rank
in each division by computing the average number of
days allocated to each category.
      3. From the Kardex files in the LAPD Accoun-
tant's Office, the monthly salary of each employee
during the time he worked in the traffic bureau was
recorded.
      4. The total months worked at a pay schedule
for each rank by division were totaled and divided
by 12 to give a man-year figure. These man-year
figures indicate the exact deployment, by rank, for
fiscal year 1967/68.
      5. The average monthly salary for each rank,
by division, was computed using the frequency and
distribution of months worked at various pay sched-
ules. On the basis of this average salary and the
average number of days worked, a salary cost per
hour worked per man was computed by rank, by division.

Vehicle Costs

      Vehicle costs were derived on a cost per mile
basis. To obtain a cost per mile figure for the
various types of vehicles used by the traffic
bureau, the following steps were taken:

1. On the basis of a 25 percent sample for each vehicle class, maintenance cost figures were obtained from the LAPD Motor Transport Division. An average maintenance cost for each vehicle type was determined.

2. A 25 percent sample of all vehicles sold in 1967/68 provided the average salvage cost and average mileage at time of salvage for each type of vehicle.

3. The cost of a new, equipped vehicle minus the salvage cost divided by the average mileage at the time of salvage determined the average cost per mile of a vehicle.

4. The average cost per mile of a vehicle plus the maintenance cost per mile yielded the total cost per mile of a vehicle. Labor costs were not included because they accrue to the Motor Transport Division.

5. Virtually the same process was followed to determine helicopter vehicle costs per flight hour.

6. On the basis of average number of miles driven (or flown) per watch, by vehicle, by division, vehicle costs could be projected over the entire year.

Office Equipment Costs

To determine the office equipment costs, an actual inventory of existing furniture and equipment was taken, exclusive of that accounted for in the administrative overhead costs. The equipment and furniture were depreciated over their useful lives (based on supply division estimates), and a cost per man per hour figure was computed for all field personnel (exclusive of personnel accounted for in the administrative overhead cost).

Administrative Overhead Costs

An administrative overhead cost was derived to apportion the overhead and administrative support costs to the field personnel, as follows:

1. All salary costs of the deputy chief, inspectors, captains, lieutenants, fixed-post positions, and clerical personnel plus their depreciated
office equipment and vehicle costs were totaled.
2. Using deployment figures for the field personnel, the overhead cost was spread proportionately
to each division. Using the average number of hours
worked by each rank in a division, the overhead cost
per hour was computed for each man.

Cost Units

By building a <u>cost unit</u>, the total hourly cost
per man was determined, as follows:
1. The administrative overhead cost per hour,
the salary cost per hour, the equipment cost per
hour, and the vehicle cost per hour were summed to
make a cost unit by division, by rank. For the Accident Investigation Division, a cost unit was compiled for each watch to take into consideration
those watches using freeway patrol cars and those
having one-man and two-man patrols.
2. The cost units were multiplied by the actual deployment (man-years) for each rank (sergeant,
policeman, parking control checker, traffic control
officer) by watch, by division. Personnel accounted
for in the administrative overhead cost were excluded.

Costing the Activities

The total costs, by rank, for each watch within
each division were multiplied by the previously determined percentage of time allocated to each activity for that rank and watch. The costs for each
watch were combined to determine the total cost per
activity for the division. (Cost estimates are
shown in Tables 3.14 and 3.15.)

Spreading the Costs

The activity costs for a division were allocated
to the programs to which they contributed. The activities that did not relate to a specific program were
allocated in the ratio of the established program
subtotals.

TABLE 3.14

Cost Estimates of Traffic Enforcement Division

Unit	Salary per Man per Hour	Overhead Cost per Man per Hour	Equip. Cost per Man per Hour	Vehicle Cost per Man per Hour	Total Cost per Man per Hour	Number of Men per Watch	Total Cost per Watch per Hour	Average Number of Hours Worked	Total Cost per Watch per Year
Freeway (day)	$6.57	$0.605	$0.005	$1.189	$8.369	49.021	$410.257	1,638.096	$720,403.51
Special enforcement unit	6.57	0.605	0.005	0.634	7.814	17.400	135.964	1,638.096	222,722.08
Surface (day)	6.57	0.605	0.005	0.612	7.792	41.072	320.033	1,638.096	524,244.78
Commercial vehicle and complaints	6.57	0.605	0.005	0.809	7.989	9.635	76.974	1,638.096	126,090.80
Drunk driving	6.57	0.605	0.005	0.718	7.898	16.041	126.692	1,638.096	207,533.66
Surface (night)	6.57	0.605	0.005	0.674	7.854	43.739	343.526	1,638.096	562,728.57
Freeway (night)	6.57	0.605	0.005	1.186	8.366	50.011	418.392	1,638.096	685,366.26
Supervision	7.16	0.584	0.005	0.600	8.349	37.583	313.836	1,696.392	532,294.56

Source: Prepared by the authors.

TABLE 3.15

Cost Estimates of Accident Investigation Division

Watch	Salary per Man per Hour	Overhead Cost per Man per Hour	Equip. Cost per Man per Hour	Vehicle Cost per Man per Hour	Total Cost per Man per Hour	Number of Men per Watch	Average Number of Hours Worked	Total Cost per Watch per Year
Day watch	$5.83	$0.611	$0.005	One man per car $0.439	$6.885	9.262	1,620.440	$303,437.761
				One man in ½ car 0.220		18.525		
PM watch	5.83	0.611	0.005	0.403	6.849	65.558	1,620.440	727,588.417
Mid-watch	5.83	0.611	0.005	One man per car 0.417	6.863	11.062	1,620.440	361,617.876
				One man in ½ car 0.209	6.655	22.125		
AM watch (surface)	5.83	0.611	0.005	0.423	6.869	35.046	1,620.440	390,089.980
AM watch (freeway)	5.83	0.611	0.005	1.229	7.675	18.914	1,620.440	235,231.011
Supervision	6.17	0.552	0.005	0.280	7.007	31.025	1,795.184	390,258.820

Source: Prepared by the authors.

156

Traffic Volume, October-June, 1964-69

Beat	Weekday Average Volume, 1964-68	Weekday Average Volume, 1968-69
1. Western Avenue	27,000	29,000
Beverly Boulevard	25,000	25,000
2. Wilshire Boulevard	28,000	30,000
La Brea Avenue	33,000	31,000
3. Hollywood Boulevard	16,000	17,000
Highland Avenue	36,000	35,000
4. Pacific Coast Highway	29,000	28,000
Avalon Boulevard	19,000	18,000
5. Santa Monica Boulevard	33,000	31,000
6. Pico Boulevard	24,000	24,000
Westwood Boulevard	21,000	18,000
7. Van Nuys Boulevard	35,000	36,000
8. Olympic Boulevard	29,000	28,000

SUPPLEMENT 3

Traffic Speed

Beat	Percentage of Vehicles, 0-5 mph above Speed Limit	Percentage of Vehicles, 5 or more mph above Speed Limit	Number of Radar Checks, of ½-hour Each
1. Western Avenue	4.0	0.5	8
Beverly Boulevard	11.0	2.0	8
2. Wilshire Boulevard	1.0	0.0	14
La Brea Avenue	15.0	5.0	10
3. Hollywood Boulevard	7.0	1.5	7
Highland Avenue	1.5	0.0	7
4. Pacific Coast Highway	6.0	0.5	7
Avalon Boulevard	9.0	1.0	7
5. Santa Monica Boulevard	1.5	0.0	4
6. Pico Boulevard	5.0	2.0	3
Westwood Boulevard	10.0	4.0	3
7. Van Nuys Boulevard	4.0	0.5	5
8. Olympic Boulevard	1.0	0.0	3

4

PROGRAM ANALYSIS
FOR POLICE
PATROL SERVICES

Much of the discussion to this point has dealt with the Los Angeles Police Department's traffic law enforcement program. This focus represents a conscious choice to confine the trial application of program budgeting to an area of police operations in which the issues are relatively tractable and the mechanics of program budgeting relatively easily demonstrable. These simplifying advantages, however, are less evident in the police program chosen for examination in this chapter--the crime deterrent (or visible) police patrol program. Indeed, some of the reasons for choosing the patrol program for analysis are, at the same time, likely to ensure that the evaluation will be difficult. Among other things, many of the common methods of police patrol operation have recently become controversial public questions. For example, although the size (per capita) of the patrol force is normally greater in a low income or a minority group residential area, patrolmen are often charged with being unresponsive to the legitimate demands of ghetto residents. Many of the controversial public issues involve equity in the distribution of police services and methods of performing police tasks.

An important reason for choosing the deterrent patrol program for evaluation is the large relative size of this program in most police budgets. An examination of program budget structures for several

cities reveals that often as much as 40 percent to
50 percent of total police operating expenditures
can be safely attributed to patrol activities. In
addition to the general crime deterrent patrol
force, other police programs also engage in visible
patrol, especially traffic law enforcement units.
And although the purposes of general patrol units
and traffic patrol units differ, their effects are
likely to overlap.

Despite the large size of the general patrol
program and the public controversy over specific patrol operations, little good information is available to assist patrol administrators in deploying
patrol inputs or to assist police chiefs in directing resources between patrol and other police programs in the most efficient manner. As a result,
few patrol administrators attempt to construct comprehensive guidelines for planning the deployment
of patrol resources. Part of the difficulty is that
attempts to evaluate the patrol program require that
operational objectives and output measures be previously agreed upon. As is the case with many public services, the output of visible police patrol
is difficult to define and quantify. An important
purpose of this study, then, is to examine the feasibility of various possible output indicators for
general patrol.

Since the goal of the visible patrol program
is the deterrence of criminal events, criminal victimization rates (the number of crimes committed
per 1,000 population) are appropriate indicators of
output. The criminal victimization rate gives the
probability of becoming the victim of a crime in
each reporting area, and thus indicates the relative
security of persons and property from crime in each
area.

Since all crimes are not equally serious, the
output of the patrol program should be a set of several criminal victimization rates comprising a separate rate for each crime category. Such a breakdown makes it possible not only to make differential
measurements of crimes of each type but also to
evaluate the differential effects of patrol on the
different crime categories.

The reported crime rate is the only available measure of the criminal victimization rate. However, an unquestioning use of the reported crime rate as a reliable measure of the rate of crimes committed is not warranted. The number of crimes may be under-reported or overreported by the public or police, and the crimes that are reported are often defined differently in city and state codes, with the result that crime rates are not comparable among different police departments. (This problem of crime reporting is discussed in detail later in this chapter.)

Even if the crime data collection problems were not serious, there are other impediments to specifying police objectives to guide patrol force deployment. For instance, it is not accurately known which crimes patrol units can and do affect. Further, police patrol is only one variable influencing crime; the social and economic makeup of each community may also be important determinants of crime rates in the community.

Finally, even if the data problem were not serious and the effect of patrol inputs on each type of crime were known, distributional issues would be involved in the efficient geographical deployment of patrol resources within a city.

While all these problems of specifying police objectives interfere with attempts to employ program budgeting to improve the allocation of patrol resources, the most serious impediment is the lack of good information on the effects of the patrol program on crime rates and other output measures. It is the task of program analysis to evaluate available information germane to the problem in hand and, when needed information is unavailable, to generate it through appropriate techniques.

In Chapter 3 an attempt was made to generate the input-output relationships for the traffic law enforcement program through the use of controlled field experiments. The experimental technique was used to determine the effect on output of both increases and decreases in traffic patrol intensity. These data were then used to evaluate, through benefit-cost analysis, the net monetary returns from alterations in the number of traffic patrolmen

on selected beats and alternative methods of carrying out enforcement with a fixed number of officers.

In this chapter an alternative technique, statistical regression analysis, is implemented in an
investigation of production relationships in the
visible patrol program. Data were collected from a
cross section of urban police agencies in California
on the magnitude of selected patrol input and output
variables as well as on social and economic conditions thought to affect the individual decision to
commit an offense. The data are analyzed by means
of multivariate linear regression equations. This
particular technique analyzes the effects on output
of the variations in visible patrol inputs and socioeconomic factors that occur among the cities in the
sample at a point in time. Fortunately, variations
in both police inputs and socioeconomic characteristics of the sample cities (the sample includes low
income cities, such as Compton, and high income
cities, such as Beverly Hills) are great enough to
yield statistically reliable estimates of the effects of these variables on police output.

As an alternative to controlled field experimentation, statistical analysis has both advantages
and weaknesses. (Many of the latter were detailed
in Chapter 3.) In general, for most police programs,
statistical analysis is a less costly method of gen-
erating information than field experiments. In addition, experimental investigations of the deterrent
patrol program encounter the special problem of the
spillover of crime (assuming that crime rates are
used as a measure of output): if the risk of apprehension increases in an area because of an experimentally augmented police presence, potential offenses may merely be deferred to a later time or
diverted to a different location; or, say, a deterred
robbery may reappear in the form of a burglary. Since
such spillovers are more likely for crimes than for
traffic accidents, crime deterrent patrol experiments
conducted in a certain area well may overstate the
influence of the patrol force.

An additional weakness of the experimental technique for a crime deterrent patrol program is caused
by the universal problem of the underreporting of

crime. And if an experimental increase in patrol force strength serves merely to increase the number of crimes reported that would otherwise have remained unreported, the effects of the patrol increase will be misstated--which may indeed happen if the larger patrol forces are able to observe more crimes or induce greater public confidence and reporting by citizens. Thus, reporting problems may seriously bias even a carefully controlled patrol experiment. These and similar problems, combined with the lack of success of the few patrol field experiments reported in the literature, suggested that an alternative method be employed to evaluate patrol operations.

The police patrol program analysis is organized within the following framework. First, production and distribution and the problems of allocative efficiency in the crime deterrent patrol program are discussed. Second, a theoretical model of the production of patrol services is formulated.[1] This theoretical model suggests that the actual, "visible" crime rate should be used as the principal output measure of the visible patrol program. The index of actual, visible crime is composed of the number of reported and unreported crimes that are thought to be deterrable by visible patrol. Alternative measures of the output of deterrent patrol are also proposed; they are arrest rates and reported total crime rates. Third, the theoretical model is tested by using the public service production function.[2] Finally, in the last two sections of the chapter, an attempt is made to demonstrate how the information derived from the statistical analysis can be used to evaluate, in benefit-cost terms, reallocations of patrol inputs (or alterations of patrol techniques).

PRODUCTION AND DISTRIBUTION OF CRIME DETERRENT PATROL SERVICES

One of the more difficult problems of program budgeting is to specify the nature of the service or commodity produced by a public agency--and

whatever the producer views as his output will be
used by him in his attempt to attain efficient combinations of inputs. In the case of the police a
certain obvious conflict seems to arise on this
point. The police agency may view itself as a producer of traffic citations, criminal arrests, cases
investigated, and so forth, which are not true final
outputs. Rather, the definition of outputs should
be consistent with the objectives of the police department and its various intermediate divisions.
In such terms outputs would include the number of
crimes deterred and the social value of the losses
thereby avoided, the number of traffic accidents
prevented, and so forth. Hence, there may be an important distinction between measures used to evaluate the work performance of patrolmen and effectiveness measures used as output indicators in a program
budgeting system. Output indicators, to be correctly
defined, must be closely aligned with the previously
agreed-upon goals of the agency so that a close measurement of overall agency efficiency can be easily
made.

     The output of the patrol division is more im-
portant than that of any other police division and
one of the most difficult to specify adequately.
In smaller cities patrolmen perform all the tasks
generally given to more specialized divisions in
larger cities. But even in large cities the crime
deterrent patrol force is considered to perform the
basic police activity, and the specialized activities of detectives and traffic patrolmen, for example, are thought of as being merely supportive.
For example, in Los Angeles approximately one-half
of all sworn officers are attached to the patrol
bureau; in Chicago approximately 70 percent. And
the proportion of input devoted to deterrent patrol
is in fact considerably greater than these figures
indicate when one takes into account other officers
whose tasks include visible street patrol; for example, much of the time of both traffic enforcement
officers and accident investigation units is spent
in deterrent activity.

     The major activity of patrol units is to per-
form deterrent patrol; the major objective is to

deter potential offenders. Visibility of patrolmen produces deterrence by increasing the objective probability of apprehension and arrest (hereafter denoted P_A) if an offense is carried out. The P_A is increased for two reasons: (1) Patrol units may be able to observe the crime in progress, and (2) patrol units can respond quickly to radio calls for service, thereby enabling them to make an arrest. Visibility also serves to increase the P_A as it is subjectively perceived by the potential criminal. The higher this subjective probability of arrest (and subsequent conviction), the lower the net expected return (or expected utility of the return) to the potential offender for any given value of the expected gain (or the expected utility of the gain). Hence, all else the same, a higher P_A should result in fewer offenses per criminal and (or) fewer persons committing crimes. The approach assumes that most potential criminals are rational insofar as they respond to the subjectively evaluated incentives for each type of crime and they behave as though they maximized the net expected return (or the utility of the net expected return) of their activities. This assumption does not hold for most crimes of violence--murder, assault, rape--but may be reasonably valid for most types of property violations--burglary, theft, and so forth. Since the crime deterrence output measure selected for the evaluation of deterrent patrol is used as a guide for the efficient allocation of resources among major police programs, the measure should not include those crimes that the police do not seem capable of deterring, that is, those crimes for which the rationality assumption clearly does not hold.[3]

Although this approach assumes that the major output of patrol is a reduction in the social costs of criminal violations, other outputs also are produced. Patrol units receive many calls for service not related to crime, to which they must respond; in addition, most motorized units are continuously visible and frequently cite traffic violators, which should affect the number of traffic accidents in somewhat the same way as motorcycle patrol does, as described in Chapter 3. These essentially secondary

outputs are not included in the output measure proposed here.

Within the patrol sector, resources should be
allocated so as to maximize the primary output.
This requires a large number of explicit resource
allocation decisions by patrol administrators in
large urban police departments.

1. One such decision relates to the optimal
allocation of patrol inputs over time. The time of
the day, the day of the week, and the season of the
year must all be considered, for neither criminal
events nor calls for service are distributed uniformly over time. An additional patrol unit should
be added during peak-load periods (nights, weekends,
and summer) if more crimes can be deterred and (or)
a greater reduction in response time can be effected
during these periods than during other periods. Of
course, additional units should not be added until
no more crimes can be deterred or response time is
reduced to the minimum technically possible. At
some point the administrator must decide that the
opportunity cost of allocating another unit to a
peak hour (or peak day or peak season) exceeds the
return for it. (That is, the optimal point occurs
where net returns are maximized.) However, despite
the widespread peak occurrence of crime during the
evening hours, national data indicate that the majority of the larger city police departments maintain
the same number of beats on the day, evening, and
night shifts.[4]

2. Another such decision relates to the optimal distribution of patrol forces within a given
city. Nearly all cities have geographical areas in
which the incidence of major crimes is greater than
in others. While the objective is to minimize the
costs of crime, a question remains whether this objective should be viewed in terms of the entire
city, thereby leaving differential crime costs in
different areas of the city, or crime costs equated
among areas within the city, thereby not necessarily
minimizing crime costs for the entire city.[5]

An illustration of one method used to deploy
patrol forces on a geographical basis is the patrol
bureau formula used by the Los Angeles Police

Department to allocate patrolmen among the city's 17 police divisions.[6] The ten factors included in the formula indicate some of the performance indicators the police consider important in setting and evaluating work standards for patrol officers. The formula assumes that the future demand for patrolmen in a police division is predicted by a series of indicators of police workload in that division in the previous six-month period. The percentage of the total available patrol officers allocated to the jth division (denoted by P_j) is given by the formula:

$$(1) \quad P_j = \frac{\Sigma X_{ij}}{\Sigma X_i}$$

where $i = 1, \ldots, 10$, and $j = 1, \ldots, 17$

and X_{1j} = selected crimes and attempts occurring in division j (weighted by a factor of 3) as percent of city total

X_{2j} = radio calls handled by patrol cars in division j (weighted by a factor of 2) as percent of city total

X_{3j} = felony arrests in division j (weighted by a factor of 2) as percent of city total

X_{4j} = misdemeanor arrests in division j as percent of city total

X_{5j} = property stolen in division j as percent of city total

X_{6j} = injury traffic accidents in division j as percent of city total

X_{7j} = stolen vehicles recovered in division j as percent of city total

X_{8j} = population in division j as percent of city total

X_{9j} = street miles in division j as percent of city total

X_{10j} = percent of population density in division j.

Since P_j sums to 100 percent, all of the fixed number of patrol officers are allocated to police

districts by the formula. Table 4.1 shows the results of the formula for one six-month period in
1968. The final column shows the percentage of the
total patrolmen available (2,495 at that time) allocated to each division.

The formula has a number of weaknesses that
are cause to raise serious questions about the resulting allocation of patrol resources. For one
thing, the formula does not determine the size of
the patrol program, that is, the number of men assigned to patrol. The size of the patrol program
is determined without the use of any measures, however imperfect, that indicate a demand for patrol
services. The formula merely distributes a fixed
pool of patrolmen among geographical police divisions. Moreover, once the manpower has been allocated, it is the responsibility of the divisional
commanders to deploy patrol units by time of day,
day of week, and beat within the rather sizable
divisions.

In addition, while only crimes thought to be
"subject to control through patrol by uniformed officers" are included in the formula, all arrests--
whether adult or juvenile, felony or misdemeanor--
are included. Since patrolmen have greater discretion to affect the number of many types of misdemeanor arrests (such as many juvenile violations)
than to affect the number of reported crimes, the
arrest figures may reflect past patrol input levels
rather than exogenous factors predicting the required level of future inputs.

Despite these objections, the formula does represent a conscious effort on the part of patrol administrators to deploy their manpower in a rational
manner. It may be that a more sophisticated analysis introduced by a fully implemented program budgeting system would provide only marginal gains, if
any, to the resulting geographical distribution.

3. In addition to the choices to be made
among alternative geographical and temporal allocations of patrol resources, there are also substitution possibilities among alternative patrol activities. Presumably both of the major tasks performed
by motorized patrol units, free patrol and response

TABLE 4.1

Patrol Bureau Formula for Crime Deterrent Patrol Allocation
(in percentages)

Factors

Divisions	Selected Crimes and Attempts X 3	Radio Calls Handled by Radio Cars X 2	Adult and Juvenile Felony Arrests X 2	Adult and Juvenile Misdemeanor Arrests	Property Loss	Fatal and Injury Traffic Accidents	Vehicles Recovered in Division of Recovery	Los Angeles City Population Affected, April 1, 1968	Street Miles, April 1, 1968	Population Density, April 1, 1968	For Comparison Only; Figs. from April 1, 1968 Patrol Bureau Formula	General Average
Central	13.2	13.4	15.0	23.0	4.9	4.7	3.2	1.2	1.6	5.6	7.1	6.1
Rampart	19.8	17.2	14.2	9.4	6.3	6.7	6.8	6.5	4.5	9.9	7.2	7.2
University	28.5	15.4	20.4	5.8	6.2	8.1	12.2	6.4	4.9	10.3	8.3	8.4
Hollenbeck	10.8	9.0	7.2	3.9	2.1	3.8	4.6	3.7	3.8	8.5	4.0	4.1
Harbor	14.1	7.0	10.4	5.1	4.4	4.5	4.5	4.4	5.2	3.8	4.4	4.5
Hollywood	21.6	16.0	13.6	6.4	13.3	8.6	5.5	6.4	7.0	4.9	7.3	7.4
Wilshire	21.9	16.0	16.6	5.3	3.8	7.5	7.0	7.2	5.5	9.6	7.8	7.2
West Los Angeles	13.8	7.8	7.8	3.6	12.4	6.0	1.9	7.2	7.9	2.4	5.0	5.1
Van Nuys	19.2	11.4	10.2	6.1	7.7	8.4	4.0	8.3	7.8	5.1	6.5	6.3
West Valley	16.2	10.6	9.4	3.9	6.4	5.8	3.9	9.0	10.2	3.4	7.0	5.6
Highland Park	11.7	9.2	4.2	2.5	2.9	3.3	4.6	5.1	5.8	5.2	3.7	3.9
77th Street	39.3	23.0	33.2	8.2	7.6	10.4	20.0	7.1	5.8	8.3	11.1	11.6
Newton Street	16.5	11.0	11.4	4.9	3.4	4.3	7.6	3.0	2.8	7.6	5.5	5.2
Venice	17.4	11.6	8.8	3.6	6.3	4.9	4.2	6.9	5.6	5.9	5.2	5.4
North Hollywood	12.6	8.4	6.0	3.6	5.6	5.4	2.7	6.0	6.3	5.2	4.6	4.4
Foothill	14.4	8.2	8.8	3.5	3.6	4.8	5.2	6.7	8.7	2.3	5.3	4.7
Devonshire	9.0	4.8	2.8	1.2	3.1	2.8	2.1	4.5	6.6	2.0		2.9
Totals	300.0	200.0	200.0	100.0	100.0	100.0	100.0	100.0	100.0	100.0	100.0	100.0

Source: Los Angeles Police Department, Office of the Commander, "Memorandum Number 10," November 3, 1968.

169

to radio calls, contribute to the deterrence of
criminal activities. To decide what percentage of
a patrol unit's time should be allocated to each
task requires knowledge of the effect on crime of
alterations in this percentage. A recent experiment
(1969) conducted by the Los Angeles County Sheriff's
Department increased the average free patrol time of
patrol units in a given district from 25 percent to
35.5 percent of the time available during the shift.
Despite this rather large increase in average free
patrol time, no significant effects on seven major
felonies were observed.[7] A more elaborate experiment conducted by the St. Louis Police Department[8]
divided all patrol units in a test district into
units that performed only free patrol and units that
only answered calls for service. In this case even
the use of ten different measures to evaluate change
failed to show any highly significant effects.

To choose among alternative strategies also requires knowledge of the separate effects of visible-
patrol-only and reduction of the time required to
respond to calls for service. Regardless of the
criterion of effectiveness that is chosen, and many
are possible, increasing the speed of response to
calls for service seems to be highly effective. A
study of the LAPD showed a very clear, positive relationship between the field response time of the
patrol unit and the probability that the crime was
cleared by an arrest; that is, faster field response
time results in more arrests and hence a greater deterrent effect. (See Table 4.2.)

Measuring the effectiveness of performing visible patrol is a more difficult issue. The possibility is very small that the patrol force will alter the probability of apprehension (and reduce the
number of violations) by actual observation of a
crime in progress. The President's Commission assumed an average duration of two minutes per crime
and was able to estimate that in Los Angeles the entire patrol force has a maximum opportunity in a
year to detect in progress only 12 percent of all
reported burglaries and only 2 percent of reported
robberies, approximately 100 burglaries and 2 robberies being reported per week.[9] These percentages

would be reduced considerably if a correction factor for unreported burglaries and robberies was applied. At any rate, an individual patrolman could
expect to observe a burglary in progress once in
every 3 months and a robbery approximately once in
every 14 years. In New York City it has been estimated that the probability of a patrol unit's directly observing any crime of one-minute duration
in Manhattan, with its high density of crimes and
persons, is 0.025, and in the low-density boroughs
of Queens and Richmond about 0.007.

TABLE 4.2

Average Field Response Time for
Crime Deterrent Patrol
(minutes)

Type of Call	All Calls	Cases with Arrests	Uncleared Crimes
All radio calls	5.23	3.40	8.00
Code 2 and 3 calls (emergency)	3.81	2.90	4.35
Other than Code 2 or 3 calls (nonemergency)	7.40	4.56	12.94

Source: President's Commission on Law Enforcement and Administration of Justice, Task Force Report: Science and Technology (Washington: Government Printing Office, 1967), pp. 92, 93.

While the chance of observing crimes in progress is small, it understates the total effect of
deterrent patrol units on the probability of apprehension. Patrol units can often observe and investigate suspicious behavior, thereby discovering
crimes; or they can investigate misdemeanors, often
leading to the discovery of major felonies. The

President's Commission analyzed 336 crimes that were
cleared by an arrest in a given period in Los Angeles. In connection with these 336 crimes, 148
arrests were made on the scene. Of the 148 arrests,
91 involved observations by patrolmen of suspicious
activity, including 25 observed crimes, 58 observations of individuals under suspicious circumstances,
and 8 suspicious vehicles.[10] Such activities serve
to increase the ability of visible patrol units to
affect the probability of field apprehension and
thus increase their deterrent effect.

Of course, not all offenders are equally susceptible to deterrence by the probability of arrest.
Some property thefts are obviously the result of
cold calculation, and many crimes of violence are
undoubtedly the result of temporary irrationality.
Consequently, it appears reasonable for the police
to attempt to allocate the greater part of resources
to the deterrence of those prohibited acts that are
subject to rational calculation by potential offenders, since the police are most likely to affect potential offenders' decision-making processes in
these cases, mainly personal property violations.
Thus, reductions in reported property crime rates
will be used as the most important measure of patrol output in this analysis, and a police service
production function will be tested to determine the
extent of the influence of the police on the criminal activity of property offenders.

A PRODUCTION MODEL FOR CRIME
DETERRENT PATROL SERVICES

Few theoretical or empirical analyses of
input-output relations in visible patrol police
programs have been undertaken to date. An attempt
will be made, then, in this section to outline some
of the more important considerations likely to be
involved in efforts to build and implement such
models. Also, a model is detailed that will be
statistically estimated later in the study.

A model to measure the effects of patrol inputs that has been recently proposed incorporates

most of the essential production relationships in-
ternal to the crime deterrent patrol program--though
it excludes from consideration the effects of environmental factors outside police control.[11] The
model assumes that the activities of motorized patrol units can be divided into two categories--re-
sponding to calls for service and conducting visible
patrol--the effects of which are quite distinct.
Visible patrol is characterized as an activity undertaken solely by the patrol unit without receiving alerts from victims, witnesses, or automatic
alarm systems. An indicator is selected to measure
the effects of free patrol time, presumed to be
separate from the effects of time spent responding
to calls for service. The proposed index of output,
Q, is defined as the ratio of "on-view" arrests in
a given area to the number of reported crimes in
that area. The index can be written conveniently as

$$(2) \qquad Q \equiv \frac{C}{R}$$

where   Q = the index of output
         C = number of on-view arrests (result-
             ing from detecting the criminal
             event)
         R = number of reported crimes in the
             area.

Although designed to measure only the effects of
free patrol time, the index nonetheless includes
the effects of responses to calls since, as shown
in Table 4.2, faster response to calls for service
results in a greater frequency of arrests, including on-view arrests. In addition, both tactics affect the number of reported crimes in a given area,
since a patrol unit that answers a call for service
is still visible and, presumably, continues to deter the commission of some crimes. The ratio C/R
is a special form of clearance rate--a traditional
police performance measure; in this case, however,
"clearances" are narrowly defined as on-view arrests. Either C or R can be used independently as
an output indicator--and will be so used later in
this study in the empirical analysis.

The interesting questions concern how the index is affected by police patrol inputs. The index of output can be related to patrol manpower and capital inputs via a production function such as the following:

$$(3) \quad Q = f \; \frac{T}{A}$$

where   A = area patrolled (square miles or street miles)

            T = patrol unit man-hours spent in Area A.

The variable, T, can be further defined as

$$(4) \quad T = n \sum_{j=1}^{n} t_j m_j$$

where   n = the number of visible patrol units in Area A

          t_j = the amount of visible patrol time per (the jth) patrol unit

          m_j = the number of patrolmen per (the jth) patrol unit.

The ratio T/A represents patrol input density measured as the number of patrol man-hours per square (or street) mile. This functional relationship can be tested empirically using either C, R, or C/R as the output measure. Testing equation (3) with statistical data would yield estimates of the marginal effectiveness of an additional patrol unit, of an increment in free patrol time, and of an additional officer per patrol unit--all of which are currently important and unresolved issues in patrol operations.[12] The changes in t represent alterations in patrol techniques; changes in n represent changes in the quantity of inputs, and changes in m can represent changes either in technique or in quantity of inputs.

Some precautions should be taken in using the production model represented by equations (2) through (4). It is possible that beat patrolmen will be able to directly alter C (and possibly R) in order to manipulate the level of their reported effectiveness. This is particularly true of less serious (Part Two) offenses, such as drunkenness or juvenile violations. In fact, for many of these violations, such as juvenile curfew violations, C may equal R. Hence, the crimes to be used to evaluate the effectiveness of patrol officers by the production model must be chosen carefully.

Though the equations represent the ideal model of patrol production relations that it would be desirable to estimate in this study, the data requirements preclude its being tested directly. In fact, direct access to daily patrol field reports would be the only guarantee that accurate data were obtained for C, n, and t.

Because data were not available, a variant of the model will be tested. The less specific but more widely applicable concept of the urban public service production function will be used to measure input-output relations in visible patrol. In this connection, it will be recalled from Chapter 3 that the production function is expressed in general form as

$$(5) \quad O = f\ (I, S, T)$$

where   O = output, the effects of visible patrol inputs
          I = inputs from the visible patrol program
          S = service conditions
          T = state of patrol technology.

A special type of clearance rate, C/R, was proposed above as a possible measure of the effects of visible patrol inputs, that is, to represent O. Unfortunately, it cannot be demonstrated statistically that it is the ideal measure since there are no data on C. Instead, a variety of output proxies will be tested to see which is the more reliable and (or) consistent estimator of the effects of deterrent patrol. The patrol input variables, too, will be measured by a number of alternative measures meant to be proxies for the ideal measures suggested in equations (2) through (4).

The variable, S, in this case represents any exogenous "service" conditions that can render

police patrol more or less efficient within the same
period and (or) area. These are factors that affect
R but cannot in turn be affected by police patrol
inputs. For example, socioeconomic characteristics
of individuals and thus of the population can increase R within one district or city relative to
others. Moreover, the effect of such demographic
variables as age, sex, income, schooling, and labor
market conditions should be isolated in order to estimate the effectiveness of patrol inputs separately.

Not only characteristics of the population but
also physical features of the city may affect the
ability of the police to alter C or R. The number
of street miles and the type of land-use patterns
in a city or sector can affect the detection probabilities, C, and the incidence of crime, R, by affecting patrol density or patrol frequencies (that
is, the number of times a patrol unit passes a certain point). The size of the street and the conditions along the roadway--such as the surface, traffic congestion, and curb-side parking--can affect C
and R by reducing the speed and mobility of the patrol unit.

The quality of patrol personnel, including administrators, and equipment may also have a significant effect on both reported and unreported crime
rates. Such quality variations would be relatively
minor if the production function was estimated for
divisions within a single urban agency over a period
of time. But if the model is estimated over several
cities at a single point in time (as it will be
here), quality is likely to vary significantly.
Subjective quality evaluations of the local agency
(that is, judgments expressed by the public) may
also be an important exogenous variable to be considered. If the general opinion of the community
is that the police are ineffective in dealing with
reported crimes, a great deal of nonreporting will
occur (altering R). But, more important, criminals
will perceive a higher probability of success under
certain circumstances, and the incentive to commit
property crimes may be increased.

Finally, if the model is estimated for a single
jurisdiction over time, some estimate of the nature

and extent of technological change may be called
for. For example, computerized communications operations may reduce the delay between the time a
call for service is received and the time a patrol
unit reaches the scene. As a result, the number of
on-view arrests may be increased; the number of reported crimes may either increase or decrease.

Before going into the statistical analysis in
the following section, however, it will be useful
to review briefly the empirical analyses of patrol
operations--both experimental and statistical--that
have been reported in the literature.

It is quite likely that a host of unreported
controlled field experiments have been performed to
determine the effects of deterrent patrol inputs.
However, those that have attracted the most attention normally have not been conducted under ideal
experimental conditions. One of the most widely reported police experiments was conducted in New York
City.[13] In this experiment, personnel strength was
increased 134 percent for four months in a single
precinct characterized by high crime rates. The experiment did not examine the effect of a change in
the level of inputs on any one type of output, nor
did it attempt any marginal additions in inputs but,
rather, more than doubled manpower in a short period.
Furthermore, it did not account for any possible external effects of the experiment, such as the spillover of crime into adjacent districts. The results
were that reported major felonies--such Part One
crimes as robbery, assault, and rape--decreased by
55.6 percent; on the other hand, reported Part Two
crimes--gambling, prostitution, drug addiction, and
so forth--increased approximately 140 percent.
Clearly, the number of reported crimes of the latter
category was affected by the presence of greater
numbers of policemen. This is often likely, for two
reasons: (1) Part Two crimes are crimes that require the voluntary involvement of the individual
"harmed." Since he is unlikely to report his own
indulgence in the prohibited activity, the nonreporting of these crimes is quite substantial. (2)
Because of the voluntary exchange characteristic of
many of these crimes, police agencies having limited

resources routinely devote only minimal resources
to deterring or suppressing these activities. Except in the case of sporadic changes in policy, most
agencies devote more resources to Part One than to
Part Two crimes. It is therefore to be expected
that when patrol man-hours are doubled, more time
will be devoted to uncovering Part Two offenses
than was before the experimental period.

The technique of saturating an area with police
personnel and equipment does not reveal the effectiveness of marginal changes in the level of inputs
and substitutes an unrealistic, never-to-be-repeated
alteration in the level of resources. The police
are merely demonstrating a known fact: placing a
policeman on every street corner can effectively deter most criminal behavior (and some legitimate behavior as well). The obvious direct and indirect
costs of such gross changes preclude consideration
of this technique as a reasonable police policy.
Yet, despite the fact that the statistical designs
of past experiments have often yielded unreliable
results, careful field experimentation can still be
a good source of information on police input-output
relationships, as the analysis in Chapter 3 attempted
to show.

A statistical analysis for estimating input-
output relations in the patrol division was carried
out by the President's Commission.[14] The commission
estimated a linear function for 11 of the geographical administrative divisions of the Los Angeles Police Department for the years 1955-65.[15] The function estimated was of the following form:

$$(6) \quad C = a + bP_t + cP^2 + dK + eK^2 + fT$$

where C = number of crimes in each division
             per year
         K = number of patrolmen assigned to
             the division annually
         P = population of the division
         T = number of years since some fixed
             year.

Although extremely limited, the model accounted
for most of the changes in the overall crime rate in

4 of the 11 divisions. Clearly, input variables
and output variables should be more specific and
more refined. Moreover, demographic variables
should be added to account for social and economic
characteristics of the populations of the divisions
that may affect crime. Unfortunately, limitations
of data preclude estimation of a model using time-
series data for a single large city such as Los Angeles. Instead, data from a cross section of Southern California cities were used to estimate the production model reported below.

A STATISTICAL ANALYSIS OF PATROL SERVICES

Linear multiple regression equations will be
used in the statistical analysis to estimate the effect of alternative combinations of independent variables on selected dependent variables. The basic
data are for a cross section of 46 independent cities in the greater Los Angeles region, including
cities in Los Angeles, Orange, San Bernardino, and
Riverside counties. Data from 6 cities that contract for police services from the Los Angeles
County Sheriff's Department are also included when
they are comparable with the other crime data, increasing the sample size to 52. Some of the data
were collected from published sources and other
data were generated by means of a letter and tele-
phone survey.

In the selection of the cities, an attempt was
made to achieve a fairly homogeneous sample. Population size ranges from a high of 151,000 (Anaheim)
to a low of 22,000 (South Pasadena); the mean population is approximately 65,000, the approximate
standard deviation being 34,000. Thus, a majority
of the cities are within the population range of
from 30,000 to 90,000.

There are several reasons for restricting the
sample to a single geographical region within a
single state. First, there seems to be a high positive correlation between population size and the
number of subfunctions (or programs) of police departments. This fact implies that cities having

relatively large populations have a relatively large
number of specialized programs and, therefore, larger
police forces per capita--and it is, in fact, demonstrated in the data presented in Table 4.3. However,
force size for cities between 10,000 and 100,000 in
population is remarkably constant. Since reported
crime rates are to be used as the primary dependent
variable and, in general, big cities have higher
crime rates than smaller ones, it was thought that
choosing a homogeneous sample of small cities would
help to reduce any spurious size-related relationship between number of policemen per capita and
crime rate.

TABLE 4.3

Police Personnel for Urban Areas (Median), 1967

Population Size	Uniformed Personnel per 1,000 Population
Over 50,000	1.79
250-500,000	1.51
100-250,000	1.42
50-100,000	1.36
25-50,000	1.33
10-25,000	1.39

Source: Municipal Yearbook, 1968 (Chicago:
City Manager's Association, 1968), p. 352, Table 2.

Second, the nature of the crime statistics published by the FBI in the Uniform Crime Reports (UCR)
virtually precludes making interstate crime rate
comparisons. Moreover, use of the FBI data for in-
tercity comparisons even within a state is subject
to some question. The FBI crime data in the UCR
are neither uniform nor precise. Different statutory definitions of similar crimes among states and
wide variation in quality and method of crime data
collection among urban police departments are the
major reasons for lack of uniformity of criminal

statistics.[16] Most observers agree that these problems are serious and that comparability of the data
among jurisdictions is extremely limited. However,
comprehensive crime data are collected for cities
within California by the state's Bureau of Criminal
Statistics.[17] While these data are collected on a
more uniform and analytically useful basis, the California definitions of certain types of crime differ
from the definitions used by the FBI. Thus, for
purposes of comparison, in the model that follows
crime rates will be computed using both the FBI and
the California data on reported crimes.

Finally, the effects of patrol inputs on crime
rates may be much easier to detect for small cities
than for, say, the huge police divisions of Los Angeles. The former more closely represent actual patrol beats and control more factors than it can ever
be hoped would be held constant in the large Los Angeles police divisions.

The Measures of Patrol Output

Although the production model expressed in
equations (2) through (4) suggests the use of the
ratio of on-view arrests to reported crimes as an
output proxy, data for the number of on-view arrests
are not available for the cities in the sample.
This somewhat restricts the scope of the output
proxy for the visible or preventive patrol production function. In the place of C/R as the output
measure, four alternative dependent variables have
been used in an attempt to determine the best output
proxy. Actually, only three different variables are
employed since two differ merely because two sources
of crime data were used: FBI and California.

Crime and Crime Indexes

The primary dependent variable is a "visible
crime index." To establish this variable, certain
criminal offenses have been selected from the crime
index of Part One offenses of the FBI and from the
major adult felonies of the state of California.

Further, somewhat arbitrarily, felonies have been
divided into two major categories: suppressible offenses and nonsuppressible offenses. Suppressible
crimes are those thought to be more susceptible to
deterrence through the activity of visible field patrol; thus the term visible crime index, because
such crimes occur mainly in public areas. The index includes the (FBI) crimes of robbery, burglary,
larceny-theft (both grand and petty), and auto
theft,[18] the state of California's definitions of
these crimes being nearly the same as the FBI's.
The one exception is that the California definition
of theft does not include instances in which losses
are under $200, whereas the FBI includes all in-
stances in which losses exceed $50. Despite the
definitional similarities the California figures
are in absolute magnitude far below the FBI figures,
presumably because the FBI includes attempts, whereas
California does not.

The crimes included in the visible index are
those of which the majority occur in public places.
Of course, other crimes are committed in public
areas, but they are excluded from the visible crime
index if fewer than 50 percent occur in public
streets or buildings. Obviously, the selection of
crimes is arbitrary; property violations constitute
the majority of the crimes included in the visible
index, while most personal injury crimes (homicide,
assault, rape) are excluded.[19] To offset any possible error that may arise from not including these
crimes, indexes of all major crimes, using both FBI
and California data, are also used as dependent
variables. (It is possible to think of these indexes as the second output proxy, but they have not
been listed as such because little reliance will be
placed on their use.[20]) The aggregated indexes are
expressed as crime rates per 1,000 population.

Each separate crime within both the FBI and
the California crime indexes is also run in a separate regression equation to determine whether police
patrol inputs have a differential effect on the individual crimes; it may be, for instance, that visible patrol will affect two of the five index crimes
but not all of them, and that an aggregate index

consequently would not reveal any significant effect of patrol inputs, whereas, conversely, a significant change in the aggregate index may result
from a very strong effect of patrol on only two
crimes.

Underreporting of Crime

It is frequently observed that the official
statistics on crimes reported to the police seriously underestimate the true population of criminal
events: "Crimes reported directly to prosecutors
usually do not show up in the police statistics.
Citizens often do not report crimes to the police.
Some crimes reported to the police never get into
the statistical system."[21] Hence, for an accurate
evaluation of the effect of patrol inputs on total
crimes, it is necessary to have an output measure
that attempts to account for the extensive underreporting in the published crime statistics.

A true figure for crime for any area is the
sum of the reported and unreported criminal events
occurring in that area in a given period of time.
This can be represented as follows:

$$(7) \quad A = U + R$$

where   A = actual crimes
        U = unreported crimes
        R = reported crimes

The hypothesis developed from the production model
outlined above predicts what will happen to A from
a change in patrol inputs; that is, the marginal
effect of patrol inputs on crime, both reported and
unreported, is expected to be negative. The theory
implies that

$$(8) \quad A = f(m, S)$$

where   m = the number of patrol units
        S = service conditions or environmental
            variables (yet to be specified)

and that $\partial A / \partial m < 0$. Although there is no predic-
tion for the separate effects of a change in m on R

or U, it might at first glance be assumed that both
R and U would change in the same direction. However, a "reporting" phenomenon may interfere with
the presumed relationship between R and A. This reporting phenomenon is caused by two separate prob-
lems--the problem of underreporting and the potential problem of a change in the extent of underreporting when police patrol is altered.

The reporting rate can be written as $r = R/A$.
It causes problems in measuring the effect of patrol
inputs on crime rates so long as some crimes go unreported; that is, so long as $r = R/A < 1$, R will
not be an accurate measure of A regardless of what
happens to r as m changes.

The second problem, called the reporting effect, occurs when r, the reporting rate, is positively related to the addition of patrol inputs.
Thus, $r = f(m)$ and $\partial r/\partial m > 0$. If the reporting
effect is significant, it will further seriously
bias attempts to use reported crimes, R, as a measure of police output. If the definition of the reporting rate is rewritten as $R = rA$, then the effect on R of a change in patrol presence can be
represented by the following equation:

$$(9) \qquad \frac{\partial R}{\partial m} = r \times \frac{\partial A}{\partial m} + A \times \frac{\partial r}{\partial m}.$$

The first term on the right-hand side is the deterrent effect, or the change in actual crime rates
from a change in patrol inputs. The second term on
the right-hand side represents the reporting effect
of a change in patrol inputs. Since the deterrent
effect is expected to be negative $\partial A/\partial m < 0$ and
the reporting effect positive $\partial r/\partial m > 0$, the sum
of the two effects is, a priori, unpredictable. If
measured by R, the outcome of an increase in police
presence will be unclear.

There are at least two reasons that the reporting rate, R/A, might rise following an increase in
patrol inputs: (1) The patrolmen may <u>discover</u>
crimes that would normally be unreported. (2) Crimes
that would normally be unreported may be reported.
(A National Crime Commission survey found that the

most frequent reason given by victims for not reporting the five property violations was "the police
would not be effective."[22] And so if an increased
presence of the police conveys a subjective evaluation by the public that the police can be more effective in solving crimes and recovering losses,
greater reporting on the part of the public may be
induced.) If either possibility occurs, then R/A
rises, U falls, and the final effect on A is uncertain.

A numerical example can be used to demonstrate
the effect of the reporting phenomenon and the need
for an output variable reflecting actual crime rates.
Assume that the following crime experience, A=100,
R=50, U=50, is reported before an increase in patrol
strength takes place in an area. After the increase
in patrol strength takes place, there are three possible results to the crime experience as measured
by R.

A=90, R=60, U=30. Here the fall in unreported
crimes by 20 is partially offset by an increase in
reported crimes by 10. (The reporting rate increases from 0.5 to 0.66.) If the reported crime
rate, R, is used as the output indicator, it will
be concluded that more police tend to induce more
crime when in fact A, the actual number of crimes,
fell. This is a case in which the reporting rate
increases and the (positive) reporting effect, in
equation (9) exceeds the size of the (negative) deterrent effect, that is

$$\left| A \frac{\partial r}{\partial m} \right| > \left| r \frac{\partial A}{\partial m} \right|$$

thus causing $\partial R / \partial m > 0$. Hence, if R is used as
the measure of output, an underestimate of the ef-
fect of patrol inputs will result.

A=90, R=50, U=40. In this case, the reduction
of unreported crimes by 10 results in the two effects' offsetting each other; that is, the absolute
value of the reporting effect just offsets the deterrent effect,

$$\left| A \frac{\partial r}{\partial m} \right| = \left| r \frac{\partial A}{\partial m} \right|$$

so that $\partial R/\partial m = 0$. However, the reporting rate
increased from 0.50 to 0.55, so that using R as the
output measure will reveal no effect from the increased patrol force when the true number of crimes
has fallen.

$\underline{A=90, R=40, U=50}$. In this final case the reporting effect is weaker than the deterrent effect;
that is,

$$\left| A \frac{\partial r}{\partial m} \right| < \left| r \frac{\partial A}{\partial m} \right|$$

so that $\partial R/\partial m < 0$. The increased police presence
deters 10 reported crimes that would otherwise be
reported. The deterrent effect of increased patrol
inputs shows up whether A or R is used as the output measure. (Note, however, that part of the reason is that the reporting rate fell from 0.5 to
0.44.)

Hence, in the instances in which the reporting
effect is operating, the use of estimated actual
crime rates rather than reported rates as the output variable increases the estimates of the effect
of patrol inputs. The use of those figures will
not permit a determination of the strengths of the
two effects, but in all cases in which A falls after
an increase in patrol resources it is certain that
the deterrent effect is involved.

Unfortunately, no estimates of A are available
that have been derived specifically for the sample
of Southern California cities. However, a national
interview survey conducted by the National Opinion
Research Center[23] yielded estimates of the extent
of underreporting on both a national and a regional
basis. The estimates from both the U.S. and the
Western regional samples will be used here to adjust
reported crime rates for nonreporting.

The adjustment will take the form of correction
factors that are defined as the reciprocal of the
reporting rate $1/r$ or A/R. To obtain the correction
factors, the U.S. and Western survey estimates of
the actual crime rate A for the ith crime type are
divided by the reported FBI crime rate for the same
crime type, R_i. The U.S. correction factor can be
written

$$C_i^{US} = \frac{A_i^{US}}{R_i^{US}}$$

and the Western correction factor

$$C_i^{W} = \frac{A_i^{West}}{R_i^{West}} .$$

The correction factors computed from the national survey are presented in Table 4.4; the factors from the Western survey are presented in Table 4.5. Although the NORC estimates are the result of the only national study of the underreporting phenomenon, they cannot be accepted with complete confidence for all purposes. The extent of underreporting may vary by community and by the income, age, race, or sex of the victim as well and be affected by a host of other influences. At best the correction factors used here give only rough approximations of actual crimes, A, for the cities in the sample.

It is important to point out how the correction factors, $C = A_i/R_i$, will be used. In the regression analysis, equations of the following general form will be estimated:

$$(10) \quad R_i = f \; (m_i, \; S_i)$$

where R_i = reported crime rate of type i
m_i = patrol input of type i
S_i = environmental variable i.

The multiple regression equation yields estimates of $\partial R_i / \partial m_i$, the effect of a change in a patrol input variable, m_i, on any reported crime rate, R_i. To obtain the desired adjusted estimate of the effect of m_i on A_i, the estimated effect of m_i on R_i obtained from the regression equation must be multiplied by the correction factor for each crime type; that is, it is presumed that $\partial A_i / \partial m_c = C_i \; x \; \partial R_i / \partial m$, where $\partial R_i / \partial m$ is the estimated regression coefficient. As Figure 4.1 shows, if the reporting rate is not affected by m (that is, r is constant), only the slope of the estimated regression line between m and R_i is

TABLE 4.4

Actual and Reported Crime Rates for the United States

Offense, i (1)	FBI Rates for Individuals, 1965 (per 100,000 population), R_i (2)	NORC[a] Rates, 1965-66 (per 100,000 population), A_i (3)	Correction Factor, C_i^{US} (4) = (3) ÷ (2)
Robbery	61.4	94.0	1.55
Burglary	299.6	949.1	3.13
Grand theft ($50 and over)	267.4	606.5	2.27
Petty theft (under $50)	n.c.	n.c.	2.70[b]
Auto theft	226.0	206.2	none
Total property crimes	793.0	1,761.8	2.22

[a]National Opinion Research Center.

[b]Taken directly from the survey results. Phillip H. Ennis, "Criminal Victimization in the U.S.: A Report of a National Survey," Field Survey II (President's Commission on Law Enforcement and Administration of Justice, Washington, D.C., 1967), Table 22, p. 42.

Note: n.c. = not calculated.

Source: President's Commission on Law Enforcement and Administration of Justice, The Challenge of Crime in a Free Society (Washington: Government Printing Office, 1967), p. 21.

TABLE 4.5

Actual and Reported Crime Rates for 13 Western States

offense, i (1)	FBI Rates for Individuals, 1965 (per 100,000 population), R_i (2)	NORC Rates, 1965-66 (per 100,000 population), A_i (3)	Correction Factor, C_i^W (4) = (3) ÷ (2)
Robbery	76.2	133.0	1.74
Burglary	894.8	1,348.0	1.51
Grand theft ($50 and over)	573.1	855.0	1.50
Petty theft (under $50)	1,800.0*	2,241.0	1.24*
Auto theft	341.2	380.0	1.11

*Authors' estimate of petty thefts for selected Los Angeles area suburban communities, 1967.

Source: Phillip H. Ennis, "Criminal Victimization in the U.S.: A Report of a National Survey," Field Survey II (President's Commission on Law Enforcement and Administration of Justice, Washington, D.C., 1967), Table 9, p. 21.

FIGURE 4.1

Effect of a Correction Factor for Reported Crimes

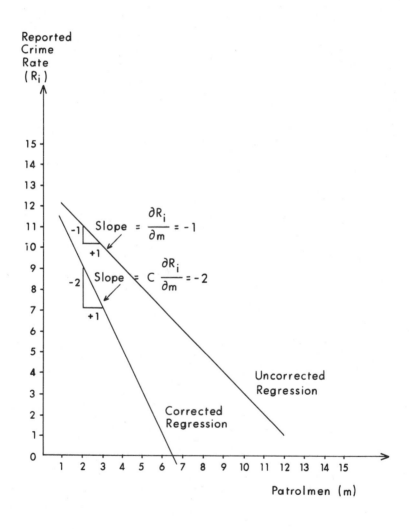

affected. The significance of neither the equation
nor the estimated coefficient, $\partial R_i / \partial m$, is affected;
only the size of the latter is changed. This correc-
tion procedure will be pursued below in the section
on evaluation and conclusions, where an attempt is
made to evaluate the significant parameter estimates
of patrol inputs with a benefit-cost analysis.

Despite this attempt to correct for underreporting, it can be shown that the effects of the
police on A will still be underestimated here if a
reporting effect is present. Dividing through equation (9) by r obtains

$$(11) \quad \frac{1}{r} \times \frac{\partial R}{\partial m} = \frac{\partial A}{\partial m} + \frac{A}{r} \frac{\partial r}{\partial m}$$

The left-hand term represents the effects on output
measured by the described correction procedure.
And, obviously, this procedure will estimate actual
crime accurately only if no reporting effect is
present; that is, $1/r \times \partial R / \partial m = \partial A / \partial m$ only if
$\partial r / \partial m = 0$. So long as the reporting effect is
present, $\partial r / \partial m > 0$, then the presumed negative effect of $\partial A / \partial m$ must be large enough to offset the
reporting effect in order for the left-hand side to
be negative. But this will mean that $\partial A / \partial m >$
$1/r \ \partial R / \partial m$. Hence, the effect of the police will
still be underestimated if the correction procedure
outlined above is used when the reporting effect is
present, and there will be a conservative bias in
the estimation of the effects of police patrol on
crime.

In the presentation of the results of the regression analysis in the section on evaluation and
conclusions the following notation will be employed
to indicate the dependent variables:

Y_8 = Robberies per 1,000 population
  $Y_{8,f}$ = FBI data
  $Y_{8,c}$ = California data
Y_9 = Burglaries per 1,000 population
  $Y_{9,f}$ = FBI data
  $Y_{9,c}$ = California data
Y_{10} = Grand thefts per 1,000 population
  $Y_{10,f}$ = FBI data
  $Y_{10,c}$ = California data

Y_{11} = Petty thefts per 1,000 population
   $Y_{11,f}$ = FBI data
   * ___ This category not included in
     California statistics
Y_{12} = Auto thefts per 1,000 population
   $Y_{12,f}$ = FBI data
   $Y_{12,c}$ = California data
Y_{13} = Total <u>Visible Crimes</u> per 1,000 population
   $Y_{13,f}$ = FBI data
   $Y_{13,c}$ = California data
Y_{14} = Total <u>all FBI Part One Crimes</u> per 1,000
     population
Y_{15} = Total <u>all California Part One Crimes</u> per
     1,000 population

Arrests as Measures of Output

In an effort to determine the most accurate
measure of patrol output, arrest rates will also be
used as dependent variables in the regression analysis. By comparing the effect of police inputs on
arrest rates with their effect on reported crimes,
it may be possible to approximate the special clearance rate, C/R, originally proposed as an ideal output proxy. Of course, since C represents on-view
arrests one must discover (or assume) the average
percentage of all arrests that are on-view to have
an exact measure of C/R.

If the percentage of all arrests that are on-
view patrol arrests cannot somehow be determined
(for example, by observation or assumption), the use
of arrest rates as an output proxy can still be justified in the context of the theoretical hypotheses
advanced above. The objective of a visible patrol
program is to deter would-be offenders, who are assumed to calculate and act on the basis of the probability of apprehension. If the subjective probability of arrest perceived by the offender closely
approximates the true risk of arrest and this risk
is accurately measured by police arrest rates (arrests per 1,000 population),[24] it can then be presumed that crimes will decrease in some proportion
to the increased arrest rates. Therefore, the arrest rates may be a reasonable measure of the deterrence produced by (that is, the output of) a

visible patrol program. Hence, in the statistical
analysis below, the following arrest rates have
been experimented with as output indicators: California adult felony arrest rates per city, adult arrests for visible crimes only, and juvenile arrest
rates. In the tables of results, arrest rates will
be designated as Y_a.

Description of the Patrol Input and
Environmental Variables

The conceptual and statistical content of the
independent variables used in the multiple regression equations can be best discussed by presenting
all of them in the following equation:

$$(12) \quad Y = \alpha + \beta_1 \times \frac{PT}{Pop} + \beta_2 \times \frac{V}{Pop} + \beta_3 \times U$$

$$+ \beta_4 \times \frac{NPT}{Pop} + \beta_5 \times PPT + \beta_6 \times \frac{SM}{Pop}$$

$$+ \beta_7 \times S + \beta_8 \times NW + \beta_9 \times \frac{W}{Pop} + \mu$$

The police patrol input variables are PT/Pop,
V/Pop, U, NPT/Pop, and PPT. The data for all these
variables were collected in a letter survey of 46
independent city police departments in the Los Angeles region.[25] In addition data were collected
from 6 contract cities serviced by the Los Angeles
County Department of the Sheriff.[26] PT/Pop: This
is the labor input variable estimated by the absolute number of sworn officers on the force who are
considered to be visible patrolmen and who are regularly assigned to patrol beat activities. It is expressed as visible patrolmen per 1,000 population.
The data include motorized and foot patrolmen as
well as accident investigation and traffic enforcement officers. Any officers are included whose primary duties require that most of their shifts be
spent patrolling surface streets.

Ideally, the labor input variable should be expressed as the number of patrol man-hours per year,
since most of the other data are expressed in annual
terms. However, the data were not collected on this

basis and the assumptions required to obtain an estimate of patrol man-hours are too unreliable to be used. Moreover, since most of these police departments have only a few patrolmen, such assumptions could substantially alter the relative importance of this variable among cities.

In accordance with the production model in equations (2) through (4), this variable should reflect only the time spent in preventive patrol, which includes answering crime-related calls, and not the time spent answering calls for services not related to crime. Again, establishing such a figure requires either unavailable data or an assumption that will permit an estimate of the "average" amount of time a patrolman spends answering crime-related calls and performing preventive patrol, say, per shift. Such assumptions and estimates can be obtained for larger cities, but using them for the small, suburb-like sample is questionable. Thus, the model will deviate from the ideal for yet another reason.

If an attempt is made to avoid these problems by estimating the number of patrolman-days per year, again it may be that the required assumptions will be unrealistic. For example, a study of St. Louis duty rosters showed that, of a total possible patrolman-days of 43,483 in a given period, only 25,225, or 58 percent, were actually devoted to patrol duties.[27] Because patrolmen in the unspecialized departments of smaller cities tend to perform a greater variety of tasks than they do in large cities like St. Louis, it would be inappropriate to estimate the number of man-days without the actual personnel data. These personnel data were not obtainable for this study--but it should be pointed out that it would be an easy task for police employees to collect such data from personnel records or, if one had knowledge of vacations, sick days, and assignment policies, to generate good approximations.

Thus, it is assumed here that the patrolmen spend all hours during their watches engaged in deterrent patrol activities. This assumption may not be as unsound as it may appear. Clearly, an element

of visibility is operating even when radio cars are
answering calls for service not related to crime
and even when they are "off the air" for lunch or
tasks relating to their equipment.

V/Pop: This variable is a proxy for the capital input of the patrol bureau. It is estimated as
the number of patrol vehicles per 1,000 population.
And again the problem arises of estimating patrol
vehicle-hours or vehicle-days--but this estimate is
relatively easy to make since many departments use
vehicles either 24 or 16 hours per day. Lacking
data, it is again assumed that all hours of vehicle
use are crime deterrent patrol hours.

Although it is often necessary to hold constant
the number of vehicles in use, it may be inappropriate to attribute a change in output to vehicles
alone, since they require patrolmen to operate them.
This seems to be a case of fixed factor proportions
and is reflected in the next input variable.

U: This is the percentage of all regularly
assigned patrol units that are one-man units; it reflects the technique of organization of men and vehicles and, at the same time, provides an estimate
of m in the model of equations (2) through (4).
There are, of course, only two real possibilities;
either one-man or two-man units. It should be
pointed out that there is some debate over the relative effectiveness of these two alternative techniques, and one of the motives for including the
percentage one-man variable in the equations is to
see how policy on this issue affects crime rates.
It seems, a priori, that one-man units could perform the task of deterrent patrol more efficiently
and at a lower cost, whereas two-man cars would be
more suited to answering calls for services in certain areas at certain times safely.

NPT: This reflects the remainder of the force,
officers who are not visible patrolmen. It is designed to hold constant any effect the activities
of the nonpatrol force may have on crime rates. It
is a service factor that can alter the effectiveness
of a patrol force of a given size. If there is a
small nonpatrol force, the implication exists that
patrolmen will be required to perform a greater

variety of duties, thus lessening their effectiveness.

PPT: This is the percentage of the total
force made up of patrolmen and is merely an alternative expression for variables PT/Pop and NPT. Needless to say, all three cannot be used in the same
regression equation.

SM/Pop: This is the number of street miles
per 1,000 population, a service condition that can
affect patrol inputs. The greater SM/Pop is, the
less effective a given number of patrol inputs is
likely to be, since more area must be patrolled and
average distances traveled to answer calls for service will be greater.[28]

S: This represents median school years completed for persons twenty-five years of age or
older.[29]

NW: This represents the percentage of the
total population that is nonwhite.

Data for all the variables are for 1968, with
the exception of S and NW. Current data on the
racial characteristics of all the sample cities
were not available. To combine the data on minori-
ties (and median school years) from the 1960 census
with the data for other variables from 1968 sources
is to assume that the relative percentage of nonwhites among the cities remained the same for the
eight-year period. This assumption is valid if
there has been a uniform relative increase in the
percentage of nonwhite residents for all cities.
The effect will be to bias the size of the regression coefficients but not their explanatory ability.
A point in favor of using these data even though potential biases are introduced is that the rate of
increase in NW is slow for Southern California
cities.

W/Pop: This is the assessed valuation of
property or "wealth" per 1,000 residents. A priori,
wealth may be either positively or negatively related to crime.

An increase in wealth in a given community may
increase the expected return to potential criminals
by increasing the amount and (or) value of theft-
susceptible property, which can be viewed as analogous to an increase in earnings, having two possible

effects on criminal activity. Since the expected
return from a given crime is higher, an individual
may commit more crimes in order to earn more. On
the other hand, the thief can earn the same amount
by committing fewer crimes (assuming all crimes are
divisible), so he may decrease his criminal activity, taking less risk. It cannot be said what individual behavior will be under such conditions or,
therefore, what will happen to the amount of crime
in a community with a change in wealth. It should
be borne in mind, however, that the effects mentioned are all related to expected return (marginal
revenue or demand). An increase in wealth may also
affect the supply response of criminals: higher
community wealth may imply better possibilities for
legitimate market employment in a community or,
more strictly, the opportunity cost of crime. From
this point of view, greater wealth would tend to
decrease the amount of crime in a given community.[30]

Per capita community income was experimented
with and, surprisingly, did not behave uniformly as
expected, even though wealth and income should be
closely related as explanatory variables.

RESULTS OF THE REGRESSION ANALYSIS

The regression equations were estimated in
linear form. Experimentation with nonlinear estimating equations yielded no substantial improvement
in the explanatory ability of the model--and because of the homogeneity of the sample of cities
there is actually no reason to believe that a nonlinear relationship between crime rates and police
inputs or other variables exists. The assumption
underlying the linear form is that the marginal
product of, say, additional patrolmen or patrol vehicles is constant throughout the entire range.
Since the range in the size of the patrol forces in
the sample is small, the assumption of a linear relationship seems reasonable.

The results presented in Tables 4.6 and 4.7
are from the most basic of the several models that
were estimated. They are the most basic in the
sense that only two police input variables are used

TABLE 4.6

Regression Equation on FBI Crime Rates per Capita in 1968, for Cities in Southern California

Dependent Variable	α	Regression Coefficients and Their t-Values						R^2
		$\frac{PT}{Pop}$	$\frac{V}{Pop}$	S	$\frac{SM}{Pop}$	NW	$\frac{W}{Pop}$	
$Y_{8,f}$	6.140	- 0.122 (0.133)	- 0.640 (0.500)	- 0.369 (2.057)	- 0.320 (2.020)	0.104 (6.035)	0.103 (0.594)	0.57
$Y_{9,f}$	36.940	- 4.440 (0.805)	3.563 (0.465)	- 1.951 (1.816)	0.098 (0.104)	0.445 (4.318)	0.540 (0.517)	0.36
$Y_{10,f}$	- 14.226	- 2.444 (0.422)	8.990 (1.116)	1.825 (1.616)	- 0.944 (0.946)	0.253 (2.333)	1.382 (1.258)	0.29
$Y_{11,f}$	26.060	- 9.368 (1.115)	15.097 (1.293)	- 1.141 (0.697)	1.666 (0.151)	0.297 (1.894)	1.231 (0.773)	0.13
$Y_{12,f}$	18.678	- 2.435 (0.857)	0.893 (0.226)	- 1.044 (1.887)	- 0.970 (1.982)	0.365 (6.857)	0.634 (1.777)	0.60
$Y_{13,f}$	74.350	- 19.368 (1.086)	27.600 (1.114)	- 2.743 (0.790)	- 0.470 (0.153)	1.468 (4.402)	4.039 (1.196)	0.33

Source: Prepared by the authors.

TABLE 4.7

Regression Equation on California Crime Rates per Capita in 1968, for Cities in Southern California

Dependent Variable	α	Regression Coefficients and Their t-Values						R^2
		$\dfrac{PT}{Pop}$	$\dfrac{V}{Pop}$	S	$\dfrac{SM}{Pop}$	NW	$\dfrac{W}{Pop}$	
$Y_{8,c}$	1.606	0.077 (0.229)	0.030 (0.065)	- 0.089 (1.229)	- 0.127 (2.080)	0.021 (3.492)	0.051 (0.820)	0.42
$Y_{9,c}$	3.367	0.028 (0.044)	- 0.793 (0.934)	- 0.188 (1.377)	- 0.284 (2.474)	0.053 (4.730)	0.510 (4.360)	0.71
$Y_{10,c}$	1.050	0.275 (0.984)	0.210 (0.556)	- 0.121 (1.998)	0.015 (0.294)	- 0.005 (1.056)	0.227 (4.395)	0.71
$Y_{12,c}$	0.439	0.364 (0.972)	- 0.382 (0.757)	- 0.008 (0.104)	- 0.155 (2.273)	0.046 (6.870)	0.176 (2.533)	0.71
$Y_{13,c}$	6.588	0.789 (0.640)	- 0.669 (0.403)	- 0.426 (1.590)	- 0.555 (2.470)	0.135 (6.141)	0.948 (4.150)	0.76

Source: Prepared by the authors.

and both are in their simplest forms. Also, the
crime rates are unadjusted for reporting phenomena.
The results in Table 4.8 introduce additional police
input variables into the model, FBI crime rates being used as output indicators. Table 4.9 presents
various aggregate total crime indexes as output
variables. In each table the regression coefficient
is presented first, with the t-value for each coefficient in parenthesis. No levels of significance
are indicated in the tables because the establishment of criteria for statistical significance can
vary among researchers. It can be pointed out, however, that if a one-tailed test of significance is
applied,[31] a t-value of 2.423 indicates statistical
significance at the 0.01 level, 1.684 at the 0.05
level, and 1.303 at the 0.10 level. In the discussions that follow the 0.05 level will be used as a
benchmark criterion.

As can be seen in Tables 4.6 and 4.7, the equations using California crime data consistently explain a greater proportion of the variation in crime
rates than those using FBI data. Unfortunately, it
cannot be inferred from the higher coefficient of
determination that the California data are superior
to the FBI data. There is no a priori reason for
selecting either of the two competing sources of
data, given a lack of knowledge of the collection
methods of the two agencies. When the "basic" equations were altered by the addition of various police
variables (compare Table 4.8 with Tables 4.6 and 4.7),
the FBI equations were substantially improved, whereas
the California equations were affected adversely, when
they were changed at all. Also, because the nonreporting correction cannot be applied to California
data, the FBI data source was relied upon most frequently in the study.

In the discussion of the results that follows
reference is made to Tables 4.6 through 4.9.

Not all the signs of the regression coefficients
confirm a priori expectations. The wealth variable
indicates that the positive effects of an increase
in wealth outweigh the negative effects. Wealthier
areas tend to experience more visible crime. This
holds uniformly throughout the models. In addition,

TABLE 4.8

Regression Equation on FBI Crime Rates per Capita in 1968, for Cities in Southern California, Employing Additional Police Input Variables

| Dependent Variable | α | Regression Coefficients and Their t-Values | | | | | | | | R^2 |
		$\frac{PT}{Pop}$	$\frac{V}{Pop}$	U	$\frac{NPT}{Pop}$	S	$\frac{SM}{Pop}$	NW	$\frac{W}{Pop}$	
$Y_{8,f}$	5.635	− 0.239 (0.254)	− 0.651 (0.510)	− 1.036 (2.515)	− 0.112 (0.222)	− 0.242 (1.190)	− 0.314 (1.706)	0.086 (4.880)	0.103 (0.561)	0.66
$Y_{9,f}$	29.974	− 4.143 (0.750)	− 2.174 (0.291)	− 5.425 (2.254)	7.673 (2.607)	− 1.034 (0.873)	− 0.069 (0.064)	0.322 (3.105)	0.306 (0.286)	0.52
$Y_{10,f}$	− 3.083	− 5.701 (0.996)	3.259 (0.422)	1.651 (0.661)	5.433 (1.779)	1.250 (1.015)	− 1.370 (1.227)	0.188 (1.748)	1.203 (1.080)	0.30
$Y_{11,f}$	1.158	− 8.435 (1.010)	10.790 (0.953)	2.202 (0.603)	14.071 (3.150)	0.416 (0.231)	1.210 (0.741)	0.343 (2.180)	− 0.021 (0.013)	0.36
$Y_{12,f}$	23.241	− 3.890 (1.389)	0.843 (0.222)	− 4.287 (3.511)	− 0.543 (0.364)	− 1.118 (1.856)	− 0.551 (1.009)	0.289 (5.502)	0.845 (1.553)	0.71
$Y_{13,f}$	55.483	− 20.050 (1.191)	*	− 10.521 (1.344)	27.489 (2.920)	− 0.517 (0.134)	− 1.030 (0.294)	1.222 (3.621)	1.628 (0.477)	0.48

*Not estimated in all equations.

Source: Prepared by the authors.

TABLE 4.9

Regression Equation on Total Crime Rates per Capita in 1968, for Cities in Southern California

Dependent Variable	α	Regression Coefficients and Their t-Values								R^2
		$\frac{PT}{Pop}$	PPT	U	$\frac{NPT}{Pop}$	S	$\frac{SM}{Pop}$	NW	$\frac{W}{Pop}$	
$Y_{13,c}$ (California, visible crimes)	6.774	0.383 (0.330)	*	- 0.790 (1.466)	- 0.075 (0.115)	- 0.405 (1.530)	- 0.441 (1.828)	0.123 (5.291)	1.006 (4.284)	0.77
Y_{15} (California, all crimes)	61.030	- 8.706 (1.033)	*	- 11.635 (2.967)	9.593 (2.037)	- 2.416 (1.253)	- 1.545 (0.879)	0.884 (5.228)	0.953 (0.557)	0.68
Y_{15}	69.855	- 4.154 (0.412)	- 14.332 (1.080)	- 11.943 (2.905)	*	- 2.365 (1.170)	- 1.266 (0.684)	0.884 (5.033)	1.160 (0.623)	0.6537
Y_{14} (FBI, all crimes)	72.226	- 11.760 (1.055)	*	- 11.015 (2.125)	12.844 (2.063)	- 2.523 (0.990)	- 2.393 (1.030)	1.021 (4.567)	1.467 (0.649)	0.60
Y_{14}	83.450	- 6.687 (0.499)	- 16.491 (0.935)	- 11.605 (2.125)	*	- 2.510 (0.938)	- 1.908 (0.776)	1.022 (4.382)	1.903 (0.769)	0.56

*Not estimated in all equations.

Source: Prepared by the authors.

wealth often becomes highly significant; although it
does not reach a significant level in Table 4.6, it
is uniformly significant for the California crime
rates in Table 4.7. Since only property crimes are
included, the positive coefficient is not an unexpected result. If personal injury crimes had also
been included in the index, the same result would
not have been expected, because economic incentives
are not so important to potential criminals in personal injury crimes.

The nonwhite variable is uniformly positive and
significant in nearly all the following cases. This
result, too, appears to have an underlying economic
rationale, because nonwhites tend to have fewer market employment opportunities and lower market wage
and salary earnings than whites, and so, ceteris
paribus, nonwhites could be expected to engage in
relatively more property violations, the opportunity
costs being lower than for whites. Thus, assuming a
certain gross expected return for a given crime, the
net expected return will be higher for nonwhites
than for whites.[32]

The SM (street miles per 1,000 population)
variable is generally negative throughout these
models but reaches acceptable levels of significance usually only when California data are used.
The a priori expectation was that greater SM/Pop
would diminish the effectiveness of a patrol force
of a given size, thereby increasing the likelihood
of crime--that, thus, SM/Pop and crime would be
positively related. That this expectation was not
sustained may be the result of the effects of a
third influence omitted from the analysis: it was
found that the cities that had greater SM/Pop also
had lower population density; and since it is fairly
well established that denser areas within large
cities tend to experience more crime, it is reasonable to suspect that SM/Pop was reflecting the effect of population density on crime. It does not
appear that the effectiveness of patrol inputs is
seriously affected in cities with more street miles.
Only if it can be assumed that the probability of a
criminal event is equal for every street mile will
more SM/Pop alter patrol output (crime) at a given

input level, and the evidence, although tentative, suggests this assumption is not tenable.

The sign of the median schooling variable, S, is not uniform throughout. However, in Table 4.6 it is negative as expected, and generally it is significant only when its sign is negative. A possible explanation of the frequent sign changes is the fact that S is the median school years completed by adults aged 25 and older. Since a large portion of most types of property violations is committed by juveniles, schooling is not reflected in S. However, in an attempt to overcome this problem use was made of a "percentage teenagers" variable, which also did not maintain a uniform sign. There are at least two variables that may help to overcome this possible source of misspecification, the school dropout rate in an area and the teenage unemployment rate. Either one may indicate the economic incentives of juveniles to commit property violations. Unfortunately, the required cross-sectional data are not available for Southern California cities.

The two patrol input variables, PT/Pop and V/Pop, are not significant in either the FBI or the California equations presented in Tables 4.6 and 4.7. Also, PT/Pop is negative in sign in Table 4.6 but positive in Table 4.7; V/Pop also reverses sign but from positive to negative. In the California equations high levels of significance were attained by all of the service-condition variables, W, NW, SM, and S--which explains the much higher coefficient of determination in the California equations.

Greater consistency of the visible patrol inputs is shown in Table 4.9 when total crime indexes (FBI and California) are used as dependent variables and alternative input measures are employed. The "percentage one-man" variable, U, is consistently negative and significant, whereas all the "percentage patrolmen," PPT, and most of the PT variables are negative but not always significant. The NPT variable, when it is positive, is significant. Of course, this latter police input measure was not included for the purpose of examining its effect per se, but for the purpose of identifying its possible influence on the visible police inputs.

The major conclusion that can be drawn from the analysis is that there is no consistent statistical support for the production function hypothesized in the first two sections of this chapter. There does not seem to be any unique relationship between the effect of deterrent patrol inputs and certain "suppressible" street crimes. Indeed, the evidence in Table 4.9 indicates that visible patrol may be able to affect all major crimes to a greater extent than any small subsample of this aggregate.

Although the findings suggest the rejection of attempts to select one of the models over any of the others, they do not necessarily suggest the conclusion that police patrol has little or no effect on the crime rate measures used; in many instances the patrol inputs have the hypothesized effect on crime rates and are either significant or very nearly so. What it does seem necessary to conclude is that the models formulated and tested here were not adequately specified. The input variables are very crude and are not good approximations of the input variables discussed in the ideal production model.

Furthermore, the output proxies used may also be criticized on the ground that the reported crime data are not reliable. As a contrast and comparison with the original models, a different production function was estimated. The only change made was the substitution of arrest rates (in per capita terms) for crime rates as the output indicator. The results for these models are presented in Table 4.10.

The regression results are as expected and fairly uniform. Except for U, the estimated patrol input coefficients are positive and generally significant. The same holds true for the W/Pop and NW variables, which are highly significant; S and SM/Pop are negative and significant. The negative sign of the "percentage one-man" patrol units variable can be readily explained. The addition of more one-man units implies a decision (intentional or not) by the police to have these units specialize more in deterrent patrol and less in answering calls for service, which results in fewer arrests.

TABLE 4.10

Regression Equation on Arrests per Capita in 1968, for Cities in Southern California

Dependent Variable	α	$\frac{PT}{Pop}$	$\frac{V}{Pop}$	U	$\frac{NPT}{Pop}$	S	$\frac{SM}{Pop}$	NW	$\frac{W}{Pop}$	R^2
					Regression Coefficients and Their t-Values					
Y_a (Total adult felony arrests, California)	15.586	1.324 (0.512)	2.522 (.699)	*	*	- 1.080 (2.140)	- 0.738 (1.648)	0.198 (4.072)	1.478 (3.010)	0.59
Y_a (Total adult felony arrests, California)	17.228	1.106 (0.503)	*	- 1.631 (1.567)	3.295 (3.055)	- 1.133 (2.419)	- 0.734 (1.716)	0.156 (3.322)	1.211 (2.706)	0.67
Y_a (Adult arrests; visible crimes, California)	8.440	1.163 (1.011)	- 0.373 (0.233)	*	*	- 0.604 (2.694)	- 0.537 (2.697)	0.111 (5.168)	0.906 (4.154)	0.73
Y_a (Adult arrests; visible crimes)	8.220	0.963 (0.900)	*	- 0.699 (1.381)	0.076 (0.145)	- 0.555 (2.435)	- 0.463 (2.228)	0.101 (4.397)	0.925 (4.247)	0.74
Y_a (Total adult felony arrests)	18.524	*	*	- 1.660 (1.615)	$\frac{PPT}{Pop}$ 3.350 (3.148)	- 1.217 (2.804)	- 0.683 (1.658)	0.161 (3.540)	1.386 (4.980)	0.67

*Not estimated in all equations.

Source: Prepared by the authors.

This explanation cannot, however, obscure the fact that the negative signs of the U coefficient are evidence against the use of arrest rates to approximate the behavior of the true indicator of patrol output--crime rates. The assumption behind the use of arrest rates as an output proxy is that additional police resources will increase both the number of arrests and the risk of apprehension, thereby reducing the number of crimes. The positive signs for most of the patrol input variables in Table 4.10 support this assumption. However, the several negative signs suggest that causality may be in a reverse direction; additional patrol inputs may first reduce the crime rate, which result, in turn, will cause the number of arrests to fall. In this event, crimes and arrests will be positively correlated--a relationship that is confirmed by the discovery of a (positive) simple correlation coefficient computed from cross-section data. If arrests are a function of the number of crimes rather than the reverse, arrest rates will not be suitable indicators of patrol output. The several positive (and significant) coefficients of patrol input variables in the regression equations support the original interpretation based on rational, maximizing behavior by potential criminals and imply that arrest rates are acceptable output proxies. However, the regression results cannot be considered conclusive and the issue deserves further research, since police administrators frequently view arrest rates as important performance indicators and, consequently, base many important resource allocation decisions upon them.

It remains an unfinished task to test a clearance rate as a proxy for patrol output as suggested by the model in equation (2). This test has not been undertaken here because data were unavailable on the number of cases cleared by on-view arrest and any alternative clearance measure would include not only the effects of patrol division inputs but also the effects of detective and traffic division inputs.

EVALUATION AND CONCLUSIONS

The results of the statistical analysis described above do not permit complete support of the patrol production models formulated; but, on the other hand, neither do they permit rejection of the technique of applying the concept of the production function to police patrol operations. The weaknesses of the empirical tests of the models were hinted at above, but it will be useful to examine some of the problems in detail.

First of all, there is little reason to believe that the model is adequately specified. Specification error in this case may arise either because of the omission of certain variables or because of the improper definition of some of the included variables. One of the omitted variables, which was unavailable but seems to be extremely important in the explanation of the cross-sectional incidence of property crimes, is the unemployment rate.[33] In addition, the effects of wealth or income may be measured more precisely by inequality of income within each community in the sample rather than by the simple assessed value per capita figure used.

In addition, the patrol input data may be improperly defined because the kind of letter survey forms by which they were collected are often subject to misinterpretation by respondents. Aside from that, the input variables seem to be merely first approximations of proper indicators of the number of men and equipment hours devoted to crime deterrent patrol only and to crime-related calls for service.

Another specification error may result from the omission of a variable to indicate the level of quality of the patrol inputs for the different departments, which could take the form of a judgment of the quality of the entire department or the quality of the sworn officers (for example, by examining departmental entrance requirements and training required). However, since no data on the municipalities in question were available, no arbitrary judgment on quality was attempted.

Another problem connected with this model is the usual one of the bias involved in the simple least-squares regression technique. This problem arises whenever the dependent variable influences the explanatory variables, thereby violating the assumption of unilateral causation from the independent to the dependent variable. For example, assume the estimating equation were presented as

$$(13) \quad Y = \alpha + \beta_1 \times \frac{PT}{Pop} + \beta_2 \times S + \beta_3 \times NW$$
$$+ \beta_4 \times W + \beta_5 \times \frac{SM}{Pop} + \mu$$

where Y = visible crime index.

The problem arises because PT/Pop, the number of patrolmen per capita, will be partially determined by crime rates and possibly by other variables exogenous to the police sector of the entire criminal justice system. Not only does the patrol variable, PT/Pop, explain the variations in crime rates, but crime rates also partially explain variations in PT/Pop. In fact, other variables in the estimating equation may also help explain PT/Pop; these variables must also be considered endogenous to the system. Thus, the functional relationship may be as follows:

$$(14) \quad \frac{PT}{Pop} = \alpha + \beta_1 \times Y + \beta_2 \times W + \beta_3$$
$$\times NW + \mu$$

which should also be estimated to obtain the least-biased regression coefficients.

Unless all endogenous variables are expressed and estimated with only exogenous variables used as explanatory variables,[34] the bilateral causation problem results in biased estimates of the estimated coefficients of the police input variables.[35] Moreover, this may account for some of the inconsistency in the sign and level of significance of the same variables. Fortunately, the bias of the estimates in this case is downward. Because of their expected negative signs, the regression coefficients are lower in size and less significant

than they would be because of the least-squares
bias (bilateral causation).[36] Thus, the effect of
the police inputs estimated in this study is less
than it would be in the estimation of the full system of simultaneous equations.

Third, there is some multicollinearity among
the explanatory variables, including the patrol input variables, and this source of error increases
the standard error of the coefficients, thus reducing the reliability of the estimated parameters.
Moreover, subsequent unreported efforts to reduce
the multicollinearity were not altogether successful.

Despite the possible sources of bias and misspecification of the model, some tentative estimates
of the effectiveness of patrol inputs can be made.
Utilizing the technique of benefit-cost analysis to
evaluate the deterrent effect of additional patrol
inputs, an implicit estimate will be made of the
value of the marginal product of certain inputs,
and an analysis will be made of the costs and benefits of altering an important technique of arranging patrol inputs--the percentages of patrol units
in one-man and two-man patrol cars.

The effects of altering the percentage of one-
man motorized patrol units will be examined for a
variety of reasons. First, although available evidence more and more strongly favors one-man units
and urban police departments are using more of
them,[37] not all departments use them in a fashion
that suggests ideal deployment, with the result
that the relative effectiveness of two-man versus
one-man units is still an interesting policy question. Second, estimating the marginal product of
an additional visible patrol officer without knowledge of the equipment-labor ratio is not a useful
exercise, especially since the sample is composed
of Southern California municipalities in which foot
patrol and other nonmotorized visible patrol methods
are uncommon. Third, the tradeoff between the two
major alternative methods of performing motorized
patrol is implicitly built into the "percentage one-
man" units variable, U, in the regression equations.
Finally, the estimated parameter of this variable
is the most consistent and uniformly significant of

all the police input variables employed in the different models.

A Benefit-Cost Evaluation of One-Man versus Two-Man Patrol Units

The formal analysis of the social benefits of
a policy change requires first an estimate of the
quantitative effect on output of the input alteration in question. Such an estimate will be obtained
by the estimated regression coefficient for the U
variable in any given equation.

The benefits attributable to a reduction in
the number of actual criminal events will first be
discussed briefly, because while the actual number
of crimes deterred by the actions of the police can
never be known or measured with certainty, the model
used assumes that the output of the patrol inputs is
deterrence or prevention. The dependent variable is
the reported crime rate (adjusted for nonreporting)
in a single year. When the estimated parameter of
an input variable is negative, the necessary interpretation of the coefficient is that it represents
the number of crimes prevented from taking place
that would have occurred in the absence of an additional unit of that input. It is assumed, therefore, that the other variables in the equation determine the number of crimes that would occur in
the absence of the police. The benefits, then, are
in the form of a saving of the costs that were prevented from being imposed on individuals whose
legal rights are violated.

The private costs incurred as a result of criminal offenses include physical damage to person or
property, monetary loss, and psychic damage. Although the monetary losses are actually transfers
and not themselves real costs, this study assumes
that the involuntary redistribution of property constitutes a social cost--and this assumption may be
justified by an appeal to society's prohibition of
these transfers. Alternatively, cost per crime
can be thought of as a real resource cost on the
basis of the assumption that the value of the loss

approximates the value of the real cost of resources
expended by offenders on each crime (that is, the
opportunity cost of the offender's time plus the
cost of his equipment). This particular element of
individual loss will be treated as the major measured benefit of the deterrence of crime in this
analysis, because although estimates of reduction
in pain and suffering and reduction in resource
costs in the form of private expenditures on protective devices are also extremely important, actual
data are unavailable.[38] The dollar loss per robbery
will, however, be adjusted by a factor to reflect
the fact that robbery (over one-half of which involves the use of firearms) has connected with it a
high probability of personal injury, unlike the
other property violations in visible crime indexes.

In addition to prevented private costs, external cost savings in the form of reduced costs for
administering the entire criminal justice system of
the state must be considered, because nonpatrol police outlays are reduced when crimes are fewer.
For major felonies, including robbery and burglary,
the investigation and apprehension costs are lowered,
as is the (prosecution) cost of court appearances
by police officers. These elements are less important for auto theft, but this crime, committed principally by juveniles, is associated with a high
rate of recidivism and rather large system costs.
As will be seen, for every 2.5 deterred auto thefts,
it can be assumed that at least one individual will
be prevented from repeating this plus other more
serious violations.

While the number of crimes will have been reduced, it is not necessarily known how many potential criminals this has deterred. This will com-
plicate the attempt to estimate the savings to various state agencies in the criminal justice system.
The reduced costs involved include the cost of judicial proceedings borne by the state, the institutional costs of incarcerated persons, and the probation and parole system costs. Savings in these
areas are necessarily substantial.

A benefit-cost evaluation of the effects of
increased police inputs represented by an increase

in U would normally require an estimate of the increase in patrol costs imposed by the change. However, for this example the U-coefficients from the
equations in Table 4.8 will be evaluated and, from
the structure of those equations, the input change
will be interpreted as not involving any addition to
direct police costs: since PT/Pop and V are held
constant in the equations, the input alteration represented by U is only a reorganization of a fixed
number of inputs. The only change is a 1 percent
increase in the proportion of one-man patrol units;
neither new patrolmen nor vehicles are added. This
resource reallocation is similar to the warnings-
only beat in the traffic endorcement experiment,
where only the technique of operation was altered,
not the number of traffic inputs.

That direct input costs are not increased
does not mean that the shift to a greater proportion of one-man cars is entirely costless. Indeed, an important reason urban police departments
deploy two-man units is that this technique affords
greater individual safety to officers during peak
crime hours. Shifting from two-man patrol units to
one-man units would, presumably, increase slightly
the probability of injury to the officer in the one-
man unit. Therefore, a small increase in (expected)
cost may result from the change. Moreover, reduced
officer safety may have some adverse effects upon
officer morale and ability to recruit new trainees
under fixed wages and working conditions. No attempt was made to estimate these potential costs.

The significant coefficients of U from Table
4.8 are presented below: it was found that U significantly reduced robberies, $Y_{8,f}$, burglaries, $Y_{9,f}$,
and auto thefts, $Y_{12,f}$.

These parameter estimates measure the effect
of $\partial R_i / \partial m_i$ discussed above, where m_i is represented by the "percentage one-man" variable, U, and
R_i is represented by robbery, burglary, and auto
theft. The deterrent effect of U, however, is somewhat indirect because of the equation used. Since
PT/Pop and V are held constant in the equation, an
officer removed from a former two-man unit is assumed to be redeployed in nonmotorized patrol. The

highly significant parameter estimates of U in the
equations imply that the loss sustained in removing
the second man in the patrol car is less than the
gain achieved deploying him differently. The interpretation is based on the assumption that the marginal product of the second man in the patrol car
is less than the marginal product of a nonmotorized
patrolman.

    The first step in evaluating the social bene-
fits of a 1 percent increase in U is to obtain the
resulting decrease in the absolute numbers of the
three crimes; each of the three estimated coefficients is multiplied by 0.01 to obtain the decrease
in the number of robberies, burglaries, and auto
thefts per 1,000 population. Then, multiplying the
reduction in crimes per capita by the mean population (approximately 65,000 or 65 (yields the mean
number of reported crimes that will be deterred by
the 1 percent change in one-man patrol units. Finally, the correction factors, both U.S. (c^{US}) and
Western (c^{W}), are applied to these figures to estimate the numbers of robberies, burglaries, and
auto thefts that are deterred. The results of this
procedure are presented in Table 4.11.

TABLE 4.11

Estimated Numbers of Crimes Deterred by
1 Percent Increase in One-Man Patrol

Offense	Using Correction Factor from West, c^{W}	Using Correction Factor from U.S., c^{US}
Robbery	- 1.172	- 1.044
Burglary	- 5.325	- 11.047
Auto theft	- 3.093	- 2.786

Source: Prepared by the authors.

Each deterred crime yields a social saving equal to the costs that would have been incurred by victims and by the state. The data presented in Table 4.12 are estimates of the average cost to individuals and the state criminal justice system for each type of crime. The table is necessarily assembled from a variety of sources; the techniques, assumptions, and sources used to obtain the final figures are discussed in detail in the supplement to this chapter.

For the offenses used in the visible crime index (1,2,3,4,5), the figures in Table 4.12 account only for the dollar value of the property transferred by the average crime. Not included are the nonpecuniary or psychic losses associated with all the property crimes. Also not included, in the particular case of robbery, are the expected costs of the probable personal injury associated with this crime. Omitting these types of loss in the estimates of the social costs of crime highlights the implicit assumption that each type of crime is of importance only in proportion to the property loss involved; it underestimates the real average cost per crime. In particular, in Table 4.12 a greater loss is attached to burglary than to robbery. However, by definition robbery involves the use or threat of force and frequently results in personal injury to the victim. Nearly 60 percent of all robberies committed in the United States involved firearms or other lethal weapons in 1966.[39] Clearly, the value of a deterred burglary should not be greater than that of a deterred robbery in the estimates of social cost.

To improve the estimates of the average personal loss of each crime in Table 4.12, a "seriousness weight" could be assigned to the average robbery transfers to adjust for the additional costs expected to arise from personal injury and to adjust for the disutility associated with this risk. Since the risk of injury associated with burglary or auto theft is negligible but that associated with robbery is high, one could, for example, weight the seriousness of a robbery as ten times that of a burglary or auto theft; in this case a dollar lost

TABLE 4.12

Social Costs for Selected Offenses

Offense	Average Value of Personal Losses per Reported Offense (1)	Average Costs to State of California Criminal Justice System per Reported Offense (2)	Total Costs per Crime = (1) + (2) (3)
Robbery	$284	$1,343	$1,627
Burglary	390	323	713
Auto theft	1,017	3,100	4,117
Grand theft	239	695	934
Petty theft	26	695	721
Homicide	93,000	7,100	100,100
Aggravated assault	200	732	932
Forcible rape	200	1,090	1,290

Source: Prepared by the authors. (See the supplement to this chapter.)

in a robbery would be assumed to involve ten times
more disutility to the victim than a dollar lost in
a burglary or auto theft. The average personal
loss per robbery in Table 4.12 would thus become
$2,840, and the total cost $4,183. (These figures
are not included in Table 4.12 because they are
merely intended to illustrate one procedure for ad-
justing robbery losses so that they will be comparable with burglary and auto theft losses.[40])

Estimates of the social saving from the additional deterred crimes represent the cost saving to
individuals and the state that would otherwise be
imposed by these offenses--and Table 4.13 presents
estimates of the social benefits stemming from the
increased "percentage one-man" patrol units. They
are obtained by multiplying the change in crimes deterred (by a 1 percent increase in U) in Table 4.11
by the social cost of each crime in Table 4.12.
(Total gross benefits are shown at the bottoms of
the two columns; the figures in parentheses are
benefit estimates when the "seriousness weight" for
robbery is applied.)

TABLE 4.13

Social Benefits of a 1 Percent
Increase in One-Man Patrol

Offense	c^W	c_{US}
Robbery	$ 1,907 (4,901)	$ 1,699 (4,367)
Burglary	3,797	7,876
Auto theft	12,734	11,470
Total gross benefits	18,438 (21,432)	21,045 (23,713)

Source: Prepared by the authors.

The argument could well be made that the average dollar loss per crime, and hence the benefit estimates, are overestimated because no account is taken of the recovery of property by the police. On the other hand, as was argued in Chapter 2, the full value of the transferred property can be considered a real cost because it approximates (assuming competition) the real resource use by criminals who commit the offense. According to this view there is no reason to adjust the average loss figures downward. If all recovered property is returned to legal owners, measuring the gross transfer loss per crime may overstate the true loss by an amount equal to the value of the restored property. Thus, a better estimate of the loss from each crime would be the net loss, which is found by deducting from the gross loss the value of all stolen property returned to the original owners. But this procedure in turn assumes that there is no loss to the owner, say, in having his car stolen and subsequently returned, no matter how long the delay between the theft and recovery. Thus, the net loss would understate the true loss. Since measurement of the true loss is difficult, both the gross loss and the net loss will be calculated in order to provide a range within which true measured benefits are likely to be.

The recovery rates used here are those of the Los Angeles Police Department averaged for the years 1967 and 1968. Of the dollar amount reported stolen, the amount recovered averaged 15.5 percent for robbery losses, 5.75 percent for burglary losses, and approximately 90 percent of vehicles taken. Table 4.14 presents estimates of the net losses for the three property crimes in column 3; the total social costs in column 4 are adjusted for the net loss.

Again, the procedure used to obtain the social benefits of a patrol change is to multiply the newly established social costs by the number of deterred crimes in Table 4.11. Both estimates of social benefits are entered in Table 4.15, in which robbery adjustment is shown in parentheses.

TABLE 4.14

Dollar Losses per Property Crime

Crime	Gross Individual Loss (1)	Loss Recovered (2)	Net Loss (3)	Total Cost = (3) + (col. 3, Table 4.10) (4)
Robbery	$284	$44	$240 (2,400)	$1,583 (3,743)
Burglary	390	22	368	691
Auto theft	1,017	915	102	3,202

Source: Prepared by the authors. (See Table 4.10.)

TABLE 4.15

Social Benefits of 1 Percent Increase in One-Man Units

Correction Factor	Low Estimates (includes recovery)	High Estimates (neglects recovery)
West	$15,437 (17,594)	$18,438 (21,432)
United States	18,305 (20,560)	21,045 (23,713)

Source: Prepared by the authors. (See Table 4.11.)

Thus, even after the numerous adjustments made in the data on losses, net benefits are sizable in all eight estimates. However, evaluating only the gain from the reduction in property violations may still understate the social saving for at least two reasons: (1) Patrol units perform many tasks not related to crime that have a positive value to the community, and (2) more important, visible patrol has some effect on other criminal activities, including personal injury crimes. Property crimes were used in the visible index merely because a majority of them seem to be affected by visible patrol. If deterrent patrol has any, even though small, effect on criminal homicides, forcible rapes, or aggravated assaults, the gain from preventing any one of these may outweigh much of the value of reduced property violations (this assumes the crimes are weighted by an index of seriousness).

Since both benefits and costs may be underestimated, it may be that the size of the bias in the estimates is small. If so, the evidence presented here leads to the conclusion that the proportion of one-man units is too small; increasing this proportion yields a net social saving. This result stems partly from the fact that the change examined involved an unmeasurable direct cost. Both the type of change and the resulting benefits are similar to those associated with the warning-only beat in the traffic experiment described in Chapter 3, but in the traffic experiment it was possible to compare this alteration with various changes in the number of traffic officers. Unfortunately, the results here do not permit similar comparisons; where such comparisons could have been made none of the coefficients of PT/Pop or U reached levels of significance high enough to support estimates of the net returns from additional patrolmen or one-man units.

Nevertheless, the results of this study have broader implications. The output measure tested was the number of deterred crimes per unit of time. The rationale for the use of this variable was the acceptance of crime deterrence as the primary objective of the police. Two major reasons were given for this assumption: (1) Crime prevention has been traditionally accepted as the major function of public police agencies, and (2) measuring output as crimes deterred or number of arrests is far easier than using any alternative output variables. But the tentative evidence presented raises questions about the uncritical acceptance of reduction of the incidence of criminal activities as the major objective of urban police departments and thus as a guide for the allocation of police resources among alternative programs. James Q. Wilson proposes that patrol policy stress should be shifted from the law enforcement function to what he calls the order maintenance function.[41] On the basis of this objective the output of patrol to be measured is not the incidence of crime or the number of arrests but the ability of the individual patrol unit to keep the peace on its assigned beat, a somewhat generalized output that involves considerable overlapping of activities. Wilson's two major arguments for this policy shift are (1) that except for certain street crimes that require a great deal of public and neighborhood support, the police cannot prevent most common crimes and (2) that problems of order maintenance (gang disturbances, family trouble, assaults, fights, drunkenness, and neighbor trouble) are more frequent than law enforcement problems (mainly felonies). This study indirectly supports his first argument by the failure to show a significant effect for patrolmen inputs under a variety of different structural equations. Marginal additions to most patrol inputs do not seem capable of affecting most crimes significantly.

It should be emphasized, however, that the inference should not be drawn from the evidence that resources now devoted to patrol should be shifted. No attempt has been made to estimate production functions for inputs in alternative police programs, and without knowledge of their effectiveness elsewhere, policy changes are not warranted. However, it may be, as Wilson suggests, that a change in the current emphasis for patrol from crime prevention activities to more general community service activities is warranted. Maintaining the peace could become the primary objective of patrol activities

while crime deterrence remained an important but
distinctly secondary goal of the organization of
police resources.

Statistical Analysis in Program Budgeting

Statistical analysis of the sort used here has
sometimes been used to project secular trends on
the basis of historical data for given variables.
For example, the St. Louis study mentioned above[42]
used bivariate linear regression analysis to project
selected variables that were thought to represent
the community's demand for police services. In that
study community demand for police services was assumed to be accurately measured by five indicators:
index crimes (St. Louis Police Department), Part One
crimes (FBI), radio calls for service, total reported traffic accidents, and personal injury and
fatal traffic accidents. Historical data on these
variables for 1948-66 (shown in Table 4.16) were employed to compute linear regression lines for each
of the five indicators (shown in Table 4.17), which
were then used to project the demand for police services in 1975 and 1980 (shown in Table 4.18).
    More elaborate projections could be devised by
investigating environmental factors that may cause
or significantly influence an observed time trend
in such selected indicators as index crimes. For
example, further examination might be warranted of
some of the nonpolice variables used in the LAPD's
patrol allocation formula or of the socioeconomic
or demographic variables tested in the production
functions above if they are highly correlated with,
say, index crimes. If any of these variables is expected to change significantly in the future, an
analysis of this change may predict a future level
of index crimes that differs greatly from the level
predicted by a simple time-trend extrapolation.
    Furthermore, statistical projections can play
an important part in the planning elements of a program budgeting system. Projections of indicators
of future exogenous demands for police or patrol
services can aid in the evaluation of a current or

TABLE 4.16

Annual Measures of Demands for Police Services
in St. Louis, 1948-66 Inclusive

Year	Index Crimes	Part One Crimes	Radio[a] Calls	Total Reported Traffic Accidents	Personal Injury and Fatal Accidents
1948	10,388	15,932	215,622	7,187	3,874
1949	10,654	16,340	272,975	7,607	4,177
1950	10,281	15,766	318,730	9,254	4,919
1951	11,701	18,075	258,766	11,127	5,151
1952	12,754	20,044	272,315	11,480	5,360
1953	14,062	22,273	282,163	10,751	4,957
1954	17,013	27,667	283,182	10,445	4,994
1955	18,327	30,511	279,167	11,032	5,109
1956	19,628	35,016	288,927	11,052	5,262
1957	21,802	37,897	338,223	12,275	5,323
1958	23,574	41,001	386,223	12,183	5,257
1959	23,175	37,121	451,165	12,674	5,741
1960	23,349	38,810	468,566	12,792	5,637
1961	20,557	35,557	489,231	13,031	5,600
1962	22,618	42,787	544,929	14,254	6,045
1963	24,792	48,746	599,556	15,248	6,366
1964	26,692	54,824	629,526[b]	18,834	7,069
1965	25,750	53,530	626,354	20,800	7,675
1966	25,798	50,940	651,575	21,347	7,542

[a]Total number of requests out of service,
directed incidents, and directed assists.

[b]Estimated.

Sources: Index Crimes: 1966 Annual Report,
Police Department, City of St. Louis; Part One
Crimes and Radio Calls: Administrative Analysis
Division, Board of Police Commissioners; Accidents:
Analysis Division, Bureau of Field Operations.

TABLE 4.17

Regression Summaries of Demands for Police Services
in St. Louis, 1948-66 Inclusive

Series	Equation[a]	Standard Error of Coefficient	R^2[b]	Current Growth Rate[a]
Index crimes	$Y = 984T - 36,986$	75	.91	3.3%
Part One crimes	$Y = 2,278T - 96,130$	145	.94	3.9%
Radio calls	$Y = 24,828T - 1,012,291$	2,104	.89	3.7%
Reported traffic accidents	$Y = 630T - 23,103$	70	.83	3.2%
Personal injury and fatal traffic accidents	$Y = 162T - 3,655$	18	.83	2.2%

[a]T represents the last two digits of the year: $T = 48, 49, \ldots, 66$.

[b]calculated as the ratio of the predicted growth during the year to the predicted value of the corresponding series for 1968.

Source: Allocation of Patrol Manpower in the St. Louis Police Department,
O.L.E.A. Grant #39 (July 1966), pp. 2-3.

TABLE 4.18

Projected Demands for Police Services in St. Louis, 1975 and 1980*

Year	Index Crimes	Part One Crimes	Radio Calls	Total Reported Traffic Accidents	Personal Injury and Fatal Traffic Accidents
1975	36,800	74,700	849,800	24,100	8,500
1980	41,700	86,100	973,900	27,300	9,300

*All calculations have been rounded to hundreds.

Source: Allocation of Patrol Manpower in the St. Louis Police Department,
O.L.E.A. Grant #39 (July 1966), pp. 2-3.

future program. For example, patrol administrators
may wish to assume that projections of crimes based
on a simple time trend will reflect true future conditions if the size of police inputs and the current
allocation of the resources remains the same; if,
however, information about the marginal products of
additional police inputs has been obtained from
previous analyses of police programs, such as the
traffic study described above, the department may
be able to reallocate inputs among alternative programs or increase resources so as to effect the
greatest possible reduction of the projected crimes.
The expected deterrent effect of more police inputs
on crimes can be applied to the projected crime
figures as the operand of any resource increase or
reallocation. Alternatively, the analyst may wish
to take the projected future "states" as given and
design the project (say, a new police station) with
no intention to alter these states.

Of course, a corollary to all planning for future environments is the financial and budgetary
implications of the projected states and any proposed program changes. (Multiyear aspects of PPBS
have generally been ignored in the program analyses
carried out here because inputs and outputs were assumed to occur simultaneously.) If they are thought
to be important in program analysis, accurate projections will be useful to predict the future financial implications of a proposed project as well as
the effects on output. However, regression analysis
has seldom, if ever, been used to evaluate alternative police programs or input arrangements directly,
as it was in this study. Unfortunately, however, to
this point the study has not shown statistical analysis to be a highly accurate analytical technique,
merely a feasible alternative to experimentation.
Its feasibility and desirability might increase if
the analytical tools were in the hands of a person
who had complete access to input-output data for a
single police department. Specifically, implemen-
tation of the model production equation proposed in
equations (2) through (4) would be facilitated by
access to time-series data for a single department.
More experimentation could be carried out with such

data as types of radio calls, clearance rates by
crime types, and actual man-hours worked per day or
year by type of program. Such experimentation could
be helpful in finding better formulas to guide resource allocation among geographical areas, seasons,
types of crimes, and so forth. Finally, cost-
effectiveness or cost-benefit analysis of the type
attempted in this chapter could be improved and facilitated by better agency data.

The direct use of statistical analysis by police agencies will inevitably be constrained both
by the quantity and by the quality of data and by
analytical capabilities. One particular constraint
on statistical analysis is the lack of availability
of adequate data (especially in continuous, annual
time series) on the environmental (or service) conditions variables (for example, percentage nonwhite,
wealth, and so forth)--and it was clear in the study
that the variables representing service conditions
explained the variation in crime rates as well as,
if not better than, the patrol inputs variables.
When possible, therefore, it is advisable to estimate police production models that include environmental conditions as explanatory variables. The
approach represented by equations (2) through (4)
and the production function approach used above are
complementary rather than competitive.

SUPPLEMENT

Sources for Column 1, Table 4.12:
Personal Losses for Selected Offenses

1. Robbery: Source of the data was the Los
Angeles Police Department, "Statistical Digest,
1967." The dollar value of all property taken by
robbers in Los Angeles in 1967 was divided by the
number of robberies that occurred.

2. Burglary: Source and method of estimation
same as for robbery, above.

3. Auto Theft: The value of personal loss of
$1,017 (given in Table 4.10) is taken from the FBI
Uniform Crime Reports, 1967 and is described as the

average value of the stolen auto at the time of the
theft.

    4. <u>Grand Theft</u>: Average value of losses
taken directly from national figures presented in
<u>Uniform Crime Reports, 1967</u>.

    5. <u>Petty Theft</u>: Source same as for grand
theft, above.

    6. <u>Homicide</u>: Data taken from U.S. Department
of Health, Education, and Welfare, <u>Motor Vehicle
Injury Prevention Program</u> (Washington: Government
Printing Office, 1966). Table A-8 from that publi-
cation, on earnings lost due to motor vehicle accidents, is reproduced below as Table 4.19, which represents the current value of expected lifetime earnings for projected motor vehicle deaths in 1968,
calculated for each five-year age bracket on the
basis of such data as 1964 life tables, 1964 labor
force participation rates, 1964 mean earnings imputed value of housewives' services, 1964 housekeeping rates, and a 3 percent discount rate. The actual homicide death rates for five-year age groups
in the <u>Uniform Crime Reports</u> corresponded fairly
closely to motor vehicle deaths; thus the average
value of lost earnings in this table was used. Age
and sex, of course, are not the sole factors in determining the value of earnings lost, but there
seems to be no a priori reason that homicide victims
will be either more or less wealthy than traffic accident victims.

    7. <u>Aggravated Assault</u>: The exact nature of
this crime is somewhat imprecise, possibly because
of the various state penal code definitions. The
President's Commission quotes at least three studies
of the injury experience for this crime (President's
Commission, <u>Task Force: Crime and Its Impact</u>, pp.
14-15). The percentage of the victims requiring
hospitalization ranged from a low of 23 percent
(from Thorsten Sellin and Marvin Wolfgang, <u>The Measurement of Delinquency</u> [New York: John Wiley,
1964] to 35 percent in the District of Columbia
(D.C. Crime Commission) to a high of 53.4 percent
in a recent St. Louis study (<u>Journal of Criminal
Law, Criminology, and Police Science</u>, December
1964). In nearly all the studies, most of the
crimes resulted in some injury.

TABLE 4.19

Motor Vehicle Fatality Losses--Total Population:
Number of Deaths and Earnings Lost, by Age, 1968
(thousands of dollars)

Age	Deaths	Earnings Lost
Under 1	283	19,081
1-4	1,330	99,928
5-14	3,660	364,170
15-24	16,600	2,190,638
25-34	6,966	910,352
35-44	4,858	497,940
45-54	5,300	375,079
55-64	4,830	180,242
65-74	3,930	59,746
75-84	2,630	16,800
85 +	479	357
Total	50,866	4,714,333

Source: U.S. Department of Health, Education,
and Welfare, Motor Vehicle Injury Prevention Program (Washington: Government Printing Office, 1966),
Table A-8, p. 26.

For those victims who are hospitalized, a loss
of one week's wages of $100 and medical costs of
$250, a total loss of $350, was assumed. For assault victims who were injured but not hospitalized,
a loss of $50 (values taken from President's Commis-
sion, Task Force: Crime and Its Impact--An Assessment, p. 45) was assumed. It was assumed further
that 50 percent of all reported California aggravated assaults (approximately 34,000) result in the
hospitalization of the victim and 50 percent result
in an injury not serious enough to require hospitalization.
The value is obtained then as follows:

$$17,000 \times \$350 + 17,000 \times \$50$$
$$= \$5,950,000 + \$850,000$$
$$= \$6,800,000 \div 34,000 = \$200.$$

8. Forcible Rape: The same injury experience
results were assumed for rape as for aggravated assault.

Sources for Column 2, Table 4.12: State of
California Criminal Justice System
Costs per Offense

Data for column 2 are from Space General Cor-
poration, Prevention and Control of Crime and Delinquency (El Monte, California, 1965). This source
provides estimates of the total costs for each crime
category of the state government of California criminal justice system. The state system includes adjudication functions; incarceration, parole, and
probation functions; and all state police functions.
Dividing the total cost of each crime by the number
of such crimes committed yields the average cost
for each crime.
Note that criminal justice system costs do not
include local law enforcement expenditures aimed
specifically at each of these crimes--and the expenditures of local law enforcement agencies (city
and county) in California are at least as great as
the expenditures by the state criminal justice system. (For example, in 1966/67, police protection
outlays for the cities and counties of Los Angeles,
San Francisco, and San Diego alone were nearly $160
million while expenditures for the state criminal
justice system were approximately $190 million.)
Unfortunately, there is no entirely satisfactory
way to find what portion of local police outlays is
devoted to criminal as against noncriminal activities or to find how crime-oriented outlays are allocated according to each crime type. Even if this
information were available, however, not all the police costs per crime could be assumed to be saved
by the deterrence of an offense. Much of total patrol expenditure continues regardless of the number
of specific crimes deterred; savings in police cost
stem mainly from programs, such as detection and
apprehension, directed toward the investigation of
unsolved crimes.
The President's Crime Commission estimated average U.S. criminal justice system costs per index

crime for 1965 and included that portion of police
costs attributable to each crime, arbitrarily charging 100 percent of detective force costs and 25 percent each of patrol force, court, and corrections
costs to index crimes. (President's Commission,
The Challenge of Crime in a Free Society [Washing-
ton: Government Printing Office, 1967], p. 265.)
For purposes of comparison the Commission's figures
are presented below.

Average U.S. Costs per Index Crime	
Robbery	$1,200
Burglary	700
Auto Theft	760
Larceny (over $50)	660
Homicide	4,900
Aggravated Assault	920
Forcible Rape	1,300

It should be noted that despite the Commission's
inclusion of police costs--and they represent 67
percent of all system costs--average costs presented
per crime are frequently lower than the estimates
derived from the California study. Also it should
be noted that no estimate of the social cost associated with the punishment received by convicted
offenders is included in the estimates of the total
social cost of each crime. These costs are particularly high for imprisonment (because of the high
foregone earnings of the incarcerated person) but
are omitted because the probability of conviction
and subsequent punishment for each crime is unknown
and because estimates of the social cost of punishment would necessarily be crude.

The two immediately preceding chapters have
dealt with production relationships in two important police programs--traffic law enforcement and
general crime deterrence. The program analyses
stressed the importance of finding the effect of
agency inputs on outputs, by either experimental or
statistical methods. But the distribution of agency
inputs and outputs among the recipients is also an
important question that a program budget should address. This question of service distribution was
introduced in Chapter 2, in which alternative criteria were suggested for the distribution of police
protection service among different geographical
areas of the same city--what can be termed intra-
jurisdictional distribution. Data for the City of
Los Angeles were used to illustrate what sort of
geographical distribution actually does take place
within a large city.

In this chapter an examination will be made of
what can be termed interjurisdictional distribution,
the distribution of police services by an agency of
a higher level government (the Los Angeles County
Sheriff's Department) among its separate political
subdivisions (cities and unincorporated areas within
the county). Information about the geographical
distribution of services among units of local government will be developed and this information will
be used to examine equity problems in the financing
of local police services in Los Angeles County.

The study demonstrates the usefulness of a program
budget format that provides data on the location of
police service recipients; it also demonstrates the
value of cost information, particularly information
on the marginal cost of police services, provided
by program analysis.

It should be noted that the intergovernmental
aspects of program budgeting are less prominent in
regard to police protection than in regard to most
other major urban governmental services. For instance, in education and welfare there is considerable state and federal involvement, both in financing the service and in making decisions about how
it should be provided. In contrast, police service
is financed and provided almost entirely at the local level. However, even at the local level there
exist distinct layers of government, notably counties and cities, and the intergovernmental relationships among these local layers of government can
give rise to difficult questions relating to the
provision and finance of police service. The question to be dealt with here is the possible inequity
that may arise when a county sheriff's department
provides to unincorporated areas police service
that incorporated cities provide for themselves,
while the sheriff's department is financed by countywide taxes. To explore this question information
is needed about the distribution of sheriff's department services among the political subdivisions
of the county, including a differentiation of services according to whether they are provided on a
countywide basis or are provided only to residents
of certain areas, such as the unincorporated areas.

Neither the appropriate level of local government (county or city) for performing specific police functions nor the level of government for financing the services will be at question here;
rather the particular question to be focused on is
whether some city residents are in fact paying
twice, first for their own municipal police service
and second for a similar service to certain other
residents of the same county.[1]

To anticipate one of the results of the study,
it appears that residents of cities that maintain

independent police departments are to a significant
extent subsidizing law enforcement service to the
unincorporated portions of Los Angeles County and
are likewise subsidizing a number of other cities
in the county, namely, those that purchase contract
law enforcement service below actual cost from the
Los Angeles County Sheriff's Department.

THE CITY-COUNTY CONFLICT OVER POLICE SERVICE FINANCE IN LOS ANGELES COUNTY

There is a long tradition of dispute between
California cities and counties on the topic of un-
just taxation of city residents by county governments to provide municipal-type services to unincorporated areas. The general issue has often been
disputed in Los Angeles County, and in regard to
law enforcement the dispute still continues. Since
1954 the controversy has become even more complicated by the county's provision of contract law enforcement, whereby the Los Angeles County Sheriff's
Department provides law enforcement services on a
fee basis to 30 of Los Angeles County's 77 cities.
In regard to contract law enforcement, the dispute
has been over the question whether contract cities
purchase police services from the county sheriff
below actual cost, the deficit being made up by
general countywide taxes.[2]

The problem of city subsidies to the unincorporated area of Los Angeles County was relatively
minor when most residents of the county lived within
incorporated cities. However, about 1930 the population of the unincorporated area began growing
much faster than the population of the cities in
the county. Between 1930 and 1950 the population
of the unincorporated area of Los Angeles County
grew by 183 percent, whereas the population of the
incorporated cities grew by only 75 percent; during
the same 20-year period the percentage of total
county population living in the unincorporated area
grew from 15 percent to 23 percent. Coincidental
with the rapid increase in the population of the
unincorporated area, the city governments in the

county became concerned about the possibility that
they were subsidizing municipal services to residents of the unincorporated area, and in 1950 the
Los Angeles Division of the League of California
Cities formed a city-county committee to investigate the possibility. In its report the committee
maintained that the county had become in some measure a municipal government for the unincorporated
urban area, providing for it services ordinarily
provided only by cities and financing these services not by special taxes on the residents of the
unincorporated area but rather by general countywide taxes. Despite the rapid urbanization of the
unincorporated area, only one new city was incorporated in Los Angeles County between 1930 and 1950
(bringing the number of cities to 45), and the city-
county committee report attributed this lack of new
incorporations to the method of financing municipal
services in the unincorporated portion of the county.
From an analysis of county expenditures for 1948/49,
the committee estimated that $9,600,000 of general
county funds was being spent for services provided
exclusively to the urban unincorporated area and
that $4,000,000 of this subsidy was for police pro-
tection.[3]

Agitation by cities for reform of city-county
fiscal relations induced the California State Legislature to investigate the problem in 1951. The Assembly Interim Committee on Municipal and County
Government made a detailed case study of Los Angeles
County; it found that, of the county sheriff's
1950/51 budget of about $8 million, approximately
$2 million was allocated to special services pro-
vided to unincorporated areas alone, while the rest
was for services of benefit to the entire county.[4]
The major portion of general county funds used to
finance the services provided exclusively to unincorporated area residents was collected from city
residents.[5] A similar situation was found in regard to public health services: five cities maintained their own health departments and at the same
time paid in county taxes two-thirds of the cost of
the Los Angeles County Health Department, which provided comparable health services to the unincorporated

area and to the cities that did not have independent health departments.[6]

As a result of its investigations in Los Angeles County, the municipal and county government
committee recommended for health services that
either the county assume all health service functions or the cities providing their own health services be relieved of county taxes for the support
of health services. For police services it recommended that the unincorporated area should be con-
stituted as a single subordinate police taxing area
or divided into several subordinate police taxing
areas and that taxes should be levied in each taxing area to finance police services that the sheriff
did not perform countywide.[7]

As a general principle, the committee in its
final report recommended that "provision be made
under the laws of the state for the establishment
of county service areas to provide extended services which the county is authorized by law to perform and which the county does not also perform on
a countywide basis, both within and without cities."[8]
As evidence that Los Angeles County was moving in the
direction of charging for special services, the
County Chief Administrative Officer was quoted as
stating: "If additional services of the type required by metropolitan areas are to be provided,
they should be financed through the formation of
local police districts or other local taxing agencies."[9]

The solution eventually achieved in the health
field was that the county government assumed countywide responsibility for health services, although
the transfer of responsibility from Los Angeles
City to Los Angeles County was not fully accomplished
until 1964.[10] However, no action was taken to form
subordinate police taxing areas in the unincorporated
portion of the county or in any way to charge the
residents of the unincorporated area for the cost
of services provided by the sheriff exclusively to
them. What did happen was a wave of new city incorporations in Los Angeles County, beginning with
the city of Lakewood in 1954. With this incorporation was inaugurated the county's now famous Lakewood Plan, or Contract Services Plan.[11]

Under the Lakewood Plan a city may purchase on contract from the county government most of the municipal services that a city is required by law to provide: parks and recreation, police and fire protection, sewers, planning and zoning, and so forth. A contract city may choose the level of each service to be provided to its citizens by the county, but it must pay the county government for each service provided according to a schedule of charges intended to represent the full cost of providing the service at the level chosen. The popularity of the Lakewood Plan was such that since 1954, 32 new incorporations have taken place, whereas none had occurred during the preceding 15 years. Each of the 32 newly incorporated cities employs at least some contract services, and 30 cities employ contract law enforcement.

THE LAKEWOOD PLAN OF CONTRACT SERVICES

The Lakewood Plan offers considerable advantages to cities that contract for government services with the county. Among these advantages, the most important are the following:

1. The Lakewood Plan allows small cities to benefit from the economies of large scale that exist in the provision of some public services. For instance, the median population of 30 cities that contracted with Los Angeles County for law enforcement in 1968 was 13,700, well below an efficient size for independent performance of many public services, including police protection.[12] Thus there can be decentralized decision making by smaller communities about the level and type of public services desired without sacrifice of the efficiency associated with larger scale.[13]

2. Services provided by a county government to each contract city can be coordinated to take into account external effects (cost and benefit spillovers) that the provision of such public services as law enforcement can have on other contract cities. In effect, the Lakewood Plan achieves a form of de facto metropolitan consolidation short of a single metropolitan government.[14]

3. The availability of governmental services
on contract from the county reduces the birth pangs
attending a new incorporation. Instead of having
to create entirely new city departments to provide
all municipal services, the city can simply con-
tinue, on a contract basis, as many as it likes of
the services that were previously provided by the
county government. However, there is the corresponding disadvantage that by making incorporation
relatively easy, the Lakewood Plan also encourages
the incorporation of tax enclaves based on a high
ratio either of assessed value or of sales to the
population in certain areas.

4. The Lakewood Plan is also a useful incentive to governmental efficiency by permitting competition between the county and an independent municipal department in the provision of a service. If
there are diseconomies of large scale in the production of a service or if a county's service is for
some other reason inefficiently provided, a contract
city always has the choice of providing the service
for itself. Thus, there can be a process of natural
selection to differentiate between services best
provided by a higher level of government and those
best provided at the most local level. Potential
competition between contract- and self-provided services is a stimulus for efficiency that is ordinarily entirely absent in the governmental sector.
However, this process is fully effective only when
the contract services are sold to cities at approximately their cost of provision, for otherwise contract services do not compete on equal terms with
self-provision of services (the problem of marginal
versus average cost is discussed below).

The coming of the Lakewood Plan and the resulting burst of city incorporations partially solved
the problem of city-county fiscal relations by eliminating much of the unincorporated area in Los Angeles County. In effect the contract cities became,
among other things, the police taxing areas that
had been recommended by the California Assembly.
The whole problem was not solved, however, for two
reasons:

1. Despite the rapid rate of incorporation,
the population of the unincorporated area actually

FIGURE 5.1

Map of the County of Los Angeles, 1968

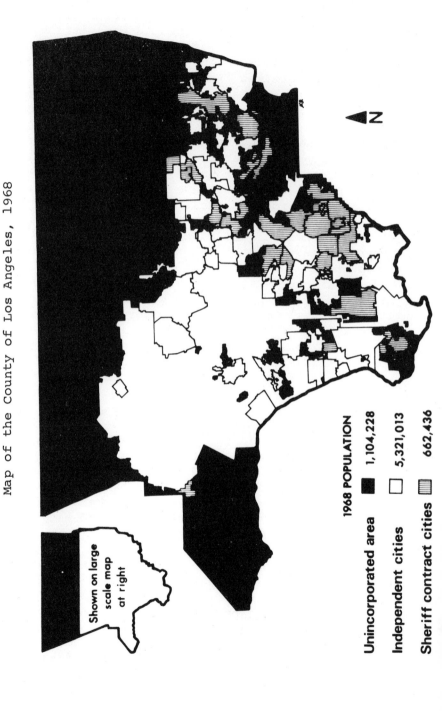

grew from 872,000 in 1950 to 1,042,000 in 1969.
And thus, the problem of financing services in the
unincorporated area grew more serious; the new incorporations merely made the problem less serious
than it would otherwise have been.

   2. Even in the newly incorporated cities that
receive and pay for contract services, the question
of subsidization from other cities that provide
their own services was not entirely eliminated.
For instance, if the contract price of the law enforcement service is below the actual cost to the
sheriff's department of the service, the contract
cities are in effect receiving a subsidy from general county funds. Thus the old problem of whether
the formerly unincorporated contract cities were
paying anything for their local police protection
was transformed into the new problem of whether
they were paying a fair price for the police protection they were purchasing on a contract basis.

THE EFFECTS OF INTRACOUNTY SUBSIDIES

   The effect on resource allocation and tax distribution of both types of potential intergovernmental subsidy within a county--from the incorporated portion to the unincorporated portion of the
county and from the rest of the county to the contract cities--can be analyzed in the same way. The
diagrammatic form of analysis used here and represented in Figure 5.2 is based on the work of Alan
Williams.[15] Williams' model was developed to explain the behavior of governments that receive subsidies by means of explicit grants-in-aid, usually
from a higher level of government, but it is applicable to an analysis of the unplanned or even un-
recognized form of interlocal subsidy being examined
here.

   The analysis assumes that the collective
decision-making behavior of a unit of government is
analogous to the conventional utility-maximizing
behavior of a single individual. For the present
purpose of analyzing expenditures for police protection, it will also be assumed that the citizenry

of the unincorporated portion of the county can be
treated as a single entity for which incentives concerning the desired level of police protection may
be analyzed in the same manner as those of city governments.

The assumed collective decision-making process
for a unit of government is shown in Figure 5.2.
It is illustrated here by police service, but it
can be applied as well to other public services.
On the vertical axis is E_p, the expenditure on police protection within each governmental unit; on
the horizontal axis is R_p, the revenue that must be
collected within that governmental unit to finance
police protection. The utility level of the government (representing its citizens) is, ceteris paribus,
a function of E_p and R_p, and indifference curves representing different levels of constant utility, I_1,
I_2, and I_3 are shown, where $I_3 > I_2 > I_1$. The indifference curves are drawn to indicate that, for a
given level of internally raised revenue, R_p, an increase in expenditure for police protection, E_p, increases the government's utility and that for a
given level of E_p, an increase in internally raised
revenue, R_p, decreases utility.

If a government is required to finance the cost
of its police protection entirely from its own resources, then the highest E_p that can be achieved
for any given R_p lies on the 45° line from the origin; that is, $E_p = R_p$. In this situation, the
utility-maximizing combination of expenditure and
revenue for police protection occurs at point A,
the tangency point of an indifference curve and the
45° expenditure-revenue constraint line, where expenditure is E_{po} and revenue is R_{po}.

Now consider the way in which an intergovernmental transfer can shift the position of the 45°
constraint line. Suppose a city government receives
from the county government a subsidy of $1.00 to be
spent on police protection for every $1.00 that the
city itself raises for police protection. Suppose
also that the subsidy is financed by taxes levied
on a countywide basis and that 15 percent of such
county taxes are collected from citizens within the
city in question: The net subsidy from sources

FIGURE 5.2

Expenditures and Internally Raised Revenues
for Local Police Services

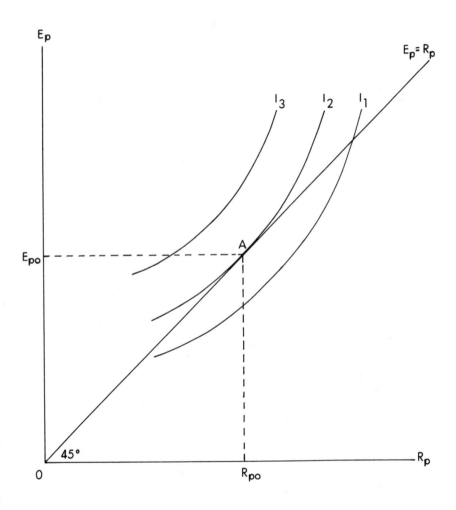

outside the city amounts to only 85¢ for every $1.15
of funds raised within the city. Such a subsidy
would raise the expenditure-revenue constraint line
as shown in Figure 5.3, where the old constraint
line, $E_p = R_p$, has been rotated counterclockwise
about the origin to the new and higher position,
$E_p = 1.74 R_p$. The new combination of expenditure,
E_{pl}, and internally raised revenue, R_{pl}, represents
changes in the city government's pattern of police
protection consumption in response to the change in
price of police services brought about by the intergovernmental subsidy. Note that with the subsidy
the amount of internally raised revenue, R_{pl}, may
be either higher or lower than the amount in the absence of a subsidy, R_{po}, depending on whether the
receiving government's demand for police protection
is price elastic or inelastic. The graph shows a
reduction in internally raised revenue from R_{po} to
R_{pl} as a result of the subsidy; so the subsidy partially substitutes for internally raised revenue.
If internally raised revenue increases as a result
of the subsidy, the grant is said to have a stimu-
lative effect.

The analysis has thus far been couched in terms
of a proportional matching grant-in-aid from a county government to a city government in order to subsidize the provision of police protection. However,
the same form of analysis can be used to investigate
the system of incentives created by the methods of
financing law enforcement service in the unincorporated area, the contract cities, and the independent
cities of Los Angeles County.

The question of police service finance in the
unincorporated area of Los Angeles County is similar
to that in many other parts of the United States and
will be discussed first. Then the further special
questions connected with financing of police service
in the contract cities will be discussed in order to
show some of the problems that may arise when subunits of a county--whether they are contract cities
or special police service districts in an unincorporated area--pay for police protection provided by
the county government.

FIGURE 5.3

Effect of Intergovernmental Subsidy

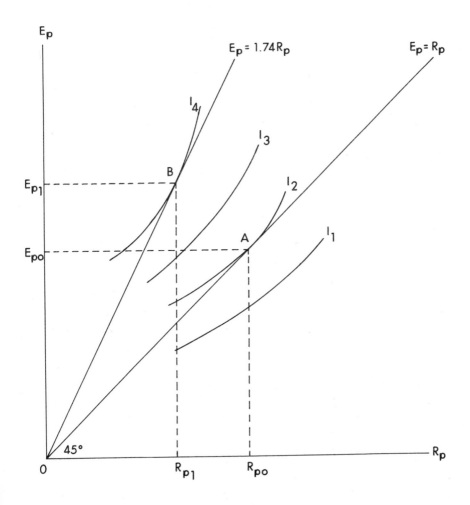

POLICE SERVICE FINANCE IN THE UNINCORPORATED
AREA OF LOS ANGELES COUNTY

A central question of police service finance in an unincorporated area is, What relationship exists between the level of police service provided and the amount of taxes levied to support this service? As pointed out previously, in Los Angeles County no tax is levied in the unincorporated area specifically to match expenditures for police protection in the unincorporated area. This procedure contrasts with the procedure for setting up special service districts or subordinate taxing areas to finance most other municipal-type services in unincorporated areas--such services as fire protection, lighting, flood control, and sewer maintenance. Rather, the expenditures of the sheriff's department are met from the county general fund, to which the unincorporated area makes no special contribution for the expense of the police service it receives. However, one significant tax is paid only by the unincorporated area into the county general fund--the sales tax. The sales tax rate is uniform throughout the county, but on sales within a municipality the local share of this tax is retained by the municipality, whereas on sales within the unincorporated area the local share of the tax goes to the county general fund. Thus, the unincorporated area's sales tax is considered its payment for municipal-type services rendered by the county government, but no explicit attempt is made to match the tax levy to the cost of municipal services provided, or vice versa.

In terms of expenditure the sheriff's department renders to the unincorporated area the single most important municipal-type service not financed by a special district charge.[16] And the most liberal estimate of the unincorporated area's payment for its police protection service would be that <u>all</u> the local sales tax revenue collected in the unincorporated area is used to pay for the services it receives from the sheriff's department. For fiscal year 1967/68 for Los Angeles County this amount was estimated to be $8,837,000,[17] which is the maximum that can be considered the unincorporated area's payment for the police service (since other municipal-type services must also be financed by the sales tax revenue). If police protection in the unincorporated area costs more than this amount, the additional cost must be drawn from the general fund, and the unincorporated area's share of any such additional cost is only its share of any resulting increases in countywide taxation.

In terms of the diagrammatic collective decision-making analysis developed above, the situation faced by residents of the unincorporated area in regard to the level of police protection is illustrated in Figure 5.4. In a system of complete self-finance, the expenditure constraint line is a 45° line from the origin: all expenditures on police service, E_p, must be financed by internally raised revenue, R_p. But for the unincorporated area under discussion, the constraint is radically altered: there is a fixed contribution, $\overline{R}_p$ (the sales tax revenue), regardless of expenditure, and any excess of expenditure over $\overline{R}_p$ is met by internally raised revenues equal only to the unincorporated area's share of any resulting increase in countywide taxation to finance general fund expenditures. Likewise, any expenditure less than $\overline{R}_p$ results in a reduction in internally raised revenue equal only to the unincorporated area's share of any resulting decrease in countywide taxation to finance general fund expenditures. Thus the slope of the new constraint line for the unincorporated area, U-U', is determined by the unincorporated area's marginal share of any such increase or decrease in countywide taxation.

Such is the set of fiscal incentives faced by the populace of the unincorporated area in making decisions about the desired level of police protection; depending on the shape of the indifference curves, the desired level of expenditures for police protection could be either greater or less than the amount of internally raised revenue (depending on whether tangency between an indifference curve and the constraint line occurs above or below point M); as drawn here, expenditure for police protection would be greater than internally raised revenue for that purpose ($E_{p1} > R_{p1}$).

FIGURE 5.4

Effects of Subsidy on an Unincorporated Area

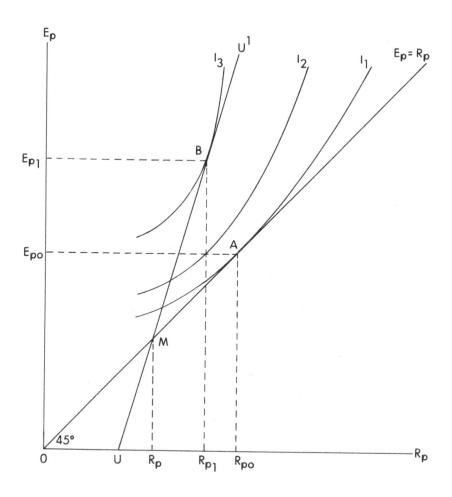

Whatever the level of police protection desired
by residents of the unincorporated area as determined by the expenditure-revenue structure described
above, there are, however, no political representatives whose sole constituency is the unincorporated
area and who make decisions in behalf of its residents alone. Rather, Los Angeles County is governed
by a five-man board of supervisors, each of whom is
elected from a district that includes both unincorporated and incorporated territory. Thus each
supervisor must represent both the conflicting interests involved--city residents paying county taxes
and unincorporated area residents receiving police
protection from the sheriff's department. Municipal
representatives have charged that county supervisors
assume an attitude in regard to the unincorporated
territory very close to the attitude of a city council toward its constituents, and the county government officials have denied the allegation.

The charge that cities are subsidizing the unincorporated area is, of course, most relevant to
those municipal-type services provided by the county
government only to the unincorporated area and financed by countywide funds. Because police protection is the most important of these services, it
will be useful to investigate the costs and sources
of revenue of the sheriff's department for police
protection in the unincorporated area of Los Angeles
County in an attempt to discover whether or not any
subsidy is involved and, if so, its possible magnitude.

POLICE SERVICE COSTS IN THE UNINCORPORATED
AREA OF LOS ANGELES COUNTY

The Los Angeles County Sheriff's Department is
the sixth largest police agency in the United States
and is the largest sheriff's department in the world.
It is well known as one of the best trained and most
progressive sheriff's departments in the country.
It is also one of the most expensive: of the 39
counties in the United States having populations
that exceed 600,000, Los Angeles County has the

highest expenditure per capita for police protection, with the exception of New York's Nassau and Suffolk Counties, in which county police departments have largely supplanted municipally provided police protection.[18]

Many of the services provided by the Los Angeles County Sheriff's Department are performed on a completely countywide basis, and such uniformly provided services will not be examined here. Only those services will be examined that are performed exclusively, or almost exclusively, in the unincorporated area and contract cities.

Although Los Angeles County is one of the five counties participating in the state-local Finances Project of the George Washington University, called the 5-5-5 project to adapt PPBS for city, county, and state governments, it has not yet presented its sheriff's department expenditure data on a client-oriented or geographical basis. Thus, the examination of police service distribution and finance must start by developing an estimate of the distribution of those services that are provided on a nonuniform basis. Services performed in the unincorporated area will be examined in this section, and services performed in the contract cities will be taken up in the next section.

It is in its police protection field activities that the sheriff's department most clearly restricts itself to operation in the unincorporated area and contract cities, these field activities being principally the services provided by the patrol division and the detective division. In all police departments the patrol division is the largest division, and it carries out all primary police functions; members of the patrol division answer calls for service from the public and engage in preventive patrol operations, either in cars or on foot or, more recently, in helicopters. Patrol is often referred to as "the backbone of the police service."[19] The detective division makes investigations of serious crimes that have been committed and attempts to apprehend criminals and recover stolen property. Of the 3,905 noncustodial members of the sheriff's department in service on July 1, 1968, 1,860 were

budgeted in the patrol division and 655 in the detective division.[20]

Although the sheriff's department has legal
authority for law enforcement throughout the county,
it does not normally act as a police agency within
the independent cities that maintain their own police departments. For instance, the "population
policed by the sheriff's department" is considered
by the department to be the combined population of
the unincorporated area and the contract cities
(1,770,645 in 1968).[21] Also, the independent cities
are identified as "cities not policed by the sheriff's department."[22]

The sheriff's published workload statistics for
the patrol division reveal an almost exclusive concentration of patrol service in the unincorporated
area and contract cities. The data on cases handled
by the 14 sheriff's department stations in the county
during 1967/68 are divided between cases handled in
the unincorporated area (approximately 56 percent)
and cases handled in the contract cities (approximately 44 percent).[23] The only section in the patrol division that reported activity also in the
noncontract (independent) cities is the vice bureau;
it reported that 16 percent of man-hours expended
were devoted to cases in noncontract cities (which
contain 75 percent of the county's population).[24]
Thus, not all the patrol division's vice bureau expenditures can be allocated to the unincorporated
area and contract cities; however, except for the
vice bureau, all other expenditures for operation
of the patrol division can reasonably be allocated
as expenditures made almost exclusively for police
protection in the unincorporated area and contract
cities.

The total expenditures of the patrol division,
minus the expenditures of the vice bureau, amounted
to $16,722,000 (exclusive of employee benefits) dur-
ing 1967/68.[25] The sheriff's department does not
itself indicate the exact share of this amount to
be allocated to the unincorporated area alone; however, the approximate share should be fairly reli-
ably indicated by the proportion of the cases
handled by the patrol division that occurs in the

unincorporated area (56 percent in 1967/68). This
figure is the only one available for breaking down
the workload statistics, but it should be an approximate indicator of breakdown of expenditures
between the two areas.[26] On the basis of this percentage, the expenditures of the patrol division,
minus the expenditures of the vice bureau, for noncountywide services provided in the unincorporated
area during fiscal 1967/68 was $9,364,000 (exclusive
of employee benefits).

To this should be added the expenditures of the
patrol division's vice bureau for the special services it provided to the unincorporated area. And
it should be noted that the reason for the disproportionately low level of vice bureau activity in
the noncontract cities is not a disproportionately
high level of morality in those cities but rather
the sheriff's department's focus on vice in the
territory it polices; it assists independent police
departments only on special request or when a case
leads sheriff's deputies across municipal boundaries.
Since the patrol division's vice bureau does provide
some service in all parts of the county (contract
cities, noncontract cities, and unincorporated area),
it is necessary to measure the level of service provided to the contract cities and unincorporated area
above the minimum level of service that is provided
everywhere in the county. Thus, the minimum level
of service that is provided on a genuinely countywide basis must first be established. The area actually receiving the lowest level of service, in
terms of man-hours expended per capita, is the noncontract city group, which contains 75 percent of
the county population; thus the service level provided in the noncontract cities can be considered
the minimum level that is provided everywhere in
the county, and any service provided above this minimum level to another area can be considered a special
benefit to the receiving area. If the unincorporated
territory had received the same countywide minimum
man-hours per capita level of vice bureau service as
the noncontract cities, only 1,623 man-hours would
have been expended in the unincorporated area; however, 25,462 man-hours actually were expended in

the unincorporated area. The excess of 23,839 man-hours was 48.3 percent of all vice bureau man-hours expended, and this fraction of the bureau's total expenditures, or $421,000, was thus allocated to the unincorporated area for service above the level provided countywide. (For details of the calculation, see Supplement 1 of this chapter.)

Therefore, an approximation of patrol division expenditures, including those of the vice bureau, for service to the unincorporated area not also provided countywide, would be $9,785,000 (exclusive of employee benefits). The inclusion of employee benefits would, of course, make the figure higher. For 1968/69, employee benefits amounted to an additional 25 percent above the salaries provided in the sheriff's budget, although in 1967/68 this figure was slightly lower; a conservative estimate is that employee benefits add 20 percent to the expenditures included in the sheriff's budget.[27] Therefore, an approximation of 1967/68 police protection expenditures for service to the unincorporated area not also provided on a countywide basis would be $11,742,000 (including employee benefits) for the patrol division alone. This amount is, by itself, greater than the revenues from the unincorporated area for all municipal-type services provided to it, by all county departments. Further, this estimate of expenditures for unincorporated area patrol division services does not include any sheriff's department overhead expenditures, such as those for administration, training, research, records and identification, or communications, all of which are required to support patrol services.

The other division of the sheriff's department most directly concerned with providing service specifically to the unincorporated area and contract cities is the detective division. The detective division does, however, also assist the police departments of the noncontract cities, chiefly the smaller ones, on a request basis when they have a need for those services of specialized investigators found only in a larger department (for homicide, arson, forgery, and so forth). Thus, since some of the smaller noncontract cities do receive detective

services from the sheriff's department, not all the
expenditures of the detective division can be allocated to the unincorporated area and contract cities
alone. It is important to note that the larger noncontract cities in the county request relatively
little such detective service because their own departments are large enough to provide most of the
necessary specialized services; for instance, the
Los Angeles Police Department (7,864 employees in
1967/68) is even larger than the sheriff's department (3,905 noncustodial employees in 1967/68).
Thus, although noncontract cities as a group do receive sheriff's detective division services, they
do not all receive them on an equal basis, and the
largest city, Los Angeles, with 41 percent of the
county's population, receives a relatively insignificant proportion of the sheriff's detective division services.

    The detective division annual workload statis-
tics are not presented on the basis of geographical
location of services rendered, and estimating the
cost of services rendered exclusively to the unincorporated area is therefore more difficult than in
the case of the patrol division. However, one
bureau of the detective division, the narcotics
bureau, does publish a breakdown of arrests by location of occurrence; on the basis of this breakdown, the noncontract cities, having 75 percent of
the county population, accounted for only 18 percent of total narcotics arrests; the unincorporated
area, having 16 percent of the county population,
accounted for 53.6 percent of narcotics arrests.
As explained above in connection with the vice bureau, the disproportionately low level of arrests
in the noncontract cities is explained not by a
lack of narcotics offenses in these cities but
rather by the fact that most of these cities have
their own narcotics detectives. If all the sheriff's detective division services were distributed
geographically in the same pattern as narcotics bureau arrests, service in the unincorporated area
well above the countywide level would be implied.

    In the absence of complete yearly workload
statistics, the best available indication of the

geographical distribution of sheriff's detective
services is a one-month compilation for December
1968 of the distribution of calls for service in
the detective division. In that month, 8,249 (25
percent) calls for service occurred in the noncontract cities, and 14,097 (43 percent) in the unincorporated area.[28] If the unincorporated area had
had the same per capita number of answered calls
for service as the noncontract cities, the number
of answered calls occurring in the unincorporated
area would have been only 1,712 instead of 14,097.
The difference between these two numbers can be considered the amount of service rendered to the unincorporated area above the level of service provided
on a genuinely countywide basis. This amount of
special service to the unincorporated area, 12,445
answered calls for detective service, represents 38
percent of the total detective workload (32,752
calls) for the month. If it is assumed that this
month is typical of the distribution of workload
during 1967/68 (which seems reasonable), the implication is that 38 percent of the expenditures of
the detective division can be allocated for exclusive service to the unincorporated area above the
level provided on a countywide basis to the 75 percent of the population served by independent police
departments.

The total expenditures of the detective division for 1967/68 were $6,998,000 (exclusive of em-
ployee benefits).[29] Therefore, 38 percent of this
amount, or $2,645,000, can be identified as expendi-
tures for the exclusive benefit of the unincorporated
area and yet financed out of countywide revenues.
If employee benefits are added to this amount, the
actual detective division expenditures for the unincorporated area were approximately $3,174,000. As
with the estimate of patrol division expenditures,
this figure does not include any allowance for overhead expenditures within the sheriff's department
attributable to the operations of the detective division. (For details of the calculation, see Supplement 2 of this chapter.)

The sum of expenditures of the patrol and the
detective divisions for exclusive service to the

unincorporated area, above the service level provided on a countywide basis, is $14,916,000 (exclu-
sive of overhead expenses). This estimate does not
include any allowance for any other sheriff's department expenditures (that is, other than those of
the patrol and detective divisions) that are not
provided on a countywide basis, although undoubtedly
some of these other expenditures also should be included.

As mentioned earlier, the sales tax revenue
collected in the unincorporated area for 1967/68
amounted to $8,837,000. Since this sales tax reve-
nue is the unincorporated area's only form of payment for municipal-type services rendered by the
county government, the sheriff's department expenditures for exclusive service to the unincorporated
area are $6,080,000 more than the taxes collected
in the unincorporated area to pay for all municipal-
type services provided to the unincorporated area by
the county government, and this excess of expenditures over tax revenues is a form of subsidy to the
unincorporated area. The estimate of a subsidy of
$6,080,000, or $5.50 per capita, is very conservative because the county government provides other
municipal-type services to the unincorporated area,
chiefly local neighborhood parks, that should also
be financed by the taxes collected only in the unincorporated area. This subsidy to the residents of
the unincorporated area is, of course, financed
mainly by taxation of city residents within Los Angeles County, who account for 84 percent of the
total county population and approximately the same
fraction of total assessed value subject to local
property taxation.

It is apparent that the existing procedure of
financing a municipal level of law enforcement service in the unincorporated area by means of countywide taxation is an unintended consequence of the
complex system of overlapping city and county governments. The unincorporated area of the county
contains more than 1 million residents, most of
whom live in urban concentrations as densely popu-
lated as the incorporated area of the county.[30]
The county government has undertaken the responsibility of providing to the residents of the

unincorporated area police service of the kind normally provided only by city governments but--per-
haps because of the difficulty of defining what are
the genuinely "countywide" services and what are
"municipal-type" services provided only to the unincorporated area--the county government has made no
specific arrangements for the unincorporated area to
pay for the municipal-type services provided by the
sheriff. There is, however, no legal requirement
that a sheriff's department must provide police protection service to the unincorporated area at a conventional municipal level. Indeed, under California
Government Code Sec. 845, there shall be no state or
public liability for failure to provide police service. In any case, the police provide many miscellaneous public services other than law enforcement,
and a sheriff's department is certainly under no
obligation to provide these other services.[31]

Other County Service Costs

An estimate has been made of the cost of sheriff's department services that are provided mainly
or exclusively to the unincorporated area. No differential allocation has been made, however, as between the unincorporated area and the cities of the
sheriff's services that the county is by state law
required to provide on a countywide basis (for example, jail service). And it may be argued that,
although there do exist sheriff's services that are
restricted to the unincorporated area and financed
by countywide taxation, the subsidy to the unincorporated area involved is compensated for by a disproportionately heavy use by city residents of
other sheriff's services or other county services,
such as welfare, that are provided on a countywide
basis.[32] However, this argument is basically inappropriate in that one of the implicit goals of put-
ting government functions on a countywide basis is
to distribute the cost of performing these functions
throughout the county. The county welfare program
is an important illustration of this: in California,
public assistance welfare services are performed exclusively by county governments, and one of the

fundamental motives for this assignment is to
achieve redistribution of income regardless of
residential jurisdiction within a county. Thus,
lower income cities with disproportionately large
numbers of welfare recipients are not disproportionately burdened with taxes to finance welfare payments, and higher income cities with few welfare
recipients do not escape taxation to finance welfare payments. The intention and the result are
that income is redistributed from higher income to
lower income residents of the county, regardless of
location of residence. Therefore, it would not be
appropriate to assign any excess of welfare expenditures over taxes collected in cities as a counter-
flow of funds compensating for the cities' subsidy
to the unincorporated area for police protection.
Doing so would be counter to the intentions behind
the establishment of welfare assistance as a countywide function.

More than 90 percent of the county budget is
expended on services provided on a uniform basis
throughout the county. And the jurisdictional distribution of revenues collected and expended to provide these services is not considered here because
there is no presumption that revenues and expenditures for these services provided on a genuinely
countywide basis should exactly balance for each
city, for all cities, or for the unincorporated territory. Depending on distribution of income and on
service conditions throughout the county, any subunit of the county may be expected to incur a deficit or a surplus in the balance of revenues and expenditures; only an overall balance is required.
But it does seem appropriate that the benefited
area should pay for services provided by the county
government to them exclusively (and self-provided
and self-financed in other portions of the county).
This principle is recognized in the existence of
subordinate taxing areas in Los Angeles County for
such other noncountywide services as fire protection, garbage disposal, lighting, sewer maintenance,
and waterworks. It is for this reason that the discussion here has been concentrated on the expenditures and revenues for sheriff's department services
that are provided on a less than countywide basis.

Although a minimum estimate has been developed
of the expenditures of the sheriff's department for
police protection provided to the residents of the
unincorporated area on a less than countywide basis,
such a calculation does not, of course, imply that
the expenditure is of no benefit to residents of incorporated cities within the county. Obviously,
criminal problems transcend municipal boundaries,
and city residents benefit from the law enforcement
service in adjacent unincorporated territory; however, the benefit spillover should also operate in
the other direction, residents of the unincorporated
area benefiting the same way from law enforcement
service provided by municipal governments. If the
existence of spillover benefits in the provision of
police protection is used to justify countywide taxation for police service in the unincorporated area,
a similar subsidy should also be made out of county
funds for municipal police departments, or perhaps
a single metropolitan police department encompassing
the whole benefit area should be formed. Available
evidence does not, however, clearly demonstrate that
benefit spillovers from police services are important enough to warrant sizable subsidies or the formation of a single police jurisdiction.[33]

Formation of Subordinate Taxing Areas

The fact that expenditures for police protection in the unincorporated area exceed taxes collected for purposes of protection does not imply
that the level of service should be reduced or that
the sheriff's department has acted improperly in
providing it. Rather, this fact argues for the formation, as the California Legislature recommended
in 1953, of one or more police protection subordinate taxing areas in the unincorporated territory
to finance the level of service that is desired by
the residents. Such subordinate taxing areas have
been formed elsewhere in California, although they
are still uncommon in the United States as a whole.[34]
A similar solution would be to relieve the cities
that provide their own police service of any county
taxation for a similar service provided to the unincorporated area by the county sheriff.[35]

Despite the desirability of establishing police service areas in the unincorporated portion of the county, the approach does not eliminate the possibility of subsidy by one jurisdiction of another, leading to the problem of establishing the appropriate price to be paid by each subordinate taxing area for the service it receives. For this to be done, the marginal cost of service provided must be defined, and overhead costs throughout the system must be allocated. And since many of the issues involved in the finance of police protection on a service area basis have already arisen in regard to the contract city program of Los Angeles County, it will be useful at this point to examine the existing method of contract law enforcement in Los Angeles County; it should provide information about ways to finance urban services not provided uniformly throughout the entire county and to reduce the fiscal exploitation of cities by unincorporated areas within a system of overlapping county and city governments.[36]

POLICE SERVICE COSTS IN THE CONTRACT CITIES OF LOS ANGELES COUNTY

In Los Angeles County 30 cities contract with the county sheriff's department for police protection. These cities range from Norwalk, having a population of 96,000, to Bradbury, having a population of about 900, and from a number of suburban bedroom communities to the highly industrialized tax enclave cities of Commerce and Industry. During 1967/68 the population of cities receiving contract police services was 662,000.

There are real advantages to the entire community from the use of contract services for police protection, the most important of which is greater efficiency than highly fragmented police jurisdictions can provide. In a consolidated system the deployment of patrol forces and the response to the crime problem can be determined on a rational communitywide basis without regard to arbitrary city lines. As the Police Task Force of the National Crime Commission noted in its recent report:

A fundamental problem confronting law enforcement today is that of fragmented crime repression efforts resulting from the large number of uncoordinated local governments and law enforcement agencies. It is not uncommon to find police units working at cross purposes in trying to solve the same or similar crimes. Although law enforcement officials speak of close cooperation among agencies, the reference often simply means a lack of conflict. There is, in fact, little cooperation on other than an informal basis, not a very effective means of meeting current needs.

Formal cooperation or consolidation is an essential ingredient in improving the quality of law enforcement. Crime is not confined within artificially created political boundaries, but, rather, extends throughout the larger community. A workable program of formal cooperation or consolidation for law enforcement services within a "common community of interests" is the desired goal for improving the quality of law enforcement at the local level.[37]

In regard to the same problem, the Los Angeles City-County Local Government Consolidation Study Commission recommended:

Every available step should be taken to improve the capacity of the Sheriff's Office to render police services of the highest order so that cities will be encouraged to utilize the police services of the Sheriff's Department. The use of the Sheriff's Department to perform municipal police services by contract is the most hopeful basis of discouraging further diffusion of the police powers of the state.[38]

If economies of large scale in the provision
of police protection result in the provision of
more efficient services by the sheriff's department
than by small independent police departments, it
would be expected that most new cities would, upon
incorporation, choose to purchase police protection
on contract from the sheriff rather than establish
independent police departments. Contract police
service has, in fact, proved popular: of the 32
cities incorporated in Los Angeles County since the
inauguration of contract police service in 1954,
only 3 have established independent police departments; and one city that previously had an independent department has since changed to contract service.

However, the decision to purchase contract law
enforcement depends not only on the efficiency with
which the sheriff provides service but also on the
method of charging for the service: if the price
charged for the service is below the long-run marginal cost of providing it, there is an additional
incentive, the subsidy, over and above the incentive
provided by the efficiency of the county service,
for contracting with the sheriff. If contract law
enforcement service is to compete on an equal basis
with independent service, its price must include
all additions to the costs of the sheriff's department associated with providing the service. But
the problems of measuring the long-run marginal
cost of the sheriff's services precisely and of
allocating fixed overhead expenditures among users
are, of course, difficult ones. They are also po-
litically controversial, since the provision of
contract law enforcement service below marginal
cost, the deficit being drawn from general county
funds, implies a subsidy to the contract cities
from the rest of the county. Because of the seriousness of this issue, it is important to examine
in detail the methods used by the sheriff's department in charging the contract cities for the police
protection services provided to them. (To anticipate one of the results of the examination, it appears that improper pricing of contract services to
suburban cities is another potential contributor to
fiscal exploitation of the central city.)

It is the sheriff's policy to charge contracting cities only "those additional costs incurred to
provide the services requested by the cities over
and above the normal staffing required by the sheriff to carry out his countywide law enforcement responsibility."[39] The additional costs are, however,
very narrowly defined. Contract cities are charged
nothing for the services of the detective division,
the technical services division (crime laboratory,
records and identification, and so forth), the administrative division, the office of business management, or the office of the sheriff. Rather, only
the operating costs of the patrol division are
charged for, and even these services are charged
for on a narrow basis. The justification presented
for excluding the costs of other divisions and offices is that they are necessary for the sheriff to
perform his countywide responsibility for law enforcement. Although these services are, of course,
theoretically available for countywide use, cities
that have their own police departments employ them
relatively little, and the largest cities make almost no use of them, as mentioned before. In practice, these services are heavily concentrated on
the areas policed by the sheriff.

The charges made to contract cities for police
protection are thus based only on the service rendered by the sheriff's patrol division. Cities may
contract for any desired level of patrol service,
the unit of service being a patrol car on 24-hour
duty seven days a week, with two eight-hour shifts
of two men each (night and morning shifts) and one
eight-hour shift of one man (day shift). The contract city can purchase whatever amount of service
it desires, above a certain minimum, and it pays accordingly. The rate charged per car has consistently been a matter of contention between the contract
cities and the independent cities, the former maintaining that the rate is too high and the latter
maintaining that the rate is too low. Between 1958
and 1969, the per car charge was increased from
$78,400 to $132,741 per year.

The per car rate is purported to be a charge
for the marginal cost of providing patrol service
to the contract cities. However, as a measure even

of this narrow cost, it appears defective for two important reasons.

First, the cost per car of patrol service in the contract cities is reduced by "credit that is allowed based on minimum staff required assuming no contract with the cities."[40] This is a substantial credit and reduces the per car price to the contract cities by an amount that is approximately 25 percent of the calculated marginal cost of providing it.[41]

If the cities did not exist, the reasoning goes, the sheriff's department would have to bear the cost of providing these services. The argument for granting the credit is that the contracting cities should be granted an allowance for what it would cost the sheriff to police them under his statutory obligations if they had not incorporated and undertaken to police themselves municipally.

There are a number of difficulties with this reasoning, the most salient of which is the factual one already mentioned, that the sheriff has no statutory obligation to provide any specific minimum level of services. Even if the contract cities were to be granted a credit for what it would cost the sheriff to provide minimum police protection to them, it seems that other cities in the county, which provide their own police services, should receive a similar allowance. No such credit is granted to the independent municipalities that maintain their own police forces. The justification given for the credit does not suggest any grounds for such preferential treatment of the contract city.

A second defect of the per car rate for patrol service is that it excludes any charge for the physical plant necessary to house the patrol force. This exclusion also is based on the assumption that a normal staff would exist in the absence of contract service. Therefore, "the overhead factors relating to utilities, grounds maintenance, special assessments, building depreciation and rent" are excluded from the patrol car cost computation.[42] None of the plant cost of the sheriff's stations is counted in the per car rate, even though most of the cases handled by several of the stations are contract cities cases--and in one station (Lakewood) 96 percent of the cases were.[43]

This discussion of the concepts used in defining the marginal cost of police protection services is intended to indicate the problems that can arise when, in an attempt to charge for services provided on a less than countywide basis, subunits of a county are required to pay the costs of services provided exclusively to them. To indicate the magnitude of the variation in charges that would be made under possible alternative concepts of the marginal cost of providing police protection services to contract cities in Los Angeles County, Table 5.1 shows the 1968/69 cost per car figures calculated by the Los Angeles County auditor-controller's office under different assumptions about the costs to be included.

The table demonstrates that the basic problem of defining the marginal cost to be charged can lead to a wide variation in interpretation. Even the full station cost does not include any charge for the sheriff's departmental and divisional overhead or for central support services, such as the records bureau, the crime laboratory, training, or headquarters detectives. (It is interesting to note that neighboring Orange County calculates contract police service costs on a basis similar to that of item 6 in Table 5.1 and that the Orange County Sheriff's Department cost per car charge is $237,684, almost identical to the figure calculated on the same basis in Los Angeles County.[44])

Even the highest figure meant to represent the marginal cost of contract law enforcement service is certainly an understatement of the actual long-run marginal cost, for it includes no charge for overhead expenditures within the sheriff's department. If the population policed on a contract basis was a very small fraction of the total population policed by the sheriff, this would not be a serious omission; however, the contract city population is equal to 60 percent of the unincorporated area population serviced by the sheriff, and such a large addition to the departmental responsibility cannot be accommodated without additional administrative expense while a fixed level of service is maintained in the unincorporated area. Some overhead expenses excluded from even the highest

TABLE 5.1

Station Costs of Los Angeles County
Sheriff's Department, 1968/69

Marginal Cost Definition	Cost per Patrol Car
1. Patrol service, recommended rate[a] (allowing "minimum staff" credit)	$132,741[c]
2. Patrol service, full marginal cost[b] (no "minimum staff" credit)	183,885
3. Special enforcement bureau[b] (patrol not assigned to station)	8,021
4. Technical services, radio unit[b]	1,969
5. Detective division at station[b]	42,158
6. Full station cost[b] (Total 2 + 3 + 4 + 5)	236,033

[a]With general county overhead charged at a rate of 8.55 percent.

[b]With general county overhead charged at a rate of 12.67 percent. (The lower overhead rate for item 1 excludes all station house maintenance and depreciation charges on the assumption that they are required for the "minimum staff.")

[c]This rate was recommended by the Chief Administrative Officer of Los Angeles County, based on the cost figures recommended by the county auditor-controller. However, the contract cities were actually charged only $119,486 per car in 1968/69; this occurred because the county had in 1963 entered into a five-year service agreement with the contract cities, and under this contract the county was not able to alter its 1968/69 per car rate to reflect the new 1968/69 method of base rate computation.

Source: Los Angeles County Auditor-Controller Office, 1968/69 Patrol Car Cost Study.

calculation of marginal cost would presumably increase almost in the same proportion as the workload
in contract cities (training, for instance) while
others would increase much less (business management). In any case, it can be confidently stated
that even the highest cost figure calculated by the
auditor-controller ($236,033 per car) is less than
the true marginal cost of providing law enforcement
service in the contract cities.

Because the sheriff's charges for contract law
enforcement are based on such a restricted concept
of the marginal cost of providing the service, the
contract cities pay, on a per capita basis, much
less for police protection than do the independent
cities of Los Angeles County. During 1967/68 the
30 contract law enforcement cities spent $9.40 per
person (employee benefits included) while the 47 independent cities spent more than $21.00 per person
(employee benefits excluded). If employee benefits
are included, the expenditure for police protection
in independent cities is approximately $25.20 per
capita.[45] If Los Angeles and Long Beach are excluded as being too large to be comparable to the
contract cities, the cost of police protection in
the remaining independent cities is $16.40 per cap-
ita, or 75 percent greater than the cost in contract
cities. This relatively low expenditure for police
protection may be one reason that 21 of the 30 contract cities levy no municipal property tax, whereas
only one of the 47 independent cities is without a
municipal property tax.[46] The relatively much higher
per capita cost of police protection in the city of
Los Angeles, $34.80 per capita in 1967/68, is partly
explained by the fact that the Los Angeles Police
Department performs for itself, at city expense,
many of the functions that the sheriff's department
performs without charge for smaller cities, both independent and contract.[47]

The foregoing discussion of the incentives
created by the methods of pricing contract law enforcement services will now be related to the
revenue-expenditure model outlined above. And it
should be noted that whereas the contract cities
have thus far been treated as a group, decisions

about the desired level of law enforcement service
are, of course, made separately by each contract
city.

It is easy to apply the proportional grant-in-
aid diagrams to the problem of determining the price
to be paid to the county government by contract
cities for contract law enforcement service. If a
contract city purchases contract law enforcement
service from the Los Angeles County Sheriff's Department at a price equal to the long-run marginal
cost of providing such service, the city may be
said to be on the 45° expenditure-constraint line
in Figure 5.5, where expenditure for police service
equals internally collected taxes to finance police
service. However, if the service of the sheriff's
department is sold to contract cities below the actual long-run marginal cost, the incentive effect
to the contracting city is the same as in the case
of a matching grant-in-aid for the provision of police services, except that receipt of the aid is,
of course, tied to purchase by the contract city of
police services from the county sheriff's department; if a city chooses to maintain its own independent police department, there is no subsidy from
the county government equivalent to the one given
by means of below-cost police protection service
provided on contract.

The data of Table 5.1 are used to indicate
graphically in Figure 5.5 the incentives provided
to contract cities to employ the law enforcement
services of the sheriff's department. If for a payment of $132,741 (the recommended 1968/69 patrol car
rate) a contract city can purchase law enforcement
services whose marginal cost is $236,033 (the full
station marginal cost calculated by the auditor-
controller), the angle of the contract city's
revenue-expenditure constraint line is changed as
shown.[48] The contract community is able to attain
a higher indifference curve and, as it is drawn,
would do so with less internally raised revenue than
in the case of complete self-financing ($R_{p1} < R_{po}$).
The deficit incurred by the county government in
providing the service ($E_{p1} - R_{p1}$) must be financed
by general county revenues; the contract city would,

FIGURE 5.5

Effects of Below-Cost Provision of Police Services

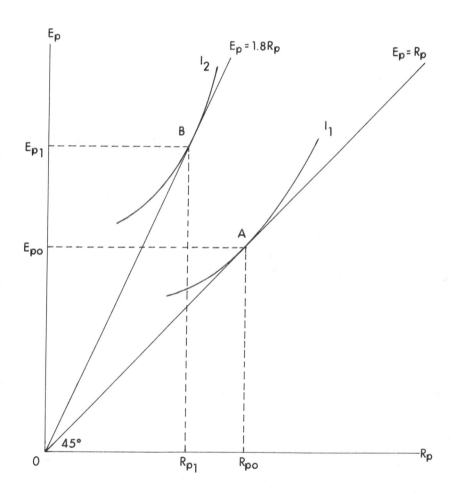

of course, contribute its share of the general revenue necessary to finance the deficit incurred in
providing contract police protection; but in Los Angeles County no contract city has more than 1.5 percent of the population or assessed valuation of the
entire county, and so each contract city can effectively neglect the marginal effect on its general
county tax liability of an increase or decrease in
contract service purchases.

The conventional justification for matching
grants-in-aid from a higher level of government to
a lower level in a federal system is, of course,
the existence of benefit spillovers in the production of some governmental services. If, for instance, law enforcement activity within one unit of
government produces benefits for residents of surrounding communities for which no charge can be
made, a higher level of government embracing the
communities among which benefit spillovers occur
may subsidize the law enforcement service of each
subunit by an amount equal to the value to other
subunits of the spillover benefit. This circumstance induces subordinate units of government to
produce the service involving such spillovers at
the level at which marginal social benefit equals
marginal social cost.

However, the justification of a county grant-
in-aid available only to cities contracting for law
enforcement service from the county sheriff's department would have to be that benefit spillovers
existed only if law enforcement was undertaken by
the sheriff's department. And there may be particular externalities associated with contract law enforcement that justify subsidizing it. Los Angeles
County is an integrated metropolitan area that has
problems of crime and public order that are a matter of communitywide concern. The high mobility of
the entire population and, in particular, of criminal offenders and victims, makes vital a coordinated policy of police protection. Such coordina-
tion may be achieved more effectively by a single
police force that serves each municipality on a contract basis than by numerous independent police
forces that are operated by independent municipalities. For example, a single centralized records

and identification division makes the data collected
in each municipality on criminals instantly available to all others, and the inclusion of an additional municipality in such a centralized system
increases the usefulness of the system to all other
users. This sort of external effect, whereby all
other contracting cities receive some benefits when
an additional city joins the contract system, may
justify a subsidy in the form of below-cost provision of service by the county sheriff's department;
but the size of the subsidy should be related to
the size of whatever external benefit is actually
present and has to be justified in those terms.
Needless to say, the existing form of subsidy ("minimum staff" credit and exclusion of all costs other
than the most obvious short-run marginal costs) is
not justified on the basis of the external benefits
associated with contract law enforcement, and the
existence of a subsidy has not been used as an argument to encourage cities to employ contract law
enforcement.

Although a small police service subsidy to contract cities of Los Angeles County by means of
below-cost sheriff services could perhaps be justified on the grounds of promoting areawide consolidation of law enforcement agencies, the policy of
making available without charge to independently
policed cities the many specialized services of the
sheriff's department actually lessens the incentive
of these small cities to enter into the contract
system. This point was made by Robert F. Wilcox in
his study of law enforcement integration in metropolitan Los Angeles:

> The present county policy of extend-
> ing police services to municipalities
> without charge should be curtailed,
> except in case of emergency; such ser-
> vices should be extended only on con-
> tract basis. In effect, the Sheriff
> now is subsidizing the small cities
> at the expense of the large, and is
> discouraging functional consolidation
> at the very point at which it should
> start. Curtailment of free services

would have the effect of forcing small
cities into a metropolitan organization.[49]

Even if the size of the subsidy to contract
cities could be justified on the basis of external
benefits of contract law enforcement, not all the
cities in Los Angeles County have equal opportunities to take advantage of it. The 45 cities that
had independent police departments prior to the introduction of contract service would undoubtedly
have political difficulty in disbanding or transferring to the sheriff their own police departments
in order to enter the contract system. During the
15 years of existence of contract law enforcement
only one city, with a population of 1,600, converted
from independent service to contract service, despite the markedly lower per capita cost of police
protection under contract service. Thus, although
all cities are nominally equally free to avail themselves of contract law enforcement service and to
benefit from the subsidy involved in its provision,
there are political obstacles to this choice except
for cities that are about to incorporate and do not
already possess an independent department.[50]

A rough minimum estimate of the amount of the
total subsidy to contract cities through underpricing of sheriff's services can be made by multiplying the per car subsidy by the total number of cars
allocated by the sheriff's department to the contract cities. The only year for which detailed
auditor-controller figures for alternative concepts
of per car costs are available is fiscal 1968/69.
In that year, the annual full station marginal cost
of contract services on a per car basis was $236,033.
The charge per car recommended by the chief administrative officer and approved by the board of supervisors as the appropriate calculation was $132,741.
Thus the annual cost per car exceeded the recommended
charge by $103,292. (See Table 5.1.) In that year
the equivalent of approximately 59 around-the-clock
law enforcement patrol car units were assigned to
the contract cities.[51] This implies that the sheriff's department station costs for contract services

exceeded revenues by approximately $6,100,000 in
1968/69, and this amount constitutes a subsidy to
the contract cities from general county revenue.[52]
Moreover, it should be noted that this estimate refers only to sheriff's department costs <u>at the station houses</u> plus a factor for general county overhead; no charge is made for the general department-
wide costs of running a modern law enforcement organization, including a training academy, crime
laboratory, headquarters staff, and so forth. Thus,
this estimate of subsidy to contract cities is undoubtedly conservative.

     Because the estimates refer to different years,
the estimate of a $6,100,000 law enforcement sub-
sidy to the contract cities in the fiscal year
1968/69 is not immediately comparable to the estimate of a $6,080,000 subsidy to the unincorporated
areas in fiscal 1967/68. However, there is reason
to believe that the subsidy to contract cities
would not have been much lower in 1967/68 than in
1968/69, because the amount of the 1968/69 subsidy
was calculated on the assumption of a contract city
payment per car of $132,392, whereas the per car
payment by contract cities was only $113,079 in
1967/68, or 15 percent less than in 1968/69. Unless the 1967/68 cost per car was more than $19,000
below the 1968/69 figure, the subsidy per car would
actually have been even higher in 1967/68 than that
used in calculating the size of the 1968/69 subsidy.
There were, however, probably fewer cars assigned
to contract cities in earlier years, for the purchases of contract services have tended to rise
over time.

     To ensure a conservative estimate of the
1967/68 subsidy to contract cities for police service, an alternative estimate can be made using the
same technique that was employed in estimating the
subsidy to the unincorporated area: calculation of
the services provided to the contract cities by the
detective and patrol divisions above the service
level provided on a countywide basis and comparison
of the cost of this exclusive service to the price
paid for it by the contract cities. On this basis,
the cost of patrol and detective services provided

to the contract cities above the level provided on
a countywide basis was $11,532,000.[53] The sheriff's
1967/68 revenue for contract law enforcement was
only $6,340,000.[54] The result is a subsidy estimate
of $5,192,000. Much of the discrepancy between this
figure and the $6,100,000 figure for 1968/69 obtained
from the auditor-controller's cost study can be attributed to the fact that the auditor-controller's
cost includes a general county overhead charge of
12.67 percent in addition to the sheriff's department costs at the station houses. If the same overhead factor is added to the costs just calculated
for the services of the patrol and detective divisions to the contract cities, the amount of the resulting subsidy is even higher than that given by
the auditor-controller's cost per car figures.[55]

The most conservative estimate of the contract
law enforcement subsidy given to the contract cities
out of general county revenue is thus $5,192,000, or
$7.80 per capita, in 1967/68. This estimated sub-
sidy to contract cities is, on a per capita basis,
even greater than the estimated subsidy received by
the unincorporated area ($5.50 per capita). Both
these figures are minimum estimates. And it may be
that the unincorporated area subsidy is more seriously underestimated than it appears to be because all
unincorporated area sales tax revenue was credited
as payment for law enforcement service. Other services provided to the unincorporated area by the
county government, such as local parks, should also
be financed by sales tax revenue, and the subsidy
attributable to law enforcement would then be
greater. The finding of such a subsidy to contract
cities demonstrates that the proper pricing of services is a crucial problem in the intergovernmental
sale of services at the local level and that serious
inequities within a county can result from setting
too low a price on any service provided by one government to another.[56]

CONCLUSION

The subsidy for law enforcement to the unincorporated area of Los Angeles County has been conservatively estimated to be $6,080,000 in 1967/68. On

a similar basis the subsidy to the cities that contract for police services from the Los Angeles
County Sheriff's Department has been estimated to
be $5,122,000. This $11,202,000 subsidy must be
financed by countywide taxation, and cities that
provide their own police protection bear a large
part of the cost of the subsidy.[57] However, it is
obvious that the larger independent cities lose
relatively more by this arrangement than do the
smaller cities because the smaller cities make more
frequent use of the specialized services provided
by the sheriff at no charge; the largest cities,
such as Los Angeles and Long Beach, whose police departments perform almost all law enforcement services for their own residents at municipal expense,
are in this situation exploited the most.

This problem of financing police protection
and other municipal-type services in urban unincorporated areas is apparently a nationwide phenomenon.
For all counties more than 100,000 in population,
69 percent of county governments provide police protection only to their unincorporated areas.[58] But,
only four states, including California, authorize
counties to provide police protection service to a
portion rather than to all of a county and to levy
a tax on the assessed value of the property within
that area to pay for such service.[59] Even for the
other counties that did report countywide provision
of police protection, it is an open question whether
the same level of service is provided by county
sheriffs within incorporated municipalities as
within unincorporated areas.[60] With regard to
other municipal-type services, 45 percent of county
governments provide libraries and 43 percent provide parks only to unincorporated areas.

As one kind of solution to the problem of financing municipal-type services in urban unincorporated areas, the Contract Services Plan of Los
Angeles County has been explored. This program
illustrates the _feasibility_ of special charges to
subareas of a county for local police protection
provided to them but not also provided on a countywide basis. However, extension of the concept of
contract law enforcement service to the problem of
police protection finance in unincorporated areas
would require the formation of one or more local

police protection subordinate taxing areas in the
unincorporated portion of a county to pay for the
cost of police protection for its residents. As
mentioned above, most states have so far failed to
make legal provision for such an arrangement.

For those counties in which the sheriff provides no police service within municipalities, the
formula for allocation of the cost of services provided on a less than countywide basis would be very
simple: The entire cost of the sheriff's department would be charged to the unincorporated police
protection subordinate taxing areas, and no question of inequity vis-à-vis municipalities would
arise. However, for counties, such as Los Angeles,
in which a sheriff's department does provide some
services on a countywide basis and other services
only to, or at a higher level in, the unincorporated
area the further problem arises of what price to
charge for noncountywide services provided only to
certain areas. The accounting problems can be considerable, particularly in regard to (1) separating
services actually provided on a countywide basis
from those provided only to certain areas, (2) measuring the marginal cost of services provided only
to certain areas, and (3) allocating the fixed
costs of the agency. The discussion of the contract law enforcement program in Los Angeles County
demonstrates the difficulty of each of these problems in practice. Analysis of the Los Angeles data
suggests that underpricing of contract law enforcement services can easily result in continued subsidies to the taxpayers of contracting cities from
the taxpayers of cities that provide their own police service. However, with a more equitable formula for pricing service, the contract service
program appears to be a desirable alternative to a
situation in which cities that provide municipal
services at their own expense must subsidize the
provision of similar services to residents of urban,
but unincorporated, areas.

When distributional information that a client-
oriented program budget would provide is not available, the unintentional intergovernmental subsidies

of the sort described here are more likely to go
unnoticed. Thus, quite aside from the goal of
greater efficiency in <u>producing</u> governmental services, an important goal of the program budgeting
effort should be to help answer the questions, Who
gets what? and Who pays for it? The answers to
these questions involve complicated considerations
of both the equity and the legality of existing
procedures. Further, the answers depend on whether
the consideration is service distribution by one
city to its police department division areas (as
described in Chapter 2) or by a county to its po-
litically separate and independent subunits. But
before one can even begin to ponder the equity or
legality of any existing arrangement, information
must be obtained about how services actually are
distributed and financed. This is the chief justification for an agency program budget format with
iteration for relevant geographical or political
subdivisions, as suggested in Table 2.5 of Chapter 2.

Allocation of Vice Bureau Expenditures

	Unincorporated Area	Contract Cities	Noncontract Cities	Total
Man-hours expended[a]	25,462	16,048	7,833	49,344
Population	1,104,228	662,436	5,321,013	7,087,677
Percent man-hours expended	51.6	32.5	15.9	100
Percent population	15.6	9.4	75	100
Man-hours expended per capita	0.0231	0.0242	0.00147	0.00682
Man-hours expended if all county served at same level as noncontract cities	1,623	974	7,833	10,430
Excess man-hours above countywide level of service	23,839	15,074	0	38,913
Excess man-hours as percent of total man-hours	48.3	30.5	0	78.8
Vice bureau expenditure 1967/68 (excluding employee benefits)[b]				$872,534
Cost of services provided above countywide level (excluding employee benefits)	$421,000	$266,000	0	
Cost of services provided above countywide level (including employee benefits)[c]	$505,200	$319,000		

[a]Los Angeles County Sheriff's Department, Statistical Summary, Fiscal Year 1967-68, p. 95.

[b]Los Angeles County Sheriff's Department, Statement of Expenditures, Fiscal Year 1967-68, p. 12.

[c]Assuming employee benefits are 20 percent of direct expenditures (see note 27, p. 335).

Allocation of Detective Division Expenditures

	Unincorporated Area	Contract Cities	Noncontract Cities	Total
Calls answered[a]	14,907	10,406	8,249	32,752
Population	1,104,228	662,436	5,321,013	7,087,677
Percent calls answered	43	32	25	100
Percent population	15.6	9.4	75	100
Calls answered per capita	0.0128	0.0157	0.00155	0.00462
Calls answered if entire county served at same level as noncontract cities	1,712	1,026	8,249	10,987
Excess of calls answered above countywide level of service	12,385	9,380	0	21,765
Excess calls answered as percent of total calls answered	37.8	28.6	0	66.4
Detective division expenditures 1967/68[b]				$6,998,404
Cost of services provided above countywide level (excluding employee benefits)	$2,645,000	$2,002,000	0	$4,647,000
Cost of services provided above countywide level (including employee benefits)[c]	$3,174,000	$2,402,000		$5,576,000

[a]Los Angeles County Sheriff's Department, Records and Data Bureau, Data Processing Section, "Statistical Reporting of Services Rendered, December 1968," July 23, 1969 (special survey prepared at the request of the authors).

[b]Los Angeles County Sheriff's Department, Statement of Expenditures, Fiscal Year 1967-68, p. 11.

[c]Assuming employee benefits are 20 percent of direct expenditures (see note 27, p. 335).

6

**SUMMARY
OF METHODOLOGY
AND FINDINGS**

GOALS OF THE POLICE

While the overall goals of the legal system
are to promote justice and social order, the more
specific goal of the police is to ensure the public
peace and security. With regard to security, the
police seek to minimize the cost of illegal actions
to society--both the harm done by criminals and the
cost of both police and private efforts to prevent
it. The objective of the police is not to reduce
the level of crime to zero but to reduce the amount
of crime to some "optimal" level below which the
cost (in terms of additional police resources) of
reducing crime further is greater than the resulting benefit (in terms of a reduction in the harm
caused by crime).

In carrying out their primary mission, the police attempt to prevent violations and to apprehend
violators of the laws that delineate individual and
property rights and that regulate public conduct.
For purposes of analysis violations dealt with by
the police force are divided into five categories:
violations of property rights, violations of individuals' rights, violations of regulations relating
to moral conduct, collective civil violations, and
traffic violations. The social costs of violations
in each of these categories are explored.

Police Program Budget Structures

The activities of the police are organized into three broad, functional groups: (1) The police attempt to <u>prevent</u> future criminal activity by altering the conditions that lead to crime. Although they cannot very well change the socioeconomic characteristics of persons or neighborhoods, they do attempt to provide information and to affect attitudes. (2) They seek to <u>deter</u> potential criminals by maintaining a conspicuous and continuous presence in the community and responding quickly to a reported crime. They do so mainly through patrol activities, usually in automobiles. (3) When prevention and deterrence fail, the police <u>investigate</u> crimes that do occur and attempt to <u>apprehend</u> individuals who have committed them. Patrol officers initiate investigations because of their ability to respond quickly, and detectives carry on the investigations if patrol officers fail to apprehend the offenders.

These three activities are directed toward minimizing the cost of crime to society. Thus, possible tradeoffs among these three methods of attaining the same goal are suggested. For example, given the existing mix of efforts directed toward prevention, deterrence, and investigation, the question may be raised whether additional police resources devoted to prevention (a school visitation program) reduce the cost of crime--in terms of individuals injured or killed and property stolen or destroyed--more or less than the same resources devoted to investigation of crime (new equipment for a crime laboratory). A police program budget not only suggests such questions but is useful also in structuring the information necessary for answering them.

In addition to these three traditional activities, the police deal with traffic law violations, collective violations (public disorders or riots), and provide public services of various sorts that are not related to crime. These activities also are reflected in the program budget in a way that relates agency cost information to basic objectives.

An organization of cost information is presented that is quite broad and includes some illus-
trative programs. This structure is closely related to the existing organizational structures of
most large urban police departments. The primary
deviation from tradition is that all traffic activities are disaggregated into the preventive, deterrence, and apprehension programs instead of being
classified as a separate traffic program. An advantage of this structure is that existing police programs can be costed-out and allocated according to
major objectives.

In another presentation programs are organized
to conform to the outputs of police agencies in the
form of protecting persons and property from three
types of crimes and of providing traffic control
and general public services. This structure has
the advantage of focusing on the broad programs of
prevention, deterrence, and apprehension. Furthermore, measuring the amount and value of protection
afforded individuals from the various types of crime
is easier because of the greater availability of
statistics by types of crime and because not all law
violations are equally important in terms of the
costs they impose.

As another alternative, it is pointed out that
police program information can be organized in
terms of recipient groups, to elucidate particular
policy decisions. Within the jurisdiction of a police department the level of police service that is
provided to different groups may vary significantly.
Though circumstances make it necessary to organize
distribution of police services by geographical
area instead of by socioeconomic category (income
class, race, and so forth), geographical location
is, in many cases, a good proxy for the socioeconomic characteristics of its residents, and in such
cases a geographical breakdown of information can
be illuminating. When police cost figures and output (service) indicators are examined on a geographical basis, it is possible to see in a rough way
who is receiving how much service at what cost.

The purpose of emphasizing the geographical
aspect of the distribution of police services is

not to advocate any one particular criterion for deciding the optimal allocation of police resources
but rather to point out that an important function
of police program budgeting is to provide data with
which to make informed decisions. Since many police services must necessarily be provided on a
geographically oriented basis and since there is
considerable ambiguity in measuring the level of
services that any area is actually receiving, it
should be useful to display cost and performance
data within a geographical breakdown corresponding
to the geographical organization of the police department. Such a breakdown also has the advantage
that it may suggest a different mix of police programs within each division. The results of a tradeoff between, say, a preventive program (community
relations) and a deterrent program (more patrol
units) may be very different in a high crime rate
area from those in a low crime rate area, and the
divisional breakdown of programs and outputs encourages specific attention to the optimal combination of programs in each area.

Estimates of Program Expenditures

The next step might have been a complete cost
analysis of program expenditures for the five major
program goals in the second presentation: (1) to
minimize injuries, deaths, and property loss caused
by criminal behavior, (2) to minimize damages caused
by violations of the moral code, (3) to minimize
damages to persons and property caused by collective
violations, (4) to minimize cost of traffic movement
and traffic accidents, and (5) to provide general
public services. This step would have required detailed examination of all current police activities
to determine which of the program categories each
activity contributed to and then allocating, or
crosswalking, the expenditures for these activities
from the line-item expenditure budget to the program budget accordingly. To obtain precise program
cost figures, however, a strenuous reformulation of
data collection techniques would have been required--

and this is one of the too infrequently mentioned
costs of constructing and presenting a program budget. This estimation of program costs is especially
difficult because most police activities contribute
to more than one program goal and there is no completely satisfactory way to allocate the joint costs
of such activities among programs.

In light of these difficulties, with the cooperation of the Los Angeles Police Department, an unusually detailed cost analysis for the traffic program was constructed, rather than a less detailed
and less accurate estimation for the full department.

A detailed program structure for the traffic
bureau of the Los Angeles Police Department is presented. The activities performed by traffic bureau
officers are categorized according to three major
subprogram objectives--accident prevention, accident
deterrence, and congestion reduction. The structure
suggests the inclusion of information on output or
performance indicators as well as the conventional
data on program expenditures, and the proposed indicators can be used in quantitative measurement of
the specified objectives of each subprogram or program element. For several of the program elements
both the indicators are included to show the difference between the output measures necessary for program analysis and the performance measures normally
used by police administrators.

Since the structure proposed for the traffic
bureau attempts to account for both the monetary
value of inputs (cost) and the physical level of
performance and (or) output, cost and effectiveness
measures are presented in a single document and can
be compared on an annual basis. Of course, it remains for administrators to assign value weights to
the incommensurable physical indicators in the budget structure.

How is the police administrator aided by this
structure? One obvious advantage is that the structure cuts across existing operating divisions, which
should be used primarily for data-collection purposes rather than for program analysis. Indeed, the
program outline highlights the fact that each division contributes to several subprograms and program
elements.

Another advantage of the program structure is that separate program elements can be evaluated, to some extent, in terms of annual costs and output levels. Thus, an administrator can observe the resulting effect on output of an alteration of resources in one program element or a shift from one to another. Because these expenditure data are calculated only on an annual basis, they may be too crude to serve as a basis for lower level decisions although they will probably suffice for higher level tradeoff decisions. Also, annual comparisons can be made within the same program element.

Integrating Program Budget Structure and Program Analysis

It is often stated that in the ideal program budget statement structure and analysis will somehow be combined. Combining the two explicitly in the budget should be carried out as far as possible, to avoid use of ad hoc analyses issued as separate program memoranda. However, it should be recognized that the possibilities are limited for incorporating program analysis into the budget document itself. Since the program budget tends to be most useful to higher level administrators for comparing the costs and outputs of major programs, the structure will be most useful for such decision makers as the police chief and major police program administrators (for example, the heads of patrol and detective bureaus). Lower level police administrators, on the other hand, will be more interested in production efficiency--achieving maximum output from a given quantity of inputs. Thus they will be concerned, for instance, not with tradeoffs between the patrol and detective divisions but with tradeoffs between vehicle and labor inputs among given patrol beats or divisions or tradeoffs between two-man and one-man patrol units. This lower level process can also be encouraged by the structure of the budget. For instance, one of the structures presented illustrates major programs subdivided by geographical divisions. They could easily be further subdivided by beats. However, analysis of the effectiveness

of additions to programs or input substitutions within programs normally requires separate memoranda.

The program structure does not by itself suggest the areas or issues for analysis; it merely
points out the dollar magnitude and goals of the
programs that will be important if policy analysis
is undertaken.

PROGRAM ANALYSIS FOR TRAFFIC
LAW ENFORCEMENT

Traffic Law Enforcement
Production Functions

Ideally, the police traffic administrator
would have complete knowledge of the effects on
traffic variables of any particular level or method
of traffic law enforcement, under all conditions.
This relationship can be expressed as a production
function, where the desired effects on traffic safety and flow (reduced accident rates and increased
speed of travel) are the outputs and police resources employed (officers, motorcycles, automobiles) are the inputs. The relationship between
inputs and outputs depends heavily on the service
conditions (weather, type of road) and on the technology of enforcement used (motorcycle patrol, unmarked cars, radar).

It is obvious that police administrators have
some relationship of this sort in mind when they
make decisions concerning how traffic laws are to
be enforced. It is usually expected that greater
expenditure for traffic law enforcement will produce more of the desired results and that how much
of these desired results are produced for any given
expenditure depends on both the particular conditions under which the services are rendered and the
enforcement technology employed. But just what the
quantitative relationship is has remained a mystery,
despite its obvious usefulness in making an efficient allocation of police resources in traffic
duties. The lack of knowledge concerning traffic
enforcement effectiveness may be explained by the

fact that a limited amount of research has been done
on the question rather than that the basic production relationships are unknowable. At the current
level of knowledge, it is almost certainly true that
the rewards to research on traffic law enforcement
production functions will be greater than the rewards of equal expenditure directly on enforcement
itself.

     Since public service outputs are usually impos-
sible to describe fully or measure accurately, output in the production function is usually represented
by one or more output indicators. Basically, the
production function shows, for a given police program, the relation between the resources used in the
program and the corresponding magnitude of the output indicator that results. Perhaps more important
for decision making, the production function also
shows how output varies in response to input changes.
Such knowledge is important because most issues of
resource allocation actually deal with marginal
changes: how much additional output will result
from an addition to a program's expenditure or how
much reduction in output will result from a reduction in program expenditure. For many purposes this
limited amount of information is enough for making
intelligent decisions about resource allocation. It
is typically much more useful to know the effect on
output of marginal variations in inputs than it is
to know the size of total output. And in many cases
measurement of changes in output may be possible
even though measurement of total output is impossible or too difficult to be feasible.

     Even without the difficult step of valuing pro-
gram output, examination of public service production functions focuses attention on whether program
output is produced as efficiently as possible. When
both inputs and outputs are valued in dollar terms,
the investigation is usually called cost-benefit
analysis; when the inputs are valued in dollar terms
but the outputs are described in physical terms, it
is called cost-effectiveness analysis. There are
many situations in which formal cost-benefit analysis
is so expensive or uncertain that the results are not
worth the cost of making the analysis but in which

simpler cost-effectiveness studies can still contribute to significant improvements.

The basic goal of a cost-effectiveness study
is to ensure that a given level of output is produced at least cost or, equivalently stated, that
for a given expenditure the maximum possible output
is produced. Cost-effectiveness analysis tells
nothing about the appropriate level of output to be
produced or of inputs to be devoted to a program,
but rather concentrates on efficient production
techniques. However, useful program analysis can
often start with a cost-effectiveness study of production techniques and only subsequently undertake
an evaluation in dollar terms of benefits produced;
indeed, too often it is simply assumed in cost-
benefit analysis that benefits are being produced
in the most efficient manner possible while in
reality the same output might be produced by a different and less costly set of inputs.

An output-oriented program budget invites both
cost-effectiveness and cost-benefit analysis of public service production, and the program analysis of
traffic law enforcement described below will contain both elements: investigation of efficient
methods of production and an attempt to ascertain
the optimum level of enforcement on a traffic beat.

The Experimental Investigation of Traffic Law Enforcement Production Functions

Traffic laws are enforced throughout Los Angeles by units of the patrol bureau; but to those
surface streets that have the greatest number of
automobile accidents the traffic bureau assigns
special motorcycle traffic law enforcement officers.
This assignment procedure is known as "selective
enforcement" and is based on the assumption that a
concentration of enforcement effort at the times
and places at which most accidents occur will produce the greatest output in terms of accident reduction.

Each motorcycle patrolman is assigned a patrol
beat of from three to six miles long. These beats,

assigned for six-month duration (winter and summer),
are semiannually reviewed to ensure that traffic enforcement officers are assigned to areas that have
experienced the greatest number of traffic accidents.
However, the specific allocation of beats among possible street segments is performed intuitively by a
clerk who works with large maps pinned to show the
number of accidents that have occurred over the previous six-month interval and the type of accident.

Unfortunately the allocation process operates
in the absence of any real knowledge of the quantitative effect of traffic law enforcement on traffic
accident rates; also, it neglects the effect that
enforcement may have on the traffic volume and on
the average speed at which traffic flows. Furthermore, there is no empirically established criterion
of what the overall level of traffic law enforcement
activity should be. The method used to measure the
need for enforcement is the enforcement index, which
is the ratio of traffic convictions to injury-
accidents occurring in the city, but no explicit
analysis has been made of what a desirable level of
the enforcement would be.

If there is a definite relationship between
the level of enforcement and the frequency of traffic accidents, comparison of similar traffic beats
that have different numbers of motorcycle officers
should reveal the successive reductions in accidents
achieved by the successive additions of motorcycle
patrol officers; then, ignoring for the moment
other benefits and costs of enforcement, by estimating the benefit of reducing accidents (in terms
of lives saved and of injuries and property damage
avoided) and the cost of enforcement (in terms of
the cost of motorcycle patrol), it should be possible to tell at what level of enforcement the marginal cost of enforcement is equal to the marginal
benefit (that is, what the optimum level of enforcement is).

The Design of the Experiment

The experiment was designed to discover the
effect of the method of patrol enforcement and of

the number of motorcycle patrol officers on such
variables as traffic accident rates and average
speed and volume of traffic--and also on one nontraffic variable, the reported crime rate, on the
patrolled street segments. Eight experimental
beats were selected, as similar as possible in
length, width, previous accident experience, volume
of traffic, and other relevant characteristics.

On the eight beats, the following methods of
patrol were employed during the experiment:

1. Visibility only (on one beat): The motor
cycle patrol officer refrained from citing traffic
law violators (except for flagrant offenses).

2. Warning only (on one beat): The officer
stopped and warned violators but did not issue citations (except for flagrant offenses).

3. Standard enforcement (on five beats): The
officer patrolled the beat and issued citations in
the same manner as before the experiment began.

The experiment was also designed to show the
effect of varying the level of manpower allocation
on each beat when the standard technique of enforcement is employed. The following manpower allocations were employed during the experiment:

1. No change: The manpower allocation remained at the preexperiment level.

2. Increased allocation: The manpower allocation was increased to a level higher than the preexperiment level.

3. Stripped allocation: The manpower allocation was reduced to zero.

The experiment was conducted during the day
watch (10 a.m. to 6 p.m.), Monday through Friday,
between October 1, 1968, and June 30, 1969. Data
for the experiment were collected on the experimental beats on total accidents (fatal, injury, and
property damage accidents); traffic citations issued; traffic violation arrests; traffic volume;
average speed (timed by radar); and crimes (reported
crimes and arrests). Data were compiled also for
the remaining hours of the week, as a control; furthermore, the same data (except for items 2, 3, and
5) are available for previous years on the same
basis.

The crime data were collected in an attempt to
determine whether the level of visibility of traffic
enforcement patrol had any effect on the crime rate
on the experimental beats, for any such nontraffic
effect should be counted among the benefits of manpower allocated to traffic law enforcement; looking
only at the effects on traffic accidents or other
traffic variables would understate the benefits of
traffic officers.

Valuation of Costs and Benefits
of Traffic Law Enforcement

Both inputs and outputs of the traffic law enforcement production process must be valued in dollar terms in order to be made comparable for a decision about whether or not benefits exceed costs at
the margin.

Cost of Traffic Law Enforcement. Data supplied
by the Los Angeles Police Department show that the
average cost of day watch motorcycle patrol is approximately $8.00 per man-hour (including salaries,
vehicle and equipment costs, and overhead). Although this is an average cost, it is probably very
close to the actual marginal cost, for it represents
mostly wages and vehicle costs for the motorcycle
officers (90 percent of the total). The marginal
cost is the crucial figure in an attempt to balance
the cost of an additional patrol unit against the
resulting additional benefit. This cost amounts to
approximately $12,000 per motorcycle unit for the
nine-month day watch.

Another possible cost, not borne by the police
department itself, may occur if stricter traffic
law enforcement results in a reduced speed of traffic flow. This must be counted as a cost of enforcement because speed is one of the primary objectives of automobile travel. The California Division
of Highways uses the figure of 3¢ per vehicle-minute
as the average value of automobile travel time, and
several other estimates of the value of travel time
cluster around the 3¢ per vehicle-minute figure.
If an increase in the level of enforcement does
alter average travel speed on the patrolled route,

the cost or benefit (per day) to the motorists of this reduction in speed is arrived at by multiplying (1) the increase or decrease in time required to traverse the beat by (2) $0.03 per minute and this by (3) volume of passenger car traffic traversing the beat per day.

Benefits of Traffic Law Enforcement. The chief benefit sought from traffic enforcement is a reduction in the number of traffic accidents. Measurement of one aspect of this benefit, property damage avoided, is not a great problem. When a property-damage-only accident is prevented, the benefit is at least equal to what it would have cost to repair such damage, which the California Division of Highways estimated, for 1964, at an average of $600 per reported accident.

The measure of benefit becomes more difficult when one moves from a consideration of property damage avoided to a consideration of injuries avoided. The California Division of Highways uses an estimate, based on survey data, of $2,100 as the direct cost of each injury-accident. But it is necessary to be mindful in using this estimate that it represents only the measurable portion of a total cost and that it is the total (measurable plus intangible) cost that is relevant for decisions about traffic safety.

The measure of benefit becomes most difficult when the issue of avoiding traffic accident fatalities is broached. Obviously no wide agreement can be expected on any specific value, but several estimates have been proposed and used in highway work. Using the direct-cost method described above, the California Division of Highways places the cost of fatalities per fatal accident in urban areas at $7,700.

However, while the direct-cost method may be appropriate for property damage or injuries, it is a questionable guide to public decisions concerning life-saving measures. At best, the direct-cost method provides an irreducible minimum estimate of the cost of a fatal accident. A study by the U.S. Department of Transportation added to the medical and property damage losses an estimate of the present discounted value (at time of death) of expected lifetime earnings. Using this concept, the Department of Transportation estimates the average total loss per fatality at $89,500. This would imply an average cost of fatalities <u>per fatal accident</u> of $89,500 times 1.15, or $102,900, based on the California average for urban areas of 1.15 fatalities per fatal accident. In a similar study, which assessed the benefits of motor vehicle injury-prevention programs, the U.S. Department of Health, Education, and Welfare estimated the average expected lifetime earnings foregone as a result of traffic fatalities at $93,000, which is very close to the Department of Transportation figure.

Although these various measures have been suggested and computed, it is obvious that no single usable estimate of the cost of a traffic fatality can be made from the available data. Rather than one of these figures, the low California Division of Highways estimate and the high Department of Transportation estimate of the cost of a traffic fatality were used to illustrate the benefit of reducing accidents, and the sensitivity of the final cost-benefit results to the varying concepts of the cost of traffic fatalities was pointed out.

Valuing the benefit of a reduction in crime is in many ways more difficult than valuing the benefit of a reduction in traffic accidents. As discussed below, we developed minimum dollar estimates of the cost of various crimes, in connection with an analysis of the effect of deterrent patrol on crime. These values are used to measure the benefit of any crime reduction that may take place as a result of traffic law enforcement patrol.

Results of the Traffic Law Enforcement Experiment

<u>Effect on Traffic Accidents</u>. On two beats the intention was to see what effect different methods of enforcement had on injury-accident experience, manpower remaining the same; only on the warning-only beat was there a reduction in the number of accidents from the average of the four preceding years. The other six beats were designed to show

the effect an increase or decrease in the number of
officers (employing the standard citation method)
had on observed injury-accident experience. One interesting overall observation can be made: On each
of the four beats on which enforcement patrol was
increased, the number of accidents either declined
(three beats) or remained the same (one beat) and
that on the beat on which enforcement was unchanged
and on the beat on which it was decreased, the number of accidents increased. The six beats on which
the number of officers was altered were ranked according to the change in the number of accidents.
An obvious rough negative rank correlation (0.829)
between the two variables was found; a greater increase in officers is associated with a greater decrease in accidents--which suggests that an increase
in the number of officers does reduce the number of
traffic injury-accidents but shows nothing about the
magnitude of the effect of traffic officers on traffic accidents.

　　For the moment assuming that the observed
changes in accidents are a result of changes in enforcement and for the moment disregarding such other
effects as those on travel speed and crime rates, an
evaluation of the traffic accident results in cost-
benefit terms was made.

　　In the absence of reliable data on property
damage and fatality accidents, it was assumed that
enforcement affects the accident-causation process
for fatality and property damage accidents in the
same way it affects that for injury-accidents and
that these other two categories of accidents will
increase or decrease in the same proportion as
injury-accidents.

　　Further, it was assumed that the ratios of
fatal/injury and property damage/injury-accidents
on each beat were the same as the citywide ratios
for surface streets. These ratios were 0.939
property damage accidents per injury-accident and
0.013 fatal accidents per injury-accident. On the
assumption that these ratios also hold for changes
in the number of accidents, an injury-accident
equivalent cost was constructed that includes, for
each injury-accident, the associated cost of 0.939

property damage accidents and 0.013 fatal accidents. The accident cost figures used were those given above ($600 per PDO accident, $2,100 per injury-accident and, for fatalities, a low estimate of $7,700 and a high estimate of $102,900 per fatality). The resulting injury-accident equivalent was a low estimate of $2,760 and a high estimate of $4,000. This injury-accident equivalent made it possible to represent the total cost of all accidents on a beat in terms of the number of injury-accidents only.

With these estimates and the $12,000 cost per patrol unit given above, a preliminary and partial evaluation of the costs and benefits of the enforcement changes was made, at this point in terms only of the cost of patrol and the cost of accidents.

An interesting result is that, on the five beats on which the number of officers was changed (and restricting the analysis to measured benefits of accident reduction versus public agency costs only--a narrow point of view often adopted in traffic safety studies), none of the changes in manpower from the status quo (either increases or decreases) appeared clearly desirable. Thus, according to this criterion, the initial allocation was better than any of the alternative manpower allocations proposed.

Next, these preliminary estimates of benefits of traffic accident reduction were subjected to tests of statistical significance to see whether they were the result of a change in the accident-causation process or a result of random variation in the number of accidents. According to these tests, four beats showed a significant change in the accident-causation process, and two beats are of particular interest because the preliminary calculation of costs and benefits showed that the change in benefits exceeded the change in costs of enforcement. These preliminary results are insufficient to judge the worth of traffic law enforcement because they refer only to a portion of total costs and benefits. But before other costs and benefits are considered, it may be useful to raise the question why the traffic accident results turned out as they did on this selection of experimental beats.

First, so far as the effect of enforcement on
accidents is concerned, manpower was obviously not
misallocated before the experiment began, because
no form of reallocation, either an increase or decrease, showed a clear increase in benefits. Apparently the previous method of determining allocation
was not grossly in error.

Another observation is prompted by the experience on the warning-only beat where the number of
accidents was reduced without any increase in the
manpower allocation. The officer on this beat could
stop motorists for any potentially dangerous violations even though the proof of violation was not incontestable. In addition, the warning-only officer
never had to lurk in a concealed location while
waiting for an incontestable citation and was thus
able to patrol the beat more visibly. While this
speculation on the possible explanation of the effectiveness of greater use of warnings would have
to be tested by further experimentation, it illustrates the potential conflict between a lower level
work measure--citations issued--and a higher level
agency goal--reduction in accidents and congestion.

The actual situation in the LAPD traffic bureau
has been somewhat exaggerated because some attention
is given to a beat's previous accident experience
and some violations are considered more serious than
others in light of that experience. However, the
fact remains that the patrolman is to a large extent
judged on the number of tickets he issues, not on
the incidence of traffic accidents along his beat.
The intermediate goal of issuing tickets has become
an end unto itself instead of being a means to the
goal of accident deterrence.

Effect on Crime Rates. Traffic law enforcement
patrol may achieve some of the crime deterrent effects produced by general patrol, though the traffic
bureau is not organizationally charged with the responsibility for doing so. And if traffic patrol
does have the effect of crime reduction, the net
benefit of traffic patrol would be underestimated
if all the cost of the patrol was charged to the
traffic program and measured only the benefit of
any traffic accident reduction. The side effect of

crime reduction should be counted as a separate and additional benefit of traffic patrol.

To estimate the effect of the experimental changes in traffic law enforcement patrol on crime, the percentage change in reported crime from the average number during the four previous years to the number during the experimental period was measured for each beat and for each of 11 separate crimes. The correlation coefficient for the percentage change in reported crime on each beat and the absolute change in the number of traffic law enforcement officers per mile on each beat was calculated. The correlation was surprisingly weak and insignificant for all crimes, except that there was a strong negative relation (0.823) between traffic law enforcement patrol and the number of robberies.

Although further research would be necessary to confirm this relationship (for robberies) or lack of relationship (for other crimes) between traffic patrol and reported crime, for the present preliminary purpose the reduction in robberies on each beat was included as one of the benefits of traffic patrol in the interest of determining what effect it had on the previous calculation of net benefit in terms of accident reduction. However, this calculation is even more tentative than was the calculation in the case of traffic accidents, for there is the possibility that robberies were not really deterred by the patrol, but rather merely diverted to other locations. If such was the case, the crime reduction benefits of the traffic patrol would be purely local, compensated for by an increase in the cost of crime elsewhere. The extent of such a diversion, if one occurred at all, is unfortunately unknown; however, the econometric study, discussed below, of the effect of general patrol on crime indicates that the total amount of crime in any city is negatively related to the number of patrol officers per capita, so that the police are at the very least able to reduce crime within their own political jurisdiction.

The correlation between the percentage change in robberies and the change in officers per mile indicated that on the average a 0.1 increase in

officers per mile leads to a 7.9 percent reduction
in the total number of robberies. Estimating the
dollar value of the social cost for a robbery is as
difficult as it is for a traffic accident; an estimate was used that is developed below ($1,600 per
robbery), which includes the cost of the goods
stolen and the subsequent cost to the criminal justice system of dealing with the robbery. Using this
dollar estimate and translating the change in number
of robberies on each beat into a change in cost of
robberies, it was found that the range on the eight
beats was from a cost of $2,820 to a benefit of $575.

Effect on Speed of Travel. During the experiment, data were obtained on perhaps the most important indicator of the effect of enforcement on
travel time--the speed distribution of moving automobiles at selected points on each beat. These
data were obtained by means of radar observations.
An immediate inference from the radar speed data is
that regardless of the level of enforcement only a
very small proportion of drivers exceeded the speed
limit on the selection of beats under study.

Because the limited evidence on speed distributions indicates very little effect of enforcement
level on the (generally small) fraction of drivers
exceeding the speed limit and because other effects
(even the direction of the effects) on traffic delay are almost impossible to measure, no attempt
was made to arrive at a dollar value estimate of
the effect of enforcement on travel time. Instead,
as a second-best solution, an estimate was made of
what the magnitude of the effect of enforcement on
average speed and travel time would have to be to
seriously affect the previous calculation of other
costs and benefits.

To estimate the social cost of a change in
traffic speed, it was necessary first to know the
volume of traffic on each beat during the experiment.
A conservative estimate of average traffic volume on
a beat during the experimental hours was 9,000 vehicles per day. The average traffic beat length was
3.7 miles. With this information and with the valuation of the cost of travel time of 3¢ per vehicle-
minute that was discussed above, it was possible to

estimate the effect on travel time cost of a change
in average steady-flow speed of traffic. For instance, a reduction in speed from 30 to 29 mph means
that it takes 0.26 minutes longer to travel the average beat. On the basis of 3¢ per vehicle-minute,
this amounts to 78¢ per vehicle, which, multiplied
by 9,000 vehicles, is a cost of $70 per day or
$13,650 during the test period.

Although the method of speed measurement available for the experiment was inadequate to detect
small changes in average speed of traffic flow, it
was possible to show that the benefit of a small reduction in travel time (or the cost of a small increase) would appreciably affect the cost-benefit
calculation. This is, of course, an indication that
the traffic bureau's expressed objective of reducing
congestion is indeed an important one, deserving
more consideration than it currently receives in
traffic patrol assignments.

Summary of Results of the Experiment

The most striking implication of the measured
results is that, with the exception of the warning-
only beat, no experimental change resulted in a
clearly demonstrated net benefit. Where manpower
was increased, the marginal measured cost exceeded
the marginal measured benefit. Where manpower was
reduced, the reduction in measured benefits exceeded
the reduction in measured costs. Such a uniformly
negative net benefit associated with the experimental changes indicates that the existing allocation
of resources to beats was superior to any reallocation that was tried and that the "saturation" technique of concentrated traffic law enforcement resources in a small area is not justified on the
basis of the measured results. In no case was the
value of the marginal product of an additional
traffic officer clearly greater than the marginal
cost when there was already one officer on a typical beat. In terms of motor officers per mile,
there was no net measured benefit from an enforcement level above approximately 0.3 officers per
mile on main surface streets.

Aside from the findings on patrol intensity, the results also indicated that a change in patrol techniques may be desirable. The warning-only beat showed a large net benefit ($23,500 low estimate, $34,000 high estimate), and this result was interpreted as possibly stemming from the inappropriate reward structure imposed on other officers whose output was, at least partially, measured by the number of citations written per day. A revision of work measurement was proposed that would make the reward structure for traffic officers more consistent with the goals of the traffic bureau. The cost-benefit calculations based on these results should not be considered evidence of the proved worth of any particular method or intensity of patrol, but rather indicators that some allocations are worth further investigation whereas other allocations are distinctly less promising for future research.

PROGRAM ANALYSIS OF CRIME DETERRENT PATROL

An examination of program budget structures for several cities reveals that as much as 40 percent to 50 percent of total operating expenditures can be safely attributed to patrol activities.

Despite the large size of the general patrol program and the public controversy over specific patrol operations, little good information is available to assist patrol administrators in deploying patrol inputs or to assist police chiefs in directing resources between patrol and other police programs in the most efficient manner. As a result, few patrol administrators attempt to construct comprehensive guidelines for planning the deployment of patrol resources. Part of the difficulty is that attempts to evaluate the patrol program require that operational objectives and output measures be previously agreed upon. As is the case with many public services, the output of visible police patrol is difficult to define and quantify. An important purpose of the study was to examine the feasibility of various possible output indicators for general patrol.

Since the goal of the visible patrol program
is the deterrence of criminal events, criminal victimization rates (the number of crimes committed
per 1,000 population) are appropriate indicators of
output. Not all offenders are equally susceptible
to deterrence by the probability of arrest attributable to patrol forces. Some property thefts are obviously the result of cold calculation, and many
crimes of violence are undoubtedly the result of
temporary irrationality. Consequently, it appears
reasonable for the police to attempt to allocate
the greater part of resources to the deterrence of
those prohibited acts that are subject to rational
calculation by potential offenders since the police
are most likely to affect the decision process of
potential offenders in these cases, mainly personal
property violations. Thus, reductions in reported
property crime rates were used as the most important
measure of patrol output in this analysis, and a police service production function was tested to determine the extent of influence of the police on
the criminal activity of property offenders. For
completeness, total reported crime rates and arrest
rates also were used in the analysis.

A Production Model for Crime
Deterrent Patrol

A model has recently been proposed that aims
to measure the effects of patrol inputs and incorporates most of the essential production relationships in the crime deterrent patrol program. The
model divides the activities of motorized patrol
units into responding to calls for service and visible patrol only. A special form of clearance rate
is the indicator selected to measure the effects of
free or visible patrol time. The proposed output
indicator is defined as the ratio of on-view arrests, C, made in a given area to the number of reported crimes in the area, R. Either the ratio,
C/R, or C or R separately could be used as output
indicators. Output is related to patrol manpower
and capital inputs via a production function

$$Q = Q\,\frac{T}{A}$$

where $Q = \frac{C}{R}$, C, or R

A = area patrolled (square miles or
street miles)

T = patrol unit man-hours spent in
area A

and the variable T is further defined as

$$T = n\sum_{j=1}^{n} t_j m_j$$

where   n = the number of visible patrol units
in area A

t_j = the amount of visible patrol time
per the jth patrol unit

m_j = the number of patrolmen per the
j^{th} patrol unit.

The ratio T/A represents patrol input density measured as the number of patrol man-hours per square
mile. Testing the proposed production function
with statistical data would yield estimates of the
marginal effectiveness of an additional patrol unit,
of an increment in free patrol time, and of an additional officer per patrol unit--all of which are
currently important and unresolved issues in patrol
operations.

Though the above equations represent the ideal
model of patrol production relations that it would
be desirable to estimate, the data requirements pre-
cluded its being tested directly. Therefore, a
less specific but more widely applicable concept of
the urban public service production function was
used to measure input-output relations in visible
patrol. That production function is expressed in
general form as

$$O = f(I, S, T)$$

where   O = output, the effects of visible
patrol inputs

I = inputs from the visible patrol
program

S = service conditions
T = state of patrol technology.

Above, a controlled field experiment was used
to discover the production function in traffic law
enforcement. Here a statistical regression analysis
based on existing data was used to discover the
input-output relations in the deterrent patrol program. A variety of output proxies was tested to see
which are the more reliable and (or) consistent es-
timators of the effects of deterrent patrol. The
patrol input variables, too, were represented by a
number of alternative measures meant to be proxies
for the ideal measures suggested in the equations
above.

A Statistical Analysis of Patrol Production

Statistical regression analysis was used to investigate production relationships in the visible
patrol program. Data were collected from a cross
section of urban police agencies on the magnitude
of selected patrol input and output variables as
well as on social and economic conditions thought
to affect the decision to commit an offense. The
data were analyzed by means of multivariate linear
regression equations. This particular technique
analyzes the effects on output of the variations in
visible patrol inputs and socioeconomic characteristics of a sample of California cities at a point in
time.

Patrol Output

The primary dependent variable was a "visible
crime index." For establishing this variable, certain criminal offenses were selected from the FBI
crime index of Part One offenses and from the felony
crime statistics collected by the California Bureau
of Criminal Statistics. Further, somewhat arbitrarily, felonies were divided into two major categories:
suppressible offenses and nonsuppressible offenses.
Suppressible crimes are those thought to be more
susceptible to deterrence through the activity of

visible field patrol; thus the visible crime index,
because such crimes occur mainly in public areas.
Visible crimes include robbery, burglary, larceny-
theft (both grand and petty), and auto theft.

The crimes included in the visible index are
those of which the majority occur in public places.
Of course, other crimes are committed in public
areas, but they are excluded from the visible crime
index if fewer than 50 percent occur in public
streets or buildings. Obviously, the selection of
crimes is arbitrary; property violations constitute
the majority of the crimes included in the visible
index, while most personal injury crimes (homicide,
assault, rape) are excluded. To offset any possible
error that might arise from not including these
crimes, a total crime index of all major crimes
(using both FBI and California data) was also used
as a dependent variable.

Each separate crime within both the FBI and
the California crime indexes was also run in a separate regression equation to determine whether police patrol inputs have a differential effect on
the individual crimes; it may be, say, that visible
patrol will affect two of the five index crimes but
not all of them.

It is frequently observed that the official
statistics on crimes reported to the police seriously underestimate the true population of criminal
events because of underreporting. In addition, the
reporting rate (ratio of reported to total crimes)
may change when the level of enforcement changes.
Both these problems bias attempts to use the reported crime rate as an adequate measure of police
output. It is shown that, in all cases, using estimated actual crime rates as output proxies improves estimates of the effect of police inputs.
Hence, it was necessary to have an output measure
designed to account for the extensive underreporting in the published crime statistics.

Unfortunately, no estimates of the actual number of crimes are available that have been derived
specifically for the sample of Southern California
cities. However, a national interview survey conducted by the National Opinion Research Center

yielded estimates of the extent of underreporting
on a national and regional basis. The estimates
from both the United States and the Western regional
sample of that survey were used to adjust the regression estimates of the effect of patrol inputs
on various reported crimes.

In an effort to determine the single most accurate measure of patrol output, arrest rates were
also used as dependent variables in the regression
analysis. The objective of a visible patrol program is to deter would-be offenders, who are assumed
to calculate and act on the basis of the probability
of apprehension. If the subjective probability of
arrest perceived by the offender closely approximates the true risk of arrest and this risk is accurately measured by police arrest rates, it can
then be presumed that crimes will decrease in some
proportion to the increased arrest rates. Therefore, the arrest rates may be a reasonable measure
of the deterrence produced by (that is, the output
of) a visible patrol program.

Patrol Input and
Environmental Variables

The conceptual and statistical content of the
independent variables used in the multiple regression equations can best be discussed by presenting
all of them in the following equation:

$$Y = \alpha + \beta_1 \times \frac{PT}{Pop} + \beta_2 \times \frac{V}{Pop} + \beta_3 \times U$$
$$+ \beta_4 \times \frac{NPT}{Pop} + \beta_5 \times PPT + \beta_6 \times \frac{SM}{Pop}$$
$$+ \beta_7 \times S + \beta_8 \times NW + \beta_9 \times \frac{W}{Pop} +$$

The police patrol input variables are PT/Pop, V/Pop,
U, NPT/Pop, and PPT.

PT/Pop is the labor input variable estimated
by the absolute number of sworn officers on the
force who are considered to be the visible patrolmen and who are regularly assigned to patrol beat
activities, expressed as visible patrolmen per
1,000 population.

V/Pop is a proxy for the capital input of the patrol bureau, estimated as the number of patrol vehicles per 1,000 population.

U is the percentage of all regularly assigned patrol units that are one-man units; it reflects the technique of organization of men and vehicles and, at the same time, provides an estimate of m in the equations of the ideal production model. It seems, a priori, that one-man units could perform the task of preventive-patrol-only more efficiently and at a lower cost, whereas two-man cars would be more suited to answering calls for services in certain areas at certain times safely.

NPT reflects the remainder of the force, officers who are not visible patrolmen, and is designed to hold constant any effect the activities of the nonpatrol force may have on crime rates.

PPT is the percentage of the total force made up of patrolmen.

SM/Pop is the number of street miles per 1,000 population, a service condition that can affect patrol inputs.

S is median school years completed by persons 25 years of age or older.

NW is the percentage of the total population that is nonwhite.

W/Pop is assessed valuation of property, or "wealth," per 1,000 residents.

Results of the Regression Analysis

The regression equations were estimated in linear form. Experimentation with nonlinear estimating equations yielded no substantial improvement in the explanatory ability of the model.

Not all the results of the regression analysis confirmed a priori expectations. The wealth variable indicates that wealthier areas tend to experience greater crime. Since only property crimes are included, this finding was not unexpected. If personal injury crimes had also been included in the index, the same result would not have been expected, because economic incentives are not so important to potential criminals in personal injury crimes.

The nonwhite variable is significant in nearly all the following cases. This result, too, appears to have an underlying economic rationale, because nonwhites tend to have fewer market job opportunities and lower market wage and salary earnings than whites. Ceteris paribus, any group with similar employment characteristics would be expected to engage in relatively more property violations.

The street miles variable is generally negative but becomes significant in the equations using California data. Instead of reflecting service conditions that make the patrol inputs more or less effective, the street miles per 1,000 population variable seems to be reflecting the effect of a third influence, population density, on crime. It does not appear, as we initially assumed, that the effectiveness of patrol inputs is seriously affected in cities having more street miles.

The sign and significance of the median schooling variable varied considerably. A possible explanation of the frequent sign changes is the fact that this is the median school years completed by adults aged 25 and older. A large percentage of property violations is committed by juveniles and these would not be reflected in the variable. However, in an attempt to overcome this problem use was made of a "percentage teenagers" variable, which also failed to generate a uniform sign. There are at least two variables capable of overcoming this possible source of misspecification, the school dropout rate in an area and the teenage unemployment rate. Either one may indicate the economic incentives of juveniles to commit property violations. Unfortunately the required cross-sectional data are not available for Southern California cities.

The patrol input variables--percentage visible patrolmen and patrol vehicles--were not consistently significant. Greater consistency of the visible patrol inputs was shown when total crime indexes (FBI and California) were used as dependent variables and alternative input measures were employed. The "percentage one-man" variable showed a consistent negative effect and was usually significant, whereas the percentage patrolmen and visible patrolmen variables were only consistently negative. The nonpatrol

force variable was positive and significant. Of
course, this latter police input measure was not
included for the purpose of examining its effect
per se, but for the purpose of identifying its possible influence on the visible police inputs.

The major conclusion that can be drawn from
this statistical evidence is that there is no consistent statistical support for the production function hypothesized. First of all, there does not
seem to be any unique relationship between the effect of preventive patrol inputs and certain "suppressible" street crimes. Indeed, the evidence indicates that visible patrol may be able to affect
all major crimes to a greater extent than it affects
any small subsample of this aggregate. Furthermore,
the correction factor for underreporting does not
seem to approximate the true amount of crime occurring in the sample cities. The extent of unreported
crime in the Southern California sample of smaller,
suburb-like cities may be much different from the
level indicated by either correction factor. Certainly the weight derived from U.S. Survey results
is too unrefined to warrant confidence in its ability to explain the true amount of crime.

Although the findings suggest the rejection of
attempts to select one of the models over any of
the others, they do not necessarily suggest the conclusion that police patrol has little or no effect
on the crime rate measures used; in many instances
the patrol inputs have the hypothesized effect on
crime rates and are either significant or very
nearly so. What it does seem necessary to conclude
is that the models formulated and tested here were
not adequately specified. The input variables are
very crude and are not good approximations of the
input variables discussed in the ideal production
model.

Furthermore, the output proxies used may be
criticized on the ground that the reported crime
data are not reliable. As a contrast and comparison with the original models, a different production function was estimated. The only change made
was the substitution of arrest rates for crime rates
as the output indicator. The results of this model

were as expected and fairly uniform. Except for the
percentage one-man variable the estimated patrol input coefficients are positive and generally significant. The same holds true for the wealth and percentage nonwhite variables, which are highly significant; median school years and street miles are negative and significant. The positive relationships
between most of the patrol input variables and arrests support the assumption that a shift (increase)
in patrol resources may affect crime by first altering (increasing) the number of arrests, thereby
changing (increasing) the individual's perception
of the risk of apprehension. Hence, arrest rates
may be an acceptable proxy for patrol output. But
the regression results are only suggestive, and
additional research is required to determine the exact relationship between patrol inputs, crimes, and
arrests.

Cost-Benefit Analysis of
One-Man Patrol Units

Despite the possible sources of bias and misspecification of the model, some tentative estimates
of the effectiveness of patrol inputs can be made.
Utilizing the technique of cost-benefit analysis to
evaluate the deterrent effect of additional patrol
inputs, an implicit estimate was made of the value
of the marginal product of certain inputs. In the
following analysis the costs and benefits of altering an important technique of arranging patrol inputs were analyzed: the percentages of patrol units
in one-man and two-man patrol cars.

The formal analysis of the social benefits requires an estimate of the physical effectiveness of
the input alteration in question. Such an estimate
was obtained by the estimated regression coefficient
for the percentage one-man variable in selected equations. The benefits are the costs that are not imposed on individuals whose legal rights are violated
and on society. The private costs incurred as a result of criminal offenses include physical damage to
person or property, monetary losses, and psychic
damages. Although the monetary losses are actually

transfers and not themselves real costs, the involuntary redistribution of property was assumed to
constitute a social cost. Although estimates of
the reduction of pain and suffering and reduction
in resource costs in the form of private expenditures on protective devices are also extremely important, actual data were unavailable. However,
the dollar loss per robbery was adjusted by a factor to reflect the fact that robbery (over half of
which involves the use of firearms) involves a high
probability of personal injury, unlike the other
property violations in the visible crime indexes.

In addition to prevented private costs, external cost savings in the form of reduced costs of administering the entire criminal justice system of
the state must be considered.

A cost-benefit evaluation of the effects of increased police inputs represented by an increase in
the percentage of one-man patrol units (U) would
normally require an estimate of the increase in patrol costs imposed by the change. However, for this
example the U-coefficients resulting from the equations were evaluated and, from the structure of
those equations, the input change was interpreted
as not involving any addition to direct police
costs. Since visible patrolmen and number of patrol vehicle variables were held constant in the
equations, the input alteration represented by
percentage-one-man units was only a reorganization
of a fixed number of inputs. The only change was a
1 percent increase in the proportion of one-man patrol units; neither new patrolmen nor vehicles were
added. This resource reallocation is similar to
the warning-only beat in the traffic enforcement
experiment; there only the technique of operation
was altered, not the number of traffic inputs.

Using the Western correction factor, it was
found that a 1 percent increase in the percentage
one-man patrol units significantly deterred 1.172
actual robberies, 5.325 burglaries, and 3.093 auto
thefts. With the U.S. correction factor the deterrence figures were 1.044 fewer robberies, 11.047
fewer burglaries, and 2.786 fewer auto thefts.

Each deterred crime yields a social saving
equal to the costs that would otherwise have been

incurred by victims and by the state. The average
cost to individuals and the state criminal justice
system for each type of crime was estimated. For
the offenses used in the visible crime index these
estimates account only for the dollar value of the
property transferred by the average crime. Not included were the nonpecuniary or psychic losses associated with all the property crimes. To improve
the estimates of the average personal loss of each
crime, a seriousness weight was assigned to the
average robbery transfers to adjust for the additional expected costs expected for personal injury
associated with this particular offense.

Estimates of the social saving were obtained
by multiplying the change in crimes deterred (by a
1 percent increase in U) by the social cost of each
crime. Total gross benefits of the change were
$18,438 (low estimate) and $21,045 (high estimate).
When the seriousness weight for robbery was applied,
the estimates were increased to $21,432 and $23,045,
respectively.

Since measurement of the true loss is difficult, the gross losses were adjusted for recovery
of property in order to provide a range within which
true measured benefits are likely to be. The result
of this adjustment was to reduce the low and the
high estimates to $17,594 and $21,432, respectively.
Thus even after numerous adjustments the estimated
net benefits of the hypothetical change are sizable.

Implications of the
Regression Results

The output measure tested was the number of deterred crimes per unit of time. The rationale for
the use of this variable was the acceptance of crime
deterrence or law enforcement as the primary objective of the police. The two major reasons given for
this assumption were that crime prevention has been
traditionally accepted as the major function of public police agencies and that measuring output as
crimes deterred or number of arrests is far easier
than using any alternative output variables.

The tentative evidence presented raises questions about the uncritical acceptance of reduction

of the incidence of criminal activities as the major
objective of urban police departments and thus as a
guide for the allocation of police resources among
alternative programs. James Q. Wilson (cited in
Chapter 4) proposes that patrol policy stress should
be shifted from the law enforcement function to what
he calls the order maintenance function. Using this
objective, the output of patrol would shift from the
incidence of crime or the number of arrests to the
ability of the individual patrol unit to "keep the
peace" on its assigned beat. Wilson's two major arguments for this policy shift are (1) that except
for certain street crimes that require a great deal
of public and neighborhood support, the police cannot prevent most common crimes and (2) that problems
of order maintenance (gang disturbances, family
trouble, assaults, fights, drunkenness, and neighbor
trouble) are more frequent than law enforcement
problems (mainly felonies). The results of the
study indirectly support his first argument because
of the failure to observe a significant effect of
the patrolmen inputs under a variety of different
structural equations. Marginal additions to most
patrol inputs did not seem capable of affecting
most crimes significantly.

It may be, as Wilson suggests, that a change
in the current emphasis of patrol from crime prevention activities to more general community service
activities is warranted. Maintaining the peace
could become the primary objective of patrol activities while crime deterrence remains an important but
distinctly secondary goal of the organization of police resource.

INTERGOVERNMENTAL ASPECTS OF THE
DISTRIBUTION OF POLICE SERVICES

The foregoing program analyses stressed the importance of finding the effect of agency inputs on
outputs, by either experimental or statistical methods. But the distribution of agency inputs and outputs among the recipients is also an important question that the program budget should address.

Information was developed about the distribution of police services by the agency of a higher level government (the Los Angeles County Sheriff's Department) among its separate political subdivisions (cities and unincorporated areas within the county), and this information was used to examine equity problems in the financing of local police services in Los Angeles County.

The intergovernmental aspects of program budgeting are less prominent in regard to police protection than in regard to most other major urban governmental services. For instance, in education and welfare there is considerable state and federal involvement, both in financing the service and in making decisions about how it should be provided. In contrast, police service is financed and provided almost entirely at the local level. However, even at the local level there exist distinct layers of government, notably counties and cities, and the intergovernmental relationships among these local layers of government can give rise to difficult questions relating to the provision and finance of police service. The question to be dealt with was the possible inequity that may arise when a county sheriff's department provides to unincorporated areas police service that incorporated cities provide for themselves, while the sheriff's department is financed by countywide taxes. To explore this question information was developed about the distribution of sheriff's department services among the political subdivisions of the county, including a differentiation of services according to whether they were provided on a countywide basis or provided only to residents of certain areas, such as the unincorporated areas.

Neither the appropriate level of local government (county or city) for performing specific police functions nor the level of government for financing the services was questioned; rather the particular question focused on was whether some city residents are in fact paying twice, first for their own municipal police service and second for a similar service to certain other residents of the same county.

The Lakewood Plan of Contract Services

A wave of new city incorporations in Los Angeles County began with the city of Lakewood in 1954. With this incorporation was inaugurated the county's now famous Contract Services Plan, or Lakewood Plan. Under the Lakewood Plan, a city may purchase on contract from Los Angeles County most of the municipal services that a city is required by law to provide: parks and recreation, police and fire protection, sewers, planning and zoning, and so forth. A contract city may choose the level of each service to be provided to its citizens by the county, but it must pay the county government for each service provided according to a schedule of charges intended to represent the full cost of providing the service at the level chosen. The popularity of the Lakewood Plan was such that since 1954, 32 new incorporations have taken place, whereas none had occurred in the preceding 15 years. Each of the 32 newly incorporated cities employs at least some contract services, and 30 cities employ contract law enforcement.

Despite the rapid rate of incorporation, the population of the unincorporated area of Los Angeles County has grown from 872,000 in 1950 to 1,042,000 in 1969. No tax is levied in the unincorporated area of Los Angeles County specifically to match expenditures for police protection in the unincorporated area. This arrangement contrasts with the procedure for setting up special service districts or subordinate taxing areas to finance most other municipal-type services in unincorporated areas (such as fire protection, lighting, flood control, and sewer maintenance). Rather, the expenditures of the sheriff's department are met from the county general fund, to which the unincorporated area makes no special contribution for the expense of the police service it receives. However, one significant tax is paid only by the unincorporated area into the county general fund--the sales tax. The sales tax rate is uniform throughout the county, but on sales within a municipality the local share of this tax is retained by the municipality, whereas on sales within the unincorporated area the local share of

the tax goes to the county general fund. Thus, the
unincorporated area's sales tax is considered to be
its payment for municipal-type services rendered by
the county government, but no explicit attempt is
made to match the tax levy to the cost of municipal
services provided, or vice versa.

In terms of expenditure, the sheriff's department renders to the unincorporated area the single
most important municipal-type service not financed
by a special district charge. The most liberal estimate of the unincorporated area's payment for its
police protection service is that all of the local
sales tax revenue collected in the unincorporated
area is used to pay for the services it receives
from the sheriff's department. For fiscal year
1967/68 this amount was estimated to be $8,837,000.
This amount is, of course, the maximum that can be
considered the unincorporated area's payment for the
police service since other municipal-type services
must also be financed by the sales tax revenue.

Geographical Distribution of
Sheriff's Police Services

Many of the services provided by the Los Angeles Sheriff's Department are performed on a completely countywide basis, and such uniformly provided services are not examined here. Only those
services are examined that are performed exclusively, or almost exclusively, in the unincorporated
area and contract cities.

Although it is one of the five counties participating in the 5-5-5 project to adapt PPBS for
city, county, and state governments, Los Angeles
County has not yet presented its sheriff's department expenditure data on a client-oriented or geographical basis. Thus, the examination of police
service distribution and finance started with development of an estimate of the distribution of those
services that are provided on a nonuniform basis.

It is in its police protection field activities
that the sheriff's department most clearly restricts
itself to operation in the unincorporated area and

contract cities, these field activities being principally the services provided by the patrol division
and the detective division.

The sheriff's published workload statistics for
the patrol division reveal an almost exclusive concentration of patrol service in the unincorporated
area and contract cities. An approximation of
1967/68 police protection expenditures for service
to the unincorporated area not also provided on a
countywide basis would be $11,742,000 (including
employee benefits) for the patrol division alone.
This estimate does not include any sheriff's department overhead expenditures, such as those for administration, training, research, records and identification, or communications, all of which are required
to support patrol services.

The detective division annual workload statistics are not presented on the basis of geographical
location of services rendered. In the absence of
such statistics, the best available indication of
the geographical distribution of detective services
is a one-month compilation for December 1968 of the
distribution of calls for service in the detective
division. Approximately $3,174,000 (including em-
ployee benefits) can be identified as expenditures
for the exclusive benefit of the unincorporated area
and yet financed out of countywide revenues.

The sum of expenditures of the patrol and the
detective divisions for exclusive service to the unincorporated area above the service level provided
on a countywide basis is $14,916,000 (exclusive of
overhead expenses). This estimate does not include
any allowance for any other sheriff's department expenditures (that is, other than those of the patrol
and detective divisions) that are not provided on a
countywide basis, although undoubtedly some of these
other expenditures also should be included.

Subsidies to Contract Cities
and Unincorporated Areas

Sales tax revenue collected in the unincorporated area for 1967/68 amounted to $8,837,000.
Since this sales tax revenue is the unincorporated

area's only form of payment for municipal-type services rendered by the county government, the sheriff's department expenditures for exclusive service
to the unincorporated area are $6,080,000 more than
the taxes collected in the unincorporated area to
pay for all municipal-type services provided to the
unincorporated area by the county government, and
this excess of expenditures over tax revenues is a
form of subsidy to the unincorporated area. The estimate of a subsidy of $6,080,000, or $5.50 per
capita, is conservative because the county government provides other municipal-type services to the
unincorporated area, chiefly local neighborhood
parks, that should also be financed by the taxes
collected only in the unincorporated area.

The charges made to contract cities for police
protection are based only on the service rendered
by the sheriff's patrol division. Cities may contract for any desired level of patrol service, the
unit of service being a patrol car on 24-hour duty
seven days a week, with two 8-hour shifts of two
men each (night and morning shifts) and one 8-hour
shift of one man (day shift). The contract city
can purchase whatever amount of service it desires,
above a certain minimum, and pay accordingly. The
rate charged per car has consistently been a matter
of contention between the contract cities and the
independent cities, the former maintaining that the
rate is too high and the latter maintaining that
the rate is too low. Between 1958 and 1969, the
per car charge was increased from $78,400 to $132,741
per year.

The per car rate is purported to be a charge
for the marginal cost of providing patrol service to
the contract cities. None of the plant cost of the
sheriff's stations is counted in the per car rate.

The basic question of defining the marginal cost
to be charged can lead to a wide variation in interpretation. Even the full station cost does not include any charge for the sheriff's departmental and
divisional overhead or for central support services,
such as the records bureau, crime laboratory, training, or headquarters detectives.

Even the highest figure meant to represent the
marginal cost of contract law enforcement service is

certainly an understatement of the actual long-run
marginal cost, for it includes no charge for overhead expenditures within the sheriff's department.
It can confidently be stated that even the highest
cost figure calculated by the Los Angeles County
Auditor-Controller ($236,033 per car) is less than
the true marginal cost of providing law enforcement
service in the contract cities. Thus, for a payment
of $132,741 (the recommended 1968/69 patrol car
rate) a contract city may purchase law enforcement
services whose marginal cost is at least $236,033
(the full station marginal cost calculated by the
auditor-controller).

A rough minimum estimate of the amount of the
total subsidy to contract cities through underpricing of sheriff's services can be made by multiplying
the per car subsidy by the total number of cars allocated by the sheriff's department to the contract
cities. The only year for which detailed auditor-
controller figures for alternative concepts of per
car costs are available is fiscal 1968/69. In that
year, the annual full station marginal cost of contract services on a per car basis was $236,033. The
charge per car recommended by the chief administrative officer and approved by the board of supervisors as the appropriate calculation was $132,741.
Thus the annual cost per car exceeded the recommended
charge by $103,292.

This estimate refers only to sheriff's department costs at the station houses plus a factor for
general county overhead. No charge is made for the
general departmentwide costs of running a modern law
enforcement organization, including a training academy, crime laboratory, headquarters staff, and so
forth. Thus, this estimate of subsidy to contract
cities is undoubtedly conservative.

Because the estimates refer to different years,
the estimate of a $6,100,000 law enforcement sub-
sidy to the contract cities in the fiscal year
1968/69 is not immediately comparable to the estimate of a $6,080,000 subsidy to the unincorporated
areas in fiscal 1967/68. However, there is reason
to believe that the subsidy to contract cities would
not have been much lower in 1967/68 than in 1968/69.

To ensure a conservative estimate of the
1967/68 subsidy to contract cities for police service an alternative estimate can be made using the
same technique that was employed in estimating the
subsidy to the unincorporated area: calculation of
the services provided to the contract cities by the
detective and patrol divisions above the service
level provided on a countywide basis and comparison
of the cost of this exclusive service with the price
paid for it by the contract cities. On this basis
the cost of patrol and detective services provided
to the contract cities above the level provided on
a countywide basis was $11,532,000. The sheriff's
1967/68 revenue for contract law enforcement was
only $6,340,000. The result is a subsidy estimate
of $5,192,000. Much of the discrepancy between
this figure and the $6,100,000 figure for 1968/69
obtained from the auditor-controller's cost study
can be attributed to the fact that the auditor-
controller's cost includes a general county overhead charge of 12.6 percent in addition to the
sheriff's department costs at the station houses.
If the same overhead factor is added to the costs
just calculated for the services of the patrol and
detective divisions to the contract cities, the
amount of the resulting subsidy is even higher than
that given by the auditor-controller's cost per car
figures.

Implications of the Intergovernmental Analysis

It is conservatively estimated that the subsidy for law enforcement to the unincorporated area
of Los Angeles County was $6,080,000 in 1967/68.
On a similar basis it was estimated that the subsidy to the cities that contract for police services
from the Los Angeles County Sheriff's Department is
$5,122,000. This $11,272,000 subsidy is financed
by countywide taxation, and cities that provide
their own police protection bear a large part of
the cost of the subsidy.

When distributional information that a client-
oriented program budget would provide is not available, the unintentional intergovernmental subsidies
of the sort described here are more likely to go
unnoticed. Thus, quite aside from the goal of
greater efficiency in producing government services,
an important goal of the program budgeting effort
should be to help answer the questions, Who gets
what? and Who pays for it? Before one can even begin to ponder the equity or legality of any existing arrangement, there is a need for information on
how services are actually distributed and financed.
This is the chief justification for an agency program budget format with iteration for relevant geographic or political subdivisions.

CHAPTER 1

1. U.S. Bureau of the Census, Current Population Reports, series P-23, Special Studies (formerly
Technical Studies), No. 27, "Trends in Social and
Economic Conditions in Metropolitan Areas" (Washington: Government Printing Office, 1969).

2. National Commission on the Causes and Prevention of Violence, Violent Crime (New York: George
Braziller, 1969), p. 35.

3. President's Commission on Law Enforcement
and Administration of Justice, Task Force Report:
Crime and Its Impact--An Assessment (Washington:
Government Printing Office, 1967), p. 55.

4. Marvin Wolfgang, "Urban Crime," in James Q.
Wilson, ed., The Metropolitan Enigma, pp. 245-81.
Also see Chapter 4 of this volume.

5. President's Commission, Task Force Report:
Crime and Its Impact, p. 55. The data refer to the
year 1965.

6. Werner Z. Hirsch, "State and Local Government Program Budgeting," Papers of the Regional
Science Association, XVIV (1966), 147-63.

7. Selma J. Mushkin, PPB for the Cities:
Problems and Next Steps," in John P. Crecine, ed.,
Financing the Metropolis (Beverly Hills: Sage Pub-
lications, 1970), pp. 265 and 266.

8. Aaron Wildavsky, "Rescuing Policy Analysis
from PPBS," in U.S. Congress, Joint Economic Committee, The Analysis and Evaluation of Public Expenditures: The PPB System, III (Washington: Government Printing Office, 1969), 843 and 844.

9. Isabel V. Sawhill, "The Role of Social Indicators and Social Reporting in Public Expenditure
Decisions," in U.S. Congress, Joint Economic Committee, The Analysis and Evaluation of Public Expenditures: The PPB System, I (Washington: Government Printing Office, 1969), p. 483.

10. Russell L. Ackoff, "Toward Quantitative
Evaluation of Urban Services," in Howard G. Schaller,

ed., _Public Expenditure Decisions in the Urban Community_ (Washington: Resources for the Future, 1963), p. 108.

11. Amitai Etzioni, _Modern Organizations_ (Englewood Cliffs, N.J.: Prentice-Hall, 1964), pp. 9 and 10.

CHAPTER 2

1. Amitai Etzioni, _Modern Organizations_ (Englewood Cliffs, N.J.: Prentice-Hall, 1964).

2. For literary purposes, the words _goal_, _mission_, and _objective_ will be used interchangeably to refer to the ends of police activities, as opposed to means. The term _objective_ is preferred when a specific measurable or operational meaning is intended. The term _output_ refers to the final product the police agency produces in pursuing its goals. Examples of police outputs are a reduction in crime, a reduction in traffic accidents, or the provision of general community services. A private sector analogy may illustrate this distinction: for instance, the goal of a baking company is maximum profits, whereas its output is loaves of bread.

3. O. W. Wilson, _Police Administration_, 2d ed. (New York: McGraw-Hill, 1963), pp. 4 and 25.

4. _Ibid_., p. 22.

5. Richard B. Hoffman, "The Transfer of Space and Computer Technology to Urban Security," _AFIPS Conference Proceedings_, XXIX (1966), 524.

6. Gordon E. Misner, "The Urban Police Mission," _Issues in Criminology_, III (Summer 1967), 37.

7. Los Angeles County Department of the Sheriff, "State of Objectives and Goals" (memorandum, n.d.).

8. City of Los Angeles, Controller, "Budget, Fiscal Year 1967/68," p. 59.

9. See, for example, Jerome Hall, _Comparative Law and Social Theory_ (Baton Rouge: Louisiana State University Press, 1963), p. 78.

10. President's Commission on Law Enforcement and Administration of Justice, _Task Force Report: Crime and Its Impact--An Assessment_ (Washington: Government Printing Office, 1967), p. 44.

11. _More valuable_ is meant in the sense that the amount the original owner would have to be paid

to be compensated for an item's loss is more than
the great amount the thief would be willing to pay
for the same item (whether used or resold by the
thief). Wealth is not intended, here, to be synonymous with welfare. In regard to illegally transferred property, measurement of welfare involves
interpersonal comparisons of utility, while measurement of wealth involves only the individual's dollar valuation of the property.

   12. This point is suggested by Gary Becker,
"Crime and Punishment: An Economic Approach,"
Journal of Political Economy, LXXVI (March–April
1968), 171.

   13. B. M. Fleisher, "The Effect of Income on
Delinquency," American Economic Review, LVI (March
1966), 118-37.

   14. This description of the incentives to
property crime sounds highly artificial. However,
much property crime is undoubtedly the product of
economic calculation. For instance, Edwin H.
Sutherland takes this position in his classic work,
The Professional Thief ([Chicago: University of
Chicago Press, 1937], p. 217):

> The profession of theft, with the char-
> acteristics which have been described,
> is organized around the effort to se-
> cure money with relative safety. In
> this respect, also, the profession of
> theft is similar to other professions
> and to other permanent groups. For
> money and safety are values inherent
> in Western civilization, and the
> methods which are used to realize these
> objectives are adjusted to the general
> culture.

   15. Any utility the arsonist or vandal may
derive from the destruction of the property is not
considered here as a benefit.

   16. In firms in which there is considerable
theft by employees, it is possible that nominal
wages will be somewhat lower as a compensation. In
such cases real wages would be the sum of "legal"
and "illegal" income.

   17. President's Commission, Task Force Report:
Crime and Its Impact, pp. 57 and 58.

18.   Ibid., p. 45.

19.   Expected cost is used in the sense of the expected value (mean of a probability distribution of the cost to an individual of a crime against his person).

20.   President's Commission, Task Force Report: Crime and Its Impact, p. 52.

21.   National Advisory Commission on Civil Disorders, Report of the National Advisory Commission on Civil Disorders (New York: Bantam Books, 1968), p. 120.

22.   California Governor's Commission on the Los Angeles Riots, Violence in the City--An End or a Beginning? (Los Angeles: Office of the Governor, 1965).

23.   It is assumed that preventing injuries or death to the perpetrator of a traffic accident him-self is, like suicide prevention, a legitimate goal of a police agency.

24.   The National Safety Council estimates that improper driving is a cause in 91 percent of all motor vehicle accidents. National Safety Council, Accident Facts (Chicago, 1968), p. 48.

25.   Ibid., p. 5.

26.   President's Commission, Task Force Report: Science and Technology (Washington: Government Printing Office, 1967).

27.   Los Angeles Police Department, "Statistical Digest" (1967), p. 2.

28.   Part One offenses are forcible rape, homicide, robbery, burglary, auto theft, aggravated assault, and larceny theft.

29.   Of course, a reporting phenomenon is encountered. Only insofar as the same percentage of total crimes is reported to the police in each division can reported crime rates be used for comparison, and even then the crimes are not weighted by seriousness.

30.   Fleisher, for instance, found income, unemployment rate, and family structure to be significant variables in explaining variations in juvenile delinquency rates among neighborhoods within a large city and among communities ("The Effect of Income on Delinquency").

31. Police agencies explicitly recognize this and often separate these crimes from those which they call repressible or suppressible crimes. The latter tend to be mainly crimes committed on the streets or in public buildings.

32. This is sometimes called the victimization rate.

33. Carl S. Shoup, "Standards for Distributing a Free Governmental Service: Crime Prevention," Public Finance, XIX, 4, 383-92.

34. The data were collected and organized by the Advance Planning Group of the LAPD and reorganized by the authors. The original table used by the LAPD is reproduced in Supplement 1 of this chapter in Table 2.8. It is constructed by allocating to each goal the tasks performed in each operating division.

35. The Philadelphia Program Budget for 1970 (Supplement 3 of this chapter) allocates all traffic expenditures to the city's transportation program. Traffic is not handled this way in the proposed Los Angeles budget because of two unique characteristics of the city: (1) Freeways inside Los Angeles City are policed by state officers and (2) the city does not control the mass transit system--and even if the city did, the "system" is virtually nonexistent.

36. Of course, some analysis involves evaluation of entirely new programs wherein both the existence and size of the program is involved.

37. U.S. Congress, Joint Economic Committee, The Analysis and Evaluation of Public Expenditures: The PPB System (a compendium of papers), 91st Cong., 1st sess., 1969, XXX, 844.

CHAPTER 3

1. Edward F. Fennessy, Jr., et al., The Technical Content of State and Community Police Traffic Services Programs (Hartford: Travellers Research Center, 1968), p. xvii.

2. Ibid., p. 135.

3. The State of the Art of Traffic Safety (Boston: A. D. Little, 1966), p. 251.

4. John A. Gardiner, Traffic and the Police, Variations in Law-Enforcement Policy (Cambridge: Harvard University Press, 1969), p. 8.

5. Ibid., pp. 158 and 159.
6. This form of public service production functions is suggested by Werner Z. Hirsch, "The Supply of Urban Public Services," in Harvey S. Perloff and Lowden Wingo, Jr., eds., Issues in Urban Economics (Baltimore: Johns Hopkins Press, 1968), pp. 485-92.
7. For example, Barna found that only one firm in four of a sample investigated made ex post facto investigations of the profitability of investment projects. Tibor Barna, Investment and Growth Policies in British Industrial Firms (Cambridge: Cambridge University Press, 1962), p. 20.
8. A good example is Martin T. Katzman, "Distribution and Production in a Big City Elementary School System," Yale Economic Essays, VIII, 1 (Spring 1968), 201-56.
9. A good example of the use of technical data to estimate the relationship between the cost of inputs and the output of criminal information is Ronald Finkles, "Analysis of the Costs of a Centralized Versus Decentralized National Inquiry System," in President's Commission on Law Enforcement and Administration of Justice, Task Force Report: Science and Technology (Washington: Government Printing Office, 1967), pp. 186-97.
10. Ronald A. Fisher, The Design of Experiments, 7th ed. (Edinburgh: Oliver and Boyd, 1960), p. 8.
11. Yet even in the field of welfare, experimentation has been strongly recommended, and an important experiment is now under way. Guy H. Orcutt and Alice G. Orcutt, "Incentive and Disincentive Experimentation for Income Maintenance Policy Purposes," American Economic Review, LVIII, 4 (September 1968), 754-72.
12. Also, an important part of this local autonomy in manpower allocation is the fact that experimental reallocations can be made with little or no attendant publicity. This is important because public knowledge of the experimental design can easily violate the element of experimental control, in which all factors other than the one under investigation should be kept the same. For instance, widespread publicity concerning increased traffic law enforcement patrols in certain areas of a city

might have definite effects on driver behavior even
if the advertised enforcement did not take place.
This suggests that there are three possible enforcement experiments: increased enforcement with publicity; increased enforcement without publicity;
and publicity of increased enforcement without any
actual increase. The results of each of the three
would be interesting, and the police are in an unusually good position to undertake any one of them.

13. For example, a study by Raymond Hooker
attempted to relate annual expenditures of the
Wyoming Highway Patrol to the annual number of
motor vehicle accidents in Wyoming by statistical
regressions. While such results are useful for
determining whether total expenditures should be
increased or decreased, they say nothing about how
such expenditures can be most efficiently used.
Raymond W. Hooker, Traffic Accident Costs and the
Effectiveness of Highway Safety Expenditures in
Wyoming (Laramie: University of Wyoming, Division
of Business and Economic Research, 1966). Hooker's
statistical techniques have been criticized by Hans
C. Joksch, "A Critique of a Study by Hooker of
Highway Patrol Effect on Accidents," Traffic Digest
and Review (June 1969).

14. Traffic regulation actually accounts for
nearly one-fourth of all nonoverhead and nonsupport
expenditures. "City of Los Angeles Budget, Fiscal
Year 1968-1969," p. 60.

15. The State of the Art of Traffic Safety,
p. 250; and Fennessy, Jr., et al., The Technical
Content of State and Community Police Traffic Services Programs, pp. xvii and 135.

16. The arrest index is the ratio of traffic
arrests to injury-accidents. It is equal to the
enforcement index (traffic convictions/injury-
accidents) times the conviction rate (traffic con-
victions/traffic arrests). Since the conviction
rate in Los Angeles in recent years has averaged
0.98 or 0.99, the enforcement and arrest indexes
are almost identical.

17. O. W. Wilson, Police Administration, 2d
ed. (New York: McGraw-Hill, 1963), p. 369.

18. Some reservations concering this sort of
experimental data will be expressed below.

19. The derivation of this figure is explained in detail in Supplement 1 of this chapter.

20. California Division of Highways, Traffic Department, "Unit Cost Factors Used in Economic Analysis" (Sacramento, February 11, 1965).

21. The methods of deriving these estimates and the resulting figures are discussed in Gerald W. Skiles, "The Quantitative Measurement of Traffic Service" (Master's thesis, UCLA, 1968), pp. 52 and 53; and James R. Nelson, "The Value of Travel Time," in Samuel B. Chase, Jr., ed., Problems in Public Expenditure Analysis (Washington: The Brookings Institution, 1968).

22. U.S. Department of Transportation, Economic Consequences of Automobile Accident Injuries, I (Washington: Government Printing Office, 1970), 2.

23. California Division of Highways, "Direct Costs of California State Highway Accidents" (1967), p. 2. This figure also includes an allowance for unreported accidents.

24. Ibid., p. 3.

25. The inclusion of damage awards and settlements makes the "direct cost" estimate something of a hybrid concept, an allowance for lost earnings being made in some cases and not in others. It would seem more logical to make an allowance for lost earnings in all cases or not in any. However, the data supplied by the California Division of Highways do not permit the deduction of damage awards and settlements. An economic loss of $2,200 per injury in 1963 was found in a study of automobile accidents in British Columbia. In that study, economic loss was defined as expenses incurred (medical and hospital expense, repair of automobiles, and other expenses resulting from the automobile accident), expected future medical expenses, and income loss. R. A. Holmes, "On the Economic Welfare of Victims of Automobile Accidents," American Economic Review (March 1970), pp. 143-52.

26. Perhaps there would be agreement on the point that individuals do not place an infinite value on their own lives, as evidenced by the many small risks (including those of driving) that people are accustomed to take daily.

27. California Division of Highways, "Direct Costs of California State Highway Accidents," p. 2. Since there may be more than one fatality per fatal accident, a lower estimate of cost per fatality is implied. In urban areas in California, the average number of fatalities per fatal accident is 1.15 (p. 14).

28. U.S. Department of Transportation, Economic Consequences of Automobile Accident Injuries, p. 27.

29. U.S. Department of Health, Education and Welfare, Motor Vehicle Injury Prevention Program (Washington: Government Printing Office, 1966). The estimate is based on calculations for each five-year age and sex group on the basis of 1964 life tables, 1964 labor force participation rates adjusted for full employment, 1964 mean earnings, 1964 imputed value of housewives' services, 1964 housekeeping rates, and an annual net effective discount rate of 3 percent. The estimate is biased downward by assuming that ages will remain at 1964 levels, but perhaps the low 3 percent discount rate compensates for this (p. 26).

30. D. J. Reynolds, "The Cost of Road Accidents," Journal of the Royal Statistical Society, CXIX, Part 4 (1956), 393-408.

31. Jacques Thedie and Claude Abraham, "Economic Aspect of Road Accidents," Traffic Engineering and Control, II, 10 (February 1961), 589-95.

32. Thomas C. Schelling, "The Life You Save May Be Your Own," in Samuel B. Chase, ed., Problems in Public Expenditure Analysis (Washington: The Brookings Institution, 1968), pp. 127-62.

33. For instance, see R. M. Michaels, "The Effects of Enforcement on Traffic Behavior," Public Roads (December 1960), pp. 109-13. For a discussion of controls, see J. W. Novak and R. P. Shumate, "The Use of 'Control Groups' in Highway Accident Research—A Field Study," Traffic Safety Research Review (June 1961).

34. This effect would be similar to the increase in certain reported crimes, particularly vice crimes, often associated with increase in deterrent patrol manpower.

35. If the two beats on which the number of officers did not vary are also included and all

eight beats are ranked according to the same variables, r = 0.834, which is significant at the 0.01
level.

36.   These crimes were theft from a motor vehicle, burglary from a motor vehicle, shoplifting,
theft of a vehicle, petty theft, grand theft, burglary, assault and battery, malicious mischief, and
rape.

37.   The formula for the length of time, T
(in minutes), required to travel 1 mile by a vehicle traveling V mph is $T = 60 \times 1/V$. The increase in T associated with a 1 mph reduction in V
is $T = 60/V-1 - 60/V = 60/V^2-V$. Thus, the effect
of a 1 mph change in speed on total travel time is
greater for lower initial speeds. For instance,
with the same traffic volume along a given road
length, the dollar benefit in terms of reduced
travel time is greater for an increase of average
speed from 20 to 21 mph than it is for an increase
from 60 to 61 mph. Urban surface street speeds
are, of course, closer to the former speed range.

CHAPTER 4
1.   The theoretical analysis of the behavior
of potential violators is developed to some extent
in Chapter 2.

2.   The production function concept is discussed, in general, in Chapter 3.

3.   An additional class of illegal acts, the
vice and moral code violations, should not be included in the measure, for quite different reasons.

4.   Kansas City Police Department, "1968 Survey
of Municipal Police Departments" (October 31, 1968),
Table 5. However, there has been a marked trend
toward increasing the number of two-man units in
peak crime periods during the evening hours and employing one-man units during days. The program
analysis below will treat this issue in greater
depth.

5.   For a discussion of this point see Chapter 2.

6.   Los Angeles Police Department, Office of
the Commander, Patrol Bureau "Memorandum Number 10,"
November 3, 1968.

7.   An unpublished report of the Los Angeles
County Sheriff, n.d.

8.   St. Louis Police Department, <u>Allocation</u>
<u>of Patrol Manpower in the St. Louis Police Depart-</u>
<u>ment</u>, O.L.E.A. Grant #39 (July 1966), I.

9.   President's Commission on Law Enforcement
and Administration of Justice, <u>Task Force Report:</u>
<u>Science and Technology</u> (Washington: Government
Printing Office, 1967), p. 12.

10.   <u>Ibid</u>., pp. 95 and 96.

11.   The discussion that follows in the text
is based in part on a model originally presented in
D. G. Olson, "Study of the Preventive Patrol Function," in <u>Allocation of Resources in the Chicago</u>
<u>Police Department</u>, third and fourth quarterly re-
ports (Chicago Police Department, Operations Research Task Force, January 1969), pp. 12-18.

12.   Of course, the change in n need not be in
units of whole patrolmen since, in principle, n
could be further divided into patrol man-hours per
unit.

13.   President's Commission, <u>Task Force Report:</u>
<u>Crime and Its Impact--An Assessment</u> (Washington:
Government Printing Office, 1967), p. 831.

14.   President's Commission, <u>Task Force Report:</u>
<u>Science and Technology</u>, pp. 18 and 19.

15.   The technique of combining cross-sectional
with time-series data is known as a pooled cross
section.

16.   An excellent review of the limitations of
the FBI data is given in State of California, Bureau of Criminal Statistics, "Crime and Delinquency
in California, 1967," pp. 17-28; see also President's Commission, <u>Task Force Report: Crime and</u>
<u>Its Impact</u>, pp. 123-37.

17.   State of California, Bureau of Criminal
Statistics, <u>Crime and Delinquency in California</u>,
<u>1967</u>.

18.   For a discussion of the definitions and
nature of each of these crimes see any recent <u>Uni-</u>
<u>form Crime Report</u>. Petty larcenies (under $50 in
value) are included even though these are not included in the FBI index of Part One offenses. The
crimes included correspond closely to those selected
crimes in the LAPD patrol bureau formula.

19.   However, robbery involves a high probability of personal injury.

20. It is probably true that regressions of
the total crime indexes will not show any significantly greater effect of police input variables
than the visible crime index alone. However, they
are included to avoid overlooking any significant
effects of police patrol.

21. Isabel V. Sawhill, "The Role of Social
Indicators and Social Reporting in Public Expendi-
ture Decisions," in U.S. Congress, Joint Economic
Committee, The Analysis and Evaluation of Public
Expenditures: The PPB System, I (Washington:
Government Printing Office, 1969), 20.

22. Phillip H. Ennis, "Criminal Victimization
in the U.S.: A Report of a National Survey," in
President's Commission, Field Survey II (Washington:
Government Printing Office, 1967), Table 26, p. 46.

23. Ibid.

24. Clearly, deterrence is produced not just
by the police but also by the entire criminal justice
system. Moreover, arrest rates may be affected by
police programs other than visible patrol. The
assumption must be made that any increase in arrest
rates is attributable only to visible patrol inputs
that appear in the regression equation.

25. The survey was conducted in December 1968
and January 1969. Only two cities failed to respond,
and two responses were not usable.

26. Personal interview in January 1969 with
Chief Parsonson of Los Angeles County Department of
Sheriff, Patrol Division.

27. Allocation of Patrol Manpower in the St.
Louis Police Department, O.L.E.A. Grant #39 (July
1966).

28. State of California, Division of Highways,
"California County Roads and City Streets--Progress
and Needs, 1965," Table 12, pp. 114-22.

29. U.S. Bureau of the Census, County and City
Data Book, 1962 (Washington: Government Printing
Office, 1962).

30. Los Angeles County Auditor, "Taxpayers'
Guide for Fiscal Year 1967/68," pp. 78-83; and State
of California, "Annual Report of the State Board of
Equalization, Fiscal Year 1965/66," Table 9, pp. A-20
and A-24.

31. The one-tailed test is appropriate because of the hypothesized negative influence of police inputs on crime.

32. This assumes that the two groups are equally "productive" in criminal activities and have equal subjective probabilities of being apprehended.

33. There is considerable evidence that both male unemployment rates (B. M. Fleisher, "The Effect of Income on Delinquency," American Economic Review, LVI [March 1966] and "The Effect of Unemployment on Delinquency," Journal of Political Economy, LXXI [December 1963]) and male labor force participation rates (L. Phillips, H. L. Votey, and D. Maxwell, "Labor Market Conditions and Economic Crimes," paper presented to Western Economic Association Meeting in Long Beach, California, August 22, 1969) significantly affect juvenile arrest rates (and, presumably, overall crime rates); participation rates are thought to have a greater effect than unemployment rates.

34. Since none of the police input variables is fixed in the conceptual formulations, all of them should be considered endogenous.

35. There are several estimating techniques to handle this source of bias. They involve estimating the model as a system of simultaneous equations; these include using the reduced forms of the original equations, using a recursive system with lagged variables of police inputs, and the two-stage least-squares technique.

36. J. Johnston, Econometric Methods (New York: McGraw-Hill, 1963), p. 234.

37. In the Municipal Yearbook (years cited) it is noted that in 1955, 20 percent of the major urban police departments reporting used one-man cars only and 20 percent used two-man cars only. In 1964, 41 percent of the cities sampled used one-man and only 5 percent two-man. The 1967 Kansas City survey (Kansas City Police Department, "1968 Survey of Municipal Police Departments") shows that approximately 50 percent of the largest U.S. cities maintain a mix of mostly one-man units on day watches. The rest of the sample is evenly divided

between all one-man or all two-man (that is, 25 percent each).

In the sample of smaller California cities,
the independent police departments used primarily
one-man units. Approximately 65 percent used that
form as opposed to 20 percent that used a mix of
one-man and two-man. Those contract cities that
purchase patrol services from the Los Angeles County
Sheriff's Department receive all one-man units during the daylight hours and all two-man during the
evening and night-time hours.

38. See Chapter 2 for a more complete discussion of the transfer versus real aspects of crime
costs and of the many costs and losses (both private
and external) associated with various offenses.

39. U.S. Federal Bureau of Investigation,
Uniform Crime Report, 1967 (Washington: Government
Printing Office, 1968), p. 15.

40. Several methods for weighting crimes to
make them comparable have been proposed. One method
(proposed in Sawhill, "The Role of Social Indicators,"
p. 480) would be to weight each crime occurring (or
weight the dollar loss) by the average length of
prison sentence for that crime type. (The length
of prison sentence would be better than the average
time served in prison since the latter reflects
factors other than "seriousness.") Sellin and
Wolfgang (Thorsten Sellin and Marvin Wolfgang, The
Measurement of Delinquency [New York: John Wiley,
1964], p. 401) suggest an elaborate scheme of
weights. In their proposed scheme a single-victim
robbery (of $100) involving a weapon and injury to
the victim would be assigned a weight of 13; a
single victim burglary (of $100) would be given a
weight of 3.

41. James Q. Wilson, Varieties of Police Behavior (Cambridge, Mass.: Harvard University Press,
1968), pp. 291-93.

42. Allocation of Patrol Manpower, pp. 2 and 3.

CHAPTER 5

1. The question who should render urban services has been investigated in a report by the
Advisory Commission on Intergovernmental Relations,

<u>Performance of Urban Functions: Local and Areawide</u>
(Washington: Government Printing Office, 1963).
The same question, and the question of separating
the financing and physical rendering of services,
has been discussed by Werner Z. Hirsch, "Local Versus Areawide Urban Government Services," <u>National</u>
<u>Tax Journal</u>, XVII, 4 (December 1964).

    2. <u>Contract law enforcement</u> refers to provi-
sion of law enforcement services on a contract basis.
<u>Contract cities</u> are cities that purchase law enforce-
ment services from Los Angeles County. <u>Independent</u>
<u>cities</u> are those that maintain their own independent
police departments.

    3. League of California Cities, Los Angeles
Division, <u>Report of the City-County Committee</u> (Los
Angeles: League of California Cities, December 13,
1950), pp. 1-4.

    4. Assembly Interim Committee on Municipal
and County Government, <u>Financing Local Government</u>
<u>in Los Angeles County</u> (Sacramento: California State
Legislature, January 17, 1953), pp. 69 and 70.

    5. <u>Ibid</u>., p. 9.

    6. <u>Ibid</u>., p. 93.

    7. <u>Ibid</u>., p. 9.

    8. Assembly Interim Committee on Municipal
and County Government, <u>Final Report</u> (Sacramento:
California State Legislature, March 27, 1953), p. 5.

    9. Assembly Interim Committee, <u>Financing Local</u>
<u>Government</u>, p. 82.

    10. Three cities still maintain independent
health departments but are compensated by the county
for the services that would ordinarily be performed
by the county. Another city (Beverly Hills) chooses
to maintain and pay for its own health department
independently of the county.

    11. A description of the Lakewood Plan of gov-
ernment is given by Samuel K. Gove, "The Lakewood
Plan," Commission Papers of the Institute of Government and Public Affairs (Urbana: University of
Illinois, Institute of Government and Public Affairs, May 1961).

    12. For instance, Hirsch suggests that "in
terms of economies of scale, governments serving
from 50,000 to 100,000 urbanites might be most

efficient." Werner Z. Hirsch, "The Supply of Urban
Public Services," in Harvey S. Perloff and Lowden
Wingo, Jr., eds., Issues in Urban Economics (Balti-
more: Johns Hopkins Press, 1968), p. 509.

    13. Criteria by which to judge the distribu-
tion of power of collective choice among political
jurisdictions are suggested by Jerome Rothenberg,
"Local Decentralization and the Theory of Optimal
Government," a paper presented at the Universities-
NBER Conference on Economics of Public Output,
April 26-27, 1968. Very similar criteria were also
discussed by Hirsch in "Urban Government Services."

    14. Winston W. Crouch, "Conflict and Co-
operation Among Local Governments in the Metropolis,"
Annals of the American Academy of Political and Social Science, CCCLIX (May 1965), 68.

    15. Alan Williams, Public Finances and Budget-
ary Policy (London: George Allen and Unwin, 1963),
pp. 171-81. This work has been further developed
by Ronald Teeples, "A Model of a Matching Grant-in-
Aid Program with External Effects," National Tax
Journal (December 1969).

    16. However, another important county service
to the unincorporated areas is the provision of local neighborhood parks.

    17. Los Angeles County, "Proposed County Bud-
get, Fiscal Year Ending 30 June 1970," p. 13.

    18. U.S. Bureau of the Census, Criminal Jus-
tice, Expenditure and Employment for Selected Large
Governmental Units, 1966/67 (Washington: Government
Printing Office, 1968), p. 25, and the President's
Commission on Law Enforcement and Administration of
Justice, Task Force Report: The Police (Washington:
Government Printing Office, 1967), pp. 103-5.

    19. O. W. Wilson, Police Administration, 2d
ed. (New York: McGraw-Hill, 1963), p. 231.

    20. Los Angeles County Department of the
Sheriff, "Assignment of Personnel, 1968/69," pp. 35
and 63. Total noncustodial personnel was found by
excluding personnel in the jail and corrections divisions.

    21. Los Angeles County Department of the
Sheriff, "Criminal Activity Report, Calendar Year
1968," p. 1.

22. Los Angeles County Department of the
Sheriff, "Biennial Report, 1965-67," p. 30.

23. Los Angeles County Department of the
Sheriff, "Statistical Summary, Fiscal Year 1967/68."
The data are presented in separate breakdowns for
each sheriff's station area, pp. 41-221. They have
been summed to show the overall breakdown.

24. Ibid., p. 45.

25. Los Angeles County Department of the
Sheriff, "Statement of Expenditures, Fiscal Year
1967/68," p. 12.

26. The coefficient of correlation between
cases handled and personnel assigned at each sheriff's station is 0.98. The coefficient of correlation between station population served and station
personnel is 0.94. Since expenditures are distributed in almost exactly the same pattern as personnel, these high correlation coefficients imply that
either cases handled or population served is a good
indicator of the breakdown of sheriff's expenditures
according to geographic location.

27. The 25 percent figure for 1968/69 was
supplied by the Los Angeles County Auditor-
Controller's Office. The 20 percent figure is recommended by the sheriff's department for application
to most police department budgets for 1967/68. (See
Los Angeles County Department of the Sheriff, Research and Development Bureau, "Preliminary Survey
of California Expenditures for Law Enforcement, Selected Cities in Los Angeles County, 1967/68 Fiscal
Year.")

28. Los Angeles County Department of the
Sheriff, Records and Data Bureau, Data Processing
Section, "Statistical Reporting of Services Rendered,
December 1968" (July 23, 1969; prepared at the re-
quest of the authors).

29. Los Angeles County Department of the
Sheriff, "Statement of Expenditures, Fiscal Year
1967/68," p. 11.

30. For instance, the unincorporated enclave
served by one sheriff's station (West Hollywood) has
a population density of 13,500 per square mile,
while the average population density of the contract
cities is 4,000 per square mile. Los Angeles County

Department of the Sheriff, "Statistical Summary, Fiscal Year 1967/68," pp. 39 and 215.

31. Misner and Hoffman's research in one city "revealed that 70.9 percent of the 'called-for services' involves miscellaneous public services, ranging anywhere from a nuisance call to assisting a resident who has been inadvertently locked out of her home." Gordon E. Misner and Richard B. Hoffman, "Police Resource Allocation," Working Paper 73 (Berkeley: University of California, Institute of Urban and Regional Development, Center for Planning and Development Research, 1967), p. 9.

32. This argument is made in a "Report Re Alleged City-Unincorporated Area Tax Inequity," prepared by Los Angeles County Chief Administrative Officer (February 5, 1965). This report mentions disproportionately heavy concentration of welfare recipients and jail bookings among residents of cities.

33. Hirsch, "Urban Government Services," p. 336

34. Only California, Maryland, New York, and South Carolina authorize counties to provide police protection services to a portion rather than to all of the county and to levy a tax on the assessed value of the property within that area to pay for such services. U.S. Bureau of the Census, 1967 Census of Governments, I, "Governmental Organization" (Washington: Government Printing Office, 1968), 314, 366, 404, and 428. This suggests that the problem described in Los Angeles is widespread.

35. This procedure has been instituted in New Castle County, Delaware. A recent reorganization act for New Castle County provides for a "local service budget" for the unincorporated area. "Under the terms of the act, the people in cities in New Castle County which are providing services that the county also provides, such as police, are not obligated to pay taxes in support of the county service." University of Delaware, Division of Urban Affairs, "Police Protection in Wilmington" (August 1967), pp. 40-41.

36. Although inequities created by county-city overlapping have to be focused on, similar problems can result from overlapping at higher

levels. For instance, the hierarchy of police organizations includes city police departments, county
sheriffs, state highway patrols, the FBI, and Inter-
pol. As an instance of the problems for cities
created by such overlapping at higher levels, until
1969 the California Highway Patrol provided all
freeway traffic law enforcement in the state except
in Los Angeles, where freeway traffic laws were enforced by the Los Angeles Police Department. This
is another clear example of a municipal government's
performing, at its own expense, a service provided
to other areas at general state expense.

37. President's Commission, Task Force Report:
The Police, p. 68.

38. Los Angeles City-County Local Government
Consolidation Study Commission, "Integration of the
Law Enforcement Services of Los Angeles County"
(June 1, 1956), page h.

39. Los Angeles County Chief Administrative
Officer, "Contract Law Enforcement Services Base
Rate" (February 27, 1969), p. 2.

40. Report to the Los Angeles County Grand
Jury by its auditors, Lybrand Ross Bros. & Mont-
gomery (September 20, 1962), p. 4.

41. Ibid.

42. Los Angeles County Chief Administrative
Officer, "Contract Law Enforcement Services Base
Rate" (memorandum, February 27, 1969), p. 4.

43. Los Angeles County Department of the
Sheriff, "Statistical Summary, Fiscal Year 1967/68,"
p. 95.

44. Orange County Office of Auditor-Controller,
"Memorandum to City Council" (July 13, 1969), p. 2.

45. California State Controller, "Annual Report of Financial Transactions Concerning Cities of
California, Fiscal Year 1967/68," pp. 98-117. The
figure for independent cities excludes employee
benefits; this significantly understates the cost
per capita. For instance, for the city of Los
Angeles, the costs of pension and retirement, health
insurance, and workmen's compensation add 35 percent
to the size of the police department budget. (See
Los Angeles City, "Budget, Fiscal Year 1967/68,"
p. 33). Los Angeles City may, however, have larger

employee benefits than other cities in the county.
The sheriff's department recommends 20 percent as
the additional amount for employee benefits. (See
Los Angeles County Department of the Sheriff, Research and Development Bureau, "Preliminary Survey
of California Expenditures for Law Enforcement, Selected Major Cities in Los Angeles County" [January 3,
1969]). This conservative estimate of 20 percent
will be used hereafter.

46.   California State Controller, "Annual Report of Financial Transactions Concerning Cities of
California, Fiscal Year 1967/68," pp. 301-03.

47.   Los Angeles City, "Budget, Fiscal Year
1967/68," p. 33.

48.   The angle of the revenue-expenditure constraint line is raised from 45^0 to 61^0 ($\tan^{-1} 1.78$).

49.   Robert I. Wilcox, Metropolitan Los Angeles,
A Study in Integration, IV, "Law Enforcement" (Los
Angeles: The Haynes Foundation, 1952), 157.

50.   One small city, Signal Hill, which was incorporated in 1924, did abandon its own independent
police and fire departments in favor of county contract service in 1959, but as a result two city
council members were recalled shortly afterward and
the new city council majority canceled the county
contract in order to restore independent police and
fire service. Winston Crouch and Beatrice Dinerman,
Southern California Metropolis (Berkeley and Los
Angeles: University of California Press, 1963),
p. 202.

51.   Los Angeles County Department of the
Sheriff, "Contract Patrol Services, 1968/69." Not
all services are purchased on an around-the-clock
basis. Some cars are purchased for 40 hours per
week, some for 56 hours per week, and some for a
full 168 hours per week; however, all cars are priced
on the same formula as an around-the-clock car. The
cars purchased on a part-time basis have been converted to full-time equivalents and summed for all
contract cities. Motorcycle units have been excluded.

52.   The actual subsidy would be even higher
because the price per car actually paid by contract
cities in 1968/69 was only $119,486 rather than the

$132,392. The actual charge was less than the higher cost figure recommended as appropriate by the county government because of a long-term contract previously negotiated with the contract cities. (See note c, Table 5.1.)

53. The calculations are identical to those performed for the unincorporated area with the data from the same sources. The expenditures of the patrol division, less the expenditures of the vice bureau, amounted to $16,722,000 (exclusive of employee benefits). Of patrol cases handled 44 percent occurred in the contract cities, and so 44 percent of the cost or $7,350,000 was allocated to them. The vice bureau of the patrol division made 15,073 more arrests in the contract cities than would have been the case if the contract cities had had the same level of arrests per capita as the independent cities. This number of arrests represented 30.5 percent of the vice bureau's total arrests, and this percentage of the vice bureau's total expenditure, or $266,000, was considered to be for exclusive service to the contract cities. Thus the total patrol division expenditure for contract service was $7,616,000 (exclusive of benefits), or $9,130,000 including employee benefits. For the detective division, the calls for service answered in the contract cities above the countywide level amounted to 28.6 percent of detective calls, and this percentage of the detective division budget of $6,998,000 (exclusive of employee benefits), or $2,002,000, was allocated to contract service ($2,402,000 inclusive of employee benefits).

54. Los Angeles County Department of the Sheriff, "Statement of Expenditures, Fiscal Year 1967/68," p. 3.

55. A 12.7 percent charge for overhead would increase the patrol and detective division costs to $13,000,000; with compensating contract city revenues of only $6,340,000, the implicit subsidy would then be $6,660,000.

56. Both these figures are only minimum estimates. It may be that the unincorporated area subsidy is more seriously underestimated because all unincorporated area sales tax revenue was credited

as payment for law enforcement service. In reality, other services, such as local parks, provided to the unincorporated area by the county government, should also be financed by sales tax revenue; therefore the subsidy attributable to law enforcement would be greater.

57. County revenues from sources other than property taxes are relatively fixed, and revenue adjustments to balance the county budget are made by varying the county property tax rate each year; thus it appears appropriate to apportion the tax burden of any increase or decrease in expenditures according to the distribution of the property tax base. Since the independent cities contain 76 percent of the total county assessed value subject to property taxation (the chief form of countywide taxation), approximately 76 percent of the total subsidy, or $8,566,000, is financed by the independent cities.

58. Victor Jones, "Urban and Metropolitan Counties," in The Municipal Year Book: 1962 (Chicago: International City Managers' Association, 1962), p. 64. Of the 303 counties having populations of more than 100,000, 40 were eliminated as being untypical for various reasons (for example, the five counties within New York City). The statistics above refer to the remaining 263 counties. (Ibid., p. 57.)

59. U.S. Bureau of the Census, 1967 Census of Governments, I, "Governmental Organization" (Washington: Government Printing Office, 1968), 314, 366, 404, and 428. Only 21 states authorize counties to provide any kind of specific service to a portion rather than to all of the county and to levy a tax on the assessed value of the property within that area to pay for such services. Only 647 of the 3,049 counties in the United States reported having such subordinate taxing districts for any kind of government service. (Ibid., p. 13.)

60. In a survey of sheriffs' departments in 11 southern states in 1967, only 12.7 percent reported that they made investigations within municipalities in all criminal cases. In 70.6 percent of the counties, the sheriff never made criminal

investigations or made them only when requested by
municipal offices or when a citizen complaint was
filed directly with the sheriff. Dana B. Bromer
and James E. Hurley, <u>A Study of Office of Sheriff
in the United States, Southern Region, 1967</u> (University, Mississippi: University of Mississippi,
Bureau of Governmental Research, 1968), p. 186.

ABOUT THE AUTHORS

DONALD C. SHOUP is Assistant Professor of Economics and Research Associate, Institute of Public Policy Studies, at the University of Michigan. He was formerly a Research Economist in the Institute of Government and Public Affairs at the University of California, Los Angeles, and Research Associate at the Institute of Public Administration, New York. Mr. Shoup is co-author (with Ruth P. Mack) of <u>Advance Land Acquisition by Local Governments</u> and author of several articles in the field of urban economics.

STEPHEN L. MEHAY is a graduate student at the University of California at Los Angeles in the Ph.D. program in economics. While at UCLA he held a fellowship from the Committee on Urban Economics of Resources for the Future and a dissertation research fellowship from the U.S. Department of Justice, National Institute of Law Enforcement and Criminal Justice. Mr. Mehay has also worked as a consultant to Public Safety Systems Incorporated in Santa Barbara, California, and taught economics at El Camino College in Torrance, California.